Gadamer

Hermeneutics, Tradition and Reason

Key Contemporary Thinkers

Published
Christopher Hookway, *Quine*

Forthcoming

Gadamer

Hermeneutics, Tradition and Reason

Georgia Warnke

Polity Press

First published 1987 by Polity Press
in association with Basil Blackwell.

Editorial Office:
Polity Press, Dales Brewery, Gwydir Street,
Cambridge CB1 2LJ, UK

Basil Blackwell Ltd
108 Cowley Road, Oxford OX4 1JF, UK

British Library Cataloguing in Publication Data
Warnke, Georgia
Gadamer : hermeneutics, tradition and
reason. — (Key contemporary thinkers).
1. Gadamer, Hans-Georg
I. Title II. Series
193   B3248.G34

ISBN 0–7456–0240–1
ISBN 0–7456–0511–7 Pbk

Typeset in Garamond
by Columns of Reading
Printed and bound in Great Britain by
Billing & Sons of Worcester

For My Parents

The ground on which the ball bounces
Is another bouncing ball.

The wheeling, whirling world
Makes no will glad.

Spinning in its spotlight darkness
It is too big for their hands.

A pitiless, purposeless Thing,
Arbitrary and unspent,

Made for no play, for no children,
But chasing only itself.

The innocent are overtaken,
They are not innocent.

They are their fathers' fathers
The past is inevitable.

Delmore Schwartz

Contents

Preface and acknowledgements

Since the publication in 1960 of Hans-Georg Gadamer's *Wahrheit und Methode*, his hermeneutics has been the focus of a great deal of philosophical attention. His ideas on understanding and interpretation have been applied to a wide-ranging series of discussions: to questions of interpretation in the study of art and literature,[1] to issues of knowledge and objectivity in the social sciences;[2] to related debates in such disciplines as theology and jurisprudence;[3] and even to re-evaluations of the project of philosophy itself.[4] None the less, Gadamer's work has less often been itself the subject of systematic interpretation or assessment and it is this omission that the present book tries to redress.[5] My concern is first to reconstruct the thread of argument that ties together Gadamer's disparate discussions of art, history and philosophy, and second to identify both its virtues and its difficulties. By doing so I hope to provide a reliable guide for the continued appropriation and discussion of his work.

Throughout the book my strategy has been to elucidate Gadamer's position by reconstructing a set of debates in which his work has participated – either actually or virtually. In the first chapter I consider his critique of the romantic hermeneutics of Schleiermacher, the Historical School and Dilthey. He argues that this tradition erred in restricting the problem of understanding to *methods* for ascertaining an agent's or author's intentions; rather, understanding remains primarily a historically situated understanding of the possible *validity* of texts or such "text-analogues" as actions, practices and social norms. In this critique of the hermeneutic tradition, Gadamer already introduces two of the important tenets of his own "philosophical hermeneutics": the possible "truth" of texts or text-analogues and the historically conditioned or prejudiced character of understanding. In chapter 2, I expand on

Gadamer's position by setting it against the intentionalist view Hirsch takes from Schleiermacher. Hirsch argues that in emphasizing the variability of textual understanding according to historical circumstances, Gadamer's position reduces to a subjectivistic glorification of an interpretive community's or tradition's prejudices. The notion of a tradition of interpretation is as central to Gadamer's view as are the ideas of truth and prejudice. The question is whether these need to be given the subjectivistic twist that Hirsch gives to them.

I take up this question in chapter 3, contrasting Gadamer's position here to a series of actual and possible criticisms. I argue that there are in fact two general objections with which Gadamer's hermeneutics must contend: not only that it is subjectivistic but that, in its attempt to avoid subjectivism, it becomes conservative. In order to provide a basis for deciding between different plausible interpretations, it takes as its standard the tradition to which it belongs and favors that interpretation which can illuminate its truth. This latter objection is similar to that which Habermas and Apel have raised and chapter 4 therefore examines their debate with Gadamer. As we shall see, Habermas and Apel stress the significance of his analysis as a critique of objectivistic positions such as Hirsch's; none the less they argue that in taking the tradition as the standard of correct interpretation, Gadamer destroys any basis upon which to assess its own rationality and that he therefore ignores the fact that traditional interpretations can be ideologically distorted. In chapter 5 I consider Richard Rorty's very different appropriation of Gadamer's work. Here the value of Gadamer's work is seen to lie in the scepticism it directs at the possibility of providing a proof for the rationality of our tradition and Rorty thus applauds Gadamer for precisely his disregard for Habermas's and Apel's "foundationalist" concerns.

In these final chapters of the book I evaluate both assessments of Gadamer's work. In my view the contrast between the two accounts suggests that Gadamer's hermeneutics might best be understood as a middle path. We are situated in history and historically conditioned. This means that our conception of rationality is subject to the limitations of the historical experiences we have inherited. At the same time, the rationality of our response to these experiences remains a constant question for us. No scepticism towards the idea of reason will permit us to avoid it; indeed, it may be that our hermeneutic understanding of others and our past can help us to a provisional answer.

I undertook the preliminary study to which this book is a distant relative while on a fellowship in Germany granted by the Deutscher Akademische Austauschdienst. The book itself was written under the auspices of the Whitney Humanities Center at Yale University and the Bunting Institute of Radcliffe College. I would like to thank all three institutions for their support. I would also like to thank Thomas McCarthy and my editor, John Thompson, for their intelligent and valuable suggestions, Paul Stern for his criticism and encouragement and Anne Janowitz for both theoretical and practical assistance. Finally, I would like to express my gratitude to Dalia Fiore who took care of my son with a competence and love that made concentration on this book possible and who is therefore largely responsible for whatever merit it may have.

Cambridge, Massachusetts

Introduction

In recent years there has been a spate of philosophical books on the limits of various philosophical approaches. In this regard, Michael Sandel's *Liberalism and the Limits of Justice*[1] and Bernard Williams's *Ethics and the Limits of Philosophy*[2] are only two of the more explicit examples. But from deconstructionist studies of the self-deception involved in claims to textual understanding to historicist accounts of scientific research, the emphasis has been on the limits of our knowledge of texts, nature, ourselves and our world. The claim is that we are always involved in interpretations and that we can have no access to anything like "the truth" about justice, the self, reality or the "moral law." Our notions of these "truths" are rather conditioned by the cultures to which we belong and the historical circumstances in which we find ourselves. Hence, we must face the fact of our finitude and the utterly contingent character of our efforts to understand.

Gadamer's work might be said to serve as the basis for this current focus on limits. For the whole of his philosophical career and culminating in his magnum opus, *Truth and Method*, his concern has been to overcome the positivistic hubris of assuming that we can develop an "objective" knowledge of the phenomena with which we are concerned. As a distinct discipline hermeneutics has its origins in nineteenth-century attempts to formulate a theory of interpretation. Questions of interpretation had been raised earlier, in particular in the Reformation's challenge to the Catholic reading of the Bible. Did an understanding of Scripture require a prior acceptance of the precepts of the Catholic faith or could it be understood on its own? If it could, was it to be read as a unified text or as a series of disparate narratives written at different times with different purposes? At the beginning of the nineteenth century, however, the philologist and theologian

F. D. E. Schleiermacher significantly expanded the scope of hermeneutic questions. The problem, as he saw it, was not just how the Bible or even classical texts were to be understood, but how meaning could be comprehended, what the methods were that would permit an objective understanding of texts and utterances of any kind. Following Schleiermacher, Wilhelm Dilthey asked even broader questions: what were the methods that would permit an objective reading of symbolic structures of any kind, including actions, social practices, norms and values? How could the understanding of meaning be raised to the same level of methodological clarity that characterized the natural sciences? How could it find as solid a basis for methodical progress?

By 1960, when Gadamer published *Truth and Method*, the consequences of this kind of question had become apparent. Dilthey had tried to establish the autonomy of the logic of the *Geisteswissenschaften* or of such studies as history, textual interpretation and the investigation of social norms, practices and institutions. That is, his desire had been to illuminate the difference between the structure of these sciences of *meaning* and the natural scientific explanation of events based on the formulation of theoretical frameworks and discovery of causal laws. Nevertheless he conceived of both kinds of study as *objective* sciences; the point of both was to develop a neutral understanding of social or human phenomena, an understanding that would be accessible to all interpreters or observers from whatever historical or cultural vantage point they might inhabit. The positivism of the mid-twentieth century differed only in denying any distinction in the logics of the natural sciences and *Geisteswissenschaften*. If both were to be objective sciences, this meant that the latter had to emulate the practices and standards of the former; what was required was an ability to explain and predict the occurrence of events by formulating and verifying causal hypotheses. Social scientific findings were to be repeatable in the same way as natural scientific experiments and in both cases objectivity was to mean an elimination of subjective intrusions: explanations were to be based on adherence to rigorous scientific methods so that the effects of differences in imagination, interpretive talent or individual perspective could be minimized. Disciplines in which the influence of talent, imagination and perspective could not be minimized, such as literary studies and art appreciation, were no longer to be viewed as cognitive disciplines at all.[3]

From Gadamer's point of view, this constellation of norms and premises is a disaster since it overlooks important differences between understanding meaning and explaining the occurrences of events, differences that Dilthey was right to emphasize. Gadamer thus reverses the positivist response to Dilthey, criticizing him not for maintaining a distinction between natural and social science but for not realizing that this distinction runs right through to the standards· of objectivity appropriate to each. In so far as positivism assumes that the natural sciences provide the model of an objective inquiry impervious to changes in historical vantage point and scientific perspective, it does not describe even them correctly. Gadamer maintains that the natural sciences are the product of a tradition of interpretation and that their norms and standards are simply the "prejudices" of this tradition. To hold them up as the muster of knowledge in general is thus to overlook the extent to which they are historically conditioned and, moreover, to refuse to recognize the existence of other historically constituted norms and standards. We shall examine the details of this argument in the substance of the book itself. The point here is that, for Gadamer, the question that Schleiermacher and Dilthey ask and positivism takes up is the wrong question. We cannot ask how the sciences of meaning are to attain the objectivity characteristic of the natural sciences because this standard of objectivity is one constituted within a certain tradition, appropriate, perhaps, for certain purposes, but not at all one that can be absolutized as a general demand.

Hermeneutics, as Gadamer conceives of it, then, is no longer to be seen as a discourse on methods of "objective" understanding as it was for the hermeneutic tradition of Schleiermacher and Dilthey. It no longer seeks to formulate a set of interpretive rules; rather, in referring to his analysis as "philosophical hermeneutics," Gadamer turns to an account of the conditions of the possiblity of understanding in general, conditions that in his view undermine faith in the ideas of both method and objectivity. Methodological approaches to both natural and human phenomena are rooted in history; they accept certain historical assumptions as to both what is to be studied and how it is to be approached. Understanding is therefore rooted in prejudice and the way in which we understand is thoroughly conditioned by the past or by what Gadamer calls "effective history." This influence of the past obtains in our aesthetic understanding, in our social and psychological self-understanding and in all forms of scientific understanding. The objectivity of our knowledge is therefore significantly curtailed by its dependence on tradition and this dependence is not one that method can in any way transcend. Anticipating the trend I noted earlier Gadamer might therefore have titled his book *Objectivity and the Limits of Method*.

By now, this analysis may seem old-hat. The positivism that prevailed in the 1950s and 1960s no longer has the force it once had and few still deny the reliance of scientific approaches on a series of historically advanced assumptions or conventions. Such theorists as Richard Rorty, whose views I shall be discussing in chapter 5, go so far as first to reject the positivistic distinction between cognitive and non-cognitive disciplines, and second to argue that natural science is itself hermeneutic. The development of hermeneutics which began with Schleiermacher and Dilthey's attempt to erect a science of meaning on a par with the natural sciences thus culminates in the claim that the natural sciences are themselves sciences of meaning; in other words, that they are themselves historically conditioned, fallible interpretations. But if *Truth and Method* thus sets itself against a positivism that is no longer generally accepted, the question arises as to whether it has anything left to say to us, post-positivists as many of us are.

In my view it has a great deal to say to us. For, if the attention *Truth and Method* pays to prejudice and the influence of the past is important, no less important is its attempt to resuscitate a dialogic conception of knowledge. Understanding (*Verstehen*) for Gadamer is primarily coming to an understanding (*Verständigung*) with others. In confronting texts, different views and perspectives, alternative life forms and world-views, we can put our own prejudices in play and learn to enrich our own point of view. Against positivism, then, Gadamer argues that an objectivity attained through scientific method is no more adequate than the prejudices it presupposes; but he also suggests that our prejudices are as much thresholds as limits, that they form perspectives from which a gradual development of our knowledge becomes possible. To this extent, Gadamer's account of understanding retains a connection to the Enlightenment. To be sure, we can no longer hope to eradicate prejudice through method. Nor can we search for an objectivity that would lift us above historical variations and subjective interpretations. None the less, in coming to an understanding with others we can learn how to amend some of our assumptions and, indeed, how to move to a richer, more developed understanding of the issues in question.

It is significant, then, that Gadamer does not refer to limits in his title. In stressing the way in which our understanding is embedded in history, his point is not simply the degree to which our history limits our knowledge and not simply the extent to which notions of truth are historically various. His point is also that history can itself aid our development and help us to cultivate what we may still call "reason."

1

Hermeneutics and history

In "Die Entstehung der Hermeneutik" the philosopher Wilhelm Dilthey characterizes the development of modern hermeneutics as a "liberation of interpretation from dogma."[1] Textual interpretation has its origins in the Greek educational system but on Dilthey's account advances in the formulation of methods of interpretation had to await the Reformation and the attack on the Church's authority to interpret the Bible. At this time Matthias Flacius, a Lutheran, criticized the Catholic emphasis on tradition in the interpretation of supposedly obscure parts of the Bible and maintained that it could be understood on its own grounds as the word of God. This attack on the Tridentine Church already disclosed what Dilthey saw as the fundamental principle of modern hermeneutic theory: texts are to be understood in their own terms rather than those of doctrine so that understanding requires not dogma but the systematic application of interpretive rules. Dilthey further credited Flacius with the first formulation of the idea of a hermeneutic circle: since Catholic teaching was no longer to serve as a guide to the Bible's meaning, the understanding of it was rather to be built up from an understanding of its individual parts. At the same time, however, it was clear that some guide was needed to the meaning of those individual parts, indeed, that they had themselves to be understood in light of the aims and composition of the Bible as a whole. Hence, it was claimed that Biblical interpretation necessarily moved in a circle, that its individual books and passages were to be understood in terms of the meaning of the whole, while the understanding of the whole was to be achieved in light of an understanding of these individual parts.

Despite the significance of Flacius's break with the canons of Tridentine interpretation, Dilthey argued that his own procedure remained problematic in so far as he overlooked the different historical circumstances under which various parts of the Bible were written. In fact, since the Protestant reading of the Bible simply assumed that it constituted a unified, self-consistent whole, what Dilthey referred to as a second "theological-hermeneutic" step criticized this reading itself as dogmatic. The importance of this step was to articulate another hermeneutic principle: the individual books of the Bible were now to be understood in light of differences in context and linguistic usage. This principle allowed G. F. Meier to extend the tenets of religious hermeneutics to the philological study of classical texts and ultimately permitted Schleiermacher to formulate the principles of a general theory of interpretation, applicable to all discourse (*Rede*). Not only classical texts and the Bible but all written works and spoken utterances could be subjected to the sophisticated scrutiny made possible by precisely formulated methods of understanding. In this way, according to Dilthey, hermeneutic theory became available as the basis for the human sciences or *Geisteswissenschaften*, as the mode of access to meaning in general – the meaning not only of texts but of signs and symbols of all sorts, social practices, historical actions and works of art.

In the second half of his major work *Truth and Method* and in related essays Hans-Georg Gadamer questions this account of the development of hermeneutics as one assisted by a successive overcoming of dogmatic prejudices and assumptions. What Dilthey sees as the liberation of interpretation from dogma signals instead a fateful "change in essence."[2] Indeed, for Gadamer, the development of hermeneutics extending from Schleiermacher through the Historical School of Ludwig von Ranke and Johann Gustav Droysen to Dilthey himself unfolds a positivistic misconception that equates understanding with a methodologically secured, "Cartesian" certainty. This "Romantic hermeneutics," as he refers to it, is therefore unable to grasp either the structure of under-standing (*Verstehen*) or its role in the human sciences. In this initial chapter I want to examine Gadamer's critique of romantic hermeneutics, showing what it reveals about his own concerns and how it reorients his hermeneutic philosophy. I shall first reconstruct an important distinction he suggests between two kinds of understanding and then turn to his interpretation of the hermeneutics of Schleiermacher, the Historical School and Dilthey. Finally, I shall look at the radical transformation of hermeneutics that he claims was effected by the work of Martin Heidegger.

CRITIQUE OF ROMANTIC HERMENEUTICS

It is common in the philosophy of history and of the social sciences to distinguish between explaining human actions and beliefs and understanding their meaning: between explaining why a given action or belief occurs or occurred and understanding what an agent is doing with a certain set of bodily movements or what belief is represented with certain words.[3] These two approaches to the study of action have been differently weighted. Some so-called "positivists" have argued that the understanding of meaning (*Verstehen*) involves simply an imaginative reconstruction of actor's intentions or purposes; although such reconstruction can be helpful in formulating a hypothesis that tries to explain the causes of action, understanding cannot count as part of the logic of science itself. The scientific aspect of the study of action consists rather in constructing explanatory hypotheses that can be incorporated into general theories of human behavior and testing them through reliable methods of empirical observation.[4] On this view the structure of science is identical in every field of research. It consists in identifying regular sequences of behavior, formulating universal laws and theories and, through them, predicting or explaining the occurrence of events. *Verstehende* or hermeneutic theorists, in contrast, have argued that history and social science cannot conform to the logic of the natural sciences because of the role an interpretive understanding plays in them. On this view, understanding *what* a given action or belief is, is itself a scientific task that necessarily precedes explaining *why* it occurs. This task involves "reading" a situation, placing bodily movements and words within the context to which they belong and hence understanding them in light of other actions and beliefs. Both the construction of explanatory hypotheses and their empirical testing thus turn out to be matters of interpretation: they rest on a specific presumption as to what the event to be explained is and therefore on an assessment of *meaning*.[5]

Gadamer's account of hermeneutic understanding is devoted to examining the conditions of this latter understanding of meaning. Throughout his work, however, he emphasizes the necessity of distinguishing between two forms of understanding: the understanding of truth-content and the understanding of intentions. The first form of understanding refers to the kind of substantive knowledge one has when one is justified in claiming that one understands Euclidean geometry or an ethical principle, for example. Here understanding means seeing the "truth" of something, grasping that the sum of the squares of the two sides of a right triangle is equal to the square of the hypotenuse, that the validity of Euclidean geometry is relativized by the discovery of other forms of geometry or that murder is wrong. Understanding in this sense involves insight into a subject-matter or, as Gadamer puts it, an understanding of *die Sache*.[6] The second sense of understanding, in contrast, involves a knowledge of conditions: the reasons why a particular person says that murder is wrong or the intentions behind someone's claiming that a geometrical proposition is true. This kind of understanding thus involves an understanding of the psychological, biographical or historical conditions behind a claim or action as opposed to a substantive understanding of the claim or action itself. What is understood is not the truth-content of a claim or the point of an action but the motives behind a certain person's making a certain claim or performing a given action.

In Gadamer's view, understanding in its strongest sense involves the first form of understanding as a substantive understanding of truth. In contrast, the second, intentional, form of understanding becomes necessary when attempts to achieve an understanding of truth fail. In other words, it is when one cannot see the point of what someone else is saying or doing that one is forced to explore the conditions under which that person says or does it: what this person might mean, given who he or she is, the circumstances of the time and so on. Alasdair MacIntyre offers a good example of the difference to which Gadamer is pointing here in claiming that "we confront a blank wall" in trying to understand the aborigine practice of carrying about "a stick or stone which is treated as if it is or embodies the soul of the individual who carries it."[7] Since we cannot make sense out of this practice or see its point, we can understand it only to the extent that we understand the conditions under which the aborigine may have thought it had a point. As Gadamer puts this point:

> The genetic formulation of the question, the goal of which is to explain a traditional opinion in terms of the historical situation, arises only where immediate insight into the truth of what is said cannot be attained because reason contradicts it.[8]

Yet we *can* be interested in genetic questions even when we accept the truth of a claim. Thus we are interested in the conditions that facilitated the Greeks' discovery of the principles of geometry, for example, just because we accept these principles for certain purposes and want to know what permitted their articulation in Greek culture at a particular time.[9] To this extent Gadamer seems to have overstated his case in claiming that genetic questions arise only when understanding in its strongest sense has failed. Moreover, it also seems to be the case that we understand in a substantive sense when we understand the *invalidity* of a claim and hence disagree with a claim or text under study. Gadamer himself sometimes makes this point. Still, he tends to associate the strong sense of understanding with an understanding of "substantive validity" and hence with an ability to agree on truth.[10] In a crucial passage he therefore writes

> Understanding (*Verständnis*) is first of all agreement (*Einverständnis*). So human beings usually understand one another immediately or they communicate (*sich verständigen*) until they reach an agreement. Reaching an understanding (*Verständigung*) is thus always: reaching an understanding about something.[11]

We shall have to examine the implications of this emphasis on agreement more thoroughly later. At this point in our discussion, however, we are interested in the way Gadamer's distinction between two forms of understanding affects his assessment of Dilthey's description of the progress of hermeneutics. In his own reconstruction of the development of hermeneutics from Schleiermacher through Dilthey, Gadamer tries to show that what Dilthey described as a liberation from dogma is instead a move from one sense of understanding, an understanding of truth-content, to the other, an understanding of conditions of genesis. Despite their differences both Tridentine Catholicism and the Protestantism of the Reformation are concerned with the truth-content of the Bible. The Bible is presumed to have normative authority for everyone and the task of hermeneutic understanding is therefore simply to help transmit the content of its normative claims. Hermeneutics thus has a largely pedagogical task: it is supposed to exhibit the truth that inheres in a given claim so that its audience can understand and learn from it. As hermeneutics develops, however, attention is redirected away from the understanding of the truth-content of a text and toward the understanding of intentions. The aim of understanding is no longer seen as a knowledge of *die Sache* — a substantive knowledge of claims to truth or normative authority. It is seen rather as insight into the historical or biographical circumstances behind their expression. The question of understanding thus becomes the genetic one: what were the conditions under which agents acted, spoke or wrote as they did? The question of the validity of their words or actions is no longer considered part of the theory of understanding. In his critique of romantic hermeneutics Gadamer traces the consequences of this omission for efforts to specify the logic of social and historical studies. He begins by examining Schleiermacher's hermeneutics.

Schleiermacher's hermeneutics

In Gadamer's view, the conceptual distance that separates Schleiermacher from his predecessors becomes clear if one looks at the account of interpretation found in the work of Spinoza and the pre-romantic hermeneuticist, Chladenius. For both of these theorists, understanding is primarily a question of understanding the truth-content of a text and, in particular, of the Bible. Moreover, both suggest that such understanding is for the most part unproblematic. One can usually read the Bible and understand the normative authority of its claims directly just as one can understand Euclidean geometry directly, without the need for explicit hermeneutic procedures. Still, Spinoza does think that an explicit procedure or "art" of understanding is required to deal with certain of the Bible's claims, such as those about miracles for example, since their truth-content is no longer self-evident. For his part, Chladenius normally associates hermeneutic understanding with an understanding of the subject-matter that a text addresses. Nevertheless, he too notes the need for an "art" or method of interpretation where students are sceptical of their teacher's account of the subject-matter and this understanding itself has to be justified. In Chladenius's view, this necessity reflects the effects of the Enlightenment, or at least the fact that students no longer trust their teachers and "want to see with their own eyes."[12] Explicit hermeneutic procedures are thus occasionally necessary because a common set of beliefs and common foundation for understanding has disappeared.[13] None the less, despite these occasional calls for an art of understanding, for both Spinoza and Chladenius the primary task of hermeneutics remains that of transmitting a substantive understanding. The method or art of hermeneutics has only a limited scope; it is relevant only where the truth of a claim is no longer clear or a particular substantive understanding itself needs to be grounded. In Schleiermacher's work, in contrast, the call for hermeneutic methods may arise at any time with regard to any form of discourse (Rede). As he writes:

Very often in the middle of a private conversation I avail myself of
hermeneutic operations if I am not satisfied with a customary degree of
understanding but seek to discover how in my friend's reflections the
transition from one thought to another has been made, or if I trace the
opinions, judgments and aspirations connected with the fact that he
expresses himself precisely so and not otherwise with regard to an object
under discussion.[14]

Thus, while both Chladenius and Spinoza see the need for hermeneutics
only where the validity of a text or interpretation is no longer self-
evident, Schleiermacher no longer associates hermeneutic understanding
with questions of validity at all. He does not contrast a "customary
degree of understanding" to a better grasp of the subject-matter at hand,
as they did. Rather he reserves this kind of substantive understanding for
dialectics and contrasts the "customary degree of understanding" to a
more detailed knowledge of the train of someone's thought, why he
expressed himself "precisely so and not otherwise." Indeed, as Gadamer
points out, in contrast to Spinoza Schleiermacher thinks that even Euclid
must be understood in this way. The focus of understanding is not
the validity of what is said but its individuality as the thought of a
particular person, expressed in a particular way at a particular time.
Schleiermacher thus differentiates two ways of practicing the "art" of
understanding:

#15 The more lax practice in the art starts from the premise that
understanding arises of itself and expresses the goal negatively: misunderstanding is to be avoided. . . .

#16 The more rigorous practice starts from the premise that misunderstand-
ing emerges of itself and that understanding must be desired and sought at
every point.[15]

The importance of this distinction between a looser and more rigorous
hermeneutic practice can be seen when it is compared to the account of
understanding that I cited earlier. As we saw, for Gadamer understanding
is primarily substantive agreement with others on truth in regard to a
subject-matter. Gadamer thus assumes with Spinoza and Chladenius that
people normally understand one another directly, that "understanding
arises of itself" or can be brought about through further communication.
Schleiermacher, however, claims that misunderstanding is the normal
case and therefore that a more rigorous hermeneutic procedure is

required. On Gadamer's view, the introduction of this rigorous practice shows that "the task of interpretation has been uprooted from the context of intelligent consensus" and as he continues, "Now it has to overcome complete alienation."[16] Still, Schleiermacher's and Gadamer's claims are not really in direct contradiction to one another since the word "understanding" refers to two different processes in each case, indeed, to the two we have already examined. Gadamer is maintaining that we can usually understand the point of what others say immediately, or by continuing to talk with them we can arrive at some kind of consensus about the subject-matter at issue. In contrast, Schleiermacher assumes that we usually have only a partial idea of what may have motivated them to say what they said. This difference signals not only a difference in degrees of alienation but also a difference in the object domain of hermeneutics itself. For Schleiermacher, the task of understanding is no longer that of facilitating a knowledge of the general truth of a claim, but rather that of achieving insight into the unique conditions behind an individual expression of the claim. The focus of hermeneutics thus shifts from general validity to individual creativity and the consequence of this shift is that questions of method move to the forefront of hermeneutic theory.

The reason for this change becomes clear if one reconsiders the original distinction between the understanding of truth-content and the understanding of intentions. As long as understanding refers to a knowledge of the validity of a text or claim – understanding Euclidean geometry for example – the method by which such understanding is accomplished is not important. Indeed, at least one mark of a good geometry teacher is that he or she can teach the same material in many different ways. The criterion of successful teaching in this case is the clarification of theorems, axioms and the like and how one clarifies these depends on the students one is teaching, the problems they have and so on. When understanding refers to the comprehension of claims to truth, it is unimportant how such understanding is accomplished. Once the focus of understanding moves from the truth of a claim to its uniqueness as a particular person's expression, however, questions of method become more significant, because seeing the validity of the claim no longer indicates the success of the process of understanding. The question now is how to arrive at a correct understanding of others' intentions and in this case understanding the truth or untruth of their remarks is no guarantee of having understood what they may have actually wanted to say. We do not have any immediate access to the intentions of others and therefore if these are to be the object of hermeneutics we require reliable interpretive methods.

Schleiermacher, in fact, notes two different methodical forms of hermeneutic practice: grammatical and psychological or technical interpretation. In grammatical interpretation, a text or mode of expression is analyzed in terms of its language, that is, in terms of its dialect, sentence structure, literary form and the like. In psychological interpretation, it is analyzed as part of the author's life history. Thus, whereas grammatical interpretation attempts to identify the precise meaning of linguistic terms, psychological interpretation focuses on the *Keimentschluss*, the core decision or basic motivation that has "moved the author to communicate."[17] The two forms of interpretation are meant to supplement and check one another in Schleiermacher's analysis; moreover, he conceives of both as applying the hermeneutic circle of part and whole. Grammatical interpretation attempts to determine the meanings of words in terms of the sentences of which they are a part and the sentences in terms of the work as a whole; finally, it places the work itself in the context of its linguistic usage and the literary genre to which it belongs. At the same time the understanding of sentences, the work, literary genre and linguistic usage is constituted by the understanding of the smaller parts that compose these larger wholes. For its part, psychological interpretation places the work in the context of the author's life and the history of the time while simultaneously building up a knowledge of these by analyzing individual experiences and projects such as the work being studied. This is also the point at which Schleiermacher introduces what Gadamer considers the most questionable part of his program, namely, the method of divination in which the interpreter "transforms himself, so to speak, into the other and seeks to comprehend the individual immediately."[18] In divination the interpreter identifies with the author whose work is being studied, imaginatively relives the experiences and thoughts that engendered the work and thereby acquires a direct and total knowledge of the individual creation in question.

Gadamer has been accused of overemphasizing the role of psychological divination in Schleiermacher's hermeneutics at the expense of grammatical interpretation and of failing to recognize the systematic context of divinatory methods.[19] It is true that Schleiermacher emphasizes the connection between divination and different comparative methods that proceed by comparing authors to general personality types and singling out their distinctive features. But Gadamer responds that his own emphasis on psychological divination in Schleiermacher's work is warranted because of its influence on Schleiermacher's heirs, particularly Dilthey. Be that as it may, Schleiermacher's inclusion of psychological divination within a system of methods and forms of interpretation does not suffice to resolve the problem Gadamer has with it.

Schleiermacher's focus on the individuality of a work or expression as opposed to its "truth-content" holds for both psychological and grammatical interpretation. Grammatical interpretation complements psychological interpretation by fixing the exact meaning of the author's words and eliciting a comprehension of the language as the author knew it, while psychological interpretation complements grammatical interpretation by exploring the life-context in which the work was generated. On both sides of hermeneutic theory, then, the goal is a precise reproduction of the meaning of a work as its author intended it. To understand the meaning of a discourse is to reconstruct the original intentions of writers or speakers by understanding their special idioms on the one hand, and the circumstances of their lives at the time on the other. In this way Schleiermacher severs hermeneutics from questions of truth and, on Gadamer's view, thereby aestheticizes the object of understanding.[20] For Schleiermacher, speech and writing of whatever type become the spontaneous overflow of genius; the task of methical understanding is to reproduce the original process of production in order to participate in an original creation. Thus, in direct contrast to the (possibly naive) commitment of pre-Romantic hermeneutics to the truth of the texts it studies, Schleiermacher sees them only as "artistic thoughts"[21]; they are understood when methods are found that bring back to life the creative processes and intentions that engendered them.

Schleiermacher's work thus already gives Gadamer's *Truth and Method* its title. On his view, the crucial shift in hermeneutics was not the one Dilthey emphasized – from dogmatic to non-dogmatic and "objective" understanding. This shift rather reflects a deeper one: a change from a focus on the possible truth of a text to a focus on method, from a consideration of the validity of a text to a preoccupation with procedures for understanding an author's intentions. Now it could be argued that there is nothing as fundamentally disastrous about this transition as Gadamer seems to intimate. Gadamer admits that hermeneutics as Schleiermacher defines it is necessary whenever the content of a text no longer makes sense and the only question that can be raised is what the author intended it to say. His objection, however, is that Schleiermacher raises this question with regard to all texts and thus considers them all simply "artistic thoughts." But the question is whether there is anything illegitimate about this procedure, given that Schleiermacher ultimately supplements hermeneutics – the study of an author's intended meaning – with dialectics – the consideration of a subject-matter.

In fact, two questions arise here. First, even if one distinguishes two forms of the understanding of meaning, is an understanding of intentions not still an important part of hermeneutics? Is it not important to ascertain both what an author was trying to say and the truth-content of what is said? Indeed, it would seem that even if one's ultimate concern is the truth of an author's ideas one still needs to understand what an author intended so that one knows that the claims one adjudicates are in fact the author's claims. The second question involves the status of method. Is there anything misguided in the application of explicit hermeneutic operations to the work of understanding and, if so, what? Certainly, methods may become more important if the object of understanding is the intention behind a text as opposed to its content. But if there is nothing objectionable about the new focus on intentions, then is there an objection to the introduction of method? In the remainder of this chaper, I shall begin to address these questions by examining Gadamer's account of the after-effects of Schleiermacher's aestheticization of hermeneutics. I shall look first at his criticisms of attempts by the historians, Ranke and Droysen, to apply hermeneutic principles to the study of history and then turn to his analysis of Wilhelm Dilthey's recourse to hermeneutics as the foundation of the human sciences in general.

The hermeneutic account of history

Gadamer suggests that it was a mistake for either Ranke or Droysen to turn to hermeneutics in their attempts to found the possibility of historical studies. That they may have had a rationale for doing so is clear: just as Schleiermacher's hermeneutic theory formed the foundation upon which literary interpretation was finally to be released from dogma, the theory was also supposed to liberate history from Hegel. Against Hegel, both Ranke and Droysen insisted that history was an empirical science and had to begin with facts rather than with speculative assumptions about the purpose of history. They therefore argued that history had to be understood on its own terms, independently of a priori principles, and in this they echoed Flacius's earlier claim that the Bible could be understood on its own, independently of Catholic principles. In addition they insisted that individual historical periods were to be understood as having their own internal meaning as opposed to a meaning deduced from Hegelian teleology. Here they followed Schleiermacher's emphasis on the uniqueness of individual expressions: each historical period was to maintain its integrity and not to be incorporated into a philosophy of history in general.[22] In Gadamer's view this attempt to transpose the principles of literary interpretation to the study of history ignored the temporal dimension of historical understanding. Indeed, despite its critique of Hegelian teleology, Gadamer thinks that the Historical School exhibited a poorer grasp of the logic of historical meaning than Hegel's own. I shall look at Gadamer's criticisms of Ranke and Droysen in turn.

Decisive for Ranke's failure to comprehend the structure of history, according to Gadamer, is his insistence that although history does not have the unity of a philosophical system, as Hegel assumed, it is none the less "not without internal connection." On the one hand, against Hegel, Ranke argues that history follows "scenes of freeedom." No event is determined in advance or required by dialectical necessity. Neither, then, is its meaning contingent upon the end-point or *telos* of history. Events and actions must be conceived rather as having meaning in themselves apart from philosophical speculation on the course of history, just as texts are seen to have meaning in themselves apart from dogmatic principles. Historical understanding is a means of clarifying the unique "free" character of individual events.

On the other hand Ranke also claims that events follow from events before them and combine themselves into cohesive wholes marking distinct historical periods. Gadamer cites the following passage from Ranke's work:

> Beside freedom stands necessity. It lies in what has already been formed, what cannot be destroyed, which is the foundation of all rising activity. What has been constitutes the connection with what is becoming. . . . A long series of events – succeeding and next to one another – in such ways bound to one another, form a century, an epoch. . . .[23]

Gadamer already sees here the influence of Schleiermacherian hermeneutics. Historical events are supposed to hang together and form a coherent, intelligible meaning among themselves. Indeed the rise of new historical periods itself depends upon "what has already been formed," upon previous periods. Hence history is itself as internally unified as a text. Having given up Hegel, however, Ranke can no longer make sense out of this unity. History is no longer seen as the working out of a divine plan or the return of spirit to itself, and yet it is still supposed to manifest the consistent unfolding of historical tendencies. On Ranke's account, the cohesiveness of history is simply a fact; certain events are bound together by historical forces to form an epoch or century and such epochs and centuries lead to others. Still, there is no longer any immanently developing content that connects them to one another. Gadamer argues that there is a contradiction here: on the one hand, "no preconception of the meaning of history is to prejudice its investigation." On the other hand "the self-evident premise of its investigation is that it forms a unity."[24] But here the Hegelian question re-emerges: if there is no immanently developing content that unifies history what does unify it?

Ranke offers no answer to this question. Instead, because he assumes that unity is simply a fact about history and that history is therefore similar to a text he also assumes that Schleiermacherian principles of textual hermeneutics have direct application. Just as a text has a beginning and an end so too does history; Ranke therefore posits God as the spectator who sees both the beginning and end of history and therefore understands the role each of its individual parts play in the meaning of the whole. Moreover, just as methods of textual interpretation are directed at clarifying the meaning of a text by placing it within the context of the author's life on the one hand, and the literary tradition to which it belongs on the other, historical understanding clarifies the individuality of historical epochs by placing them within universal history. No historical period is to be judged differently than any other; rather all are to be seen as individualities in their own right, as expressions of the variablity of human life in general. Ranke writes "I imagine the Deity – if I may venture this observation – as surveying all of historical humanity in its totality since no time lies before it and finding it all of equal value."[25] Indeed, for him the legitimacy of historical understanding depends upon the degree to which historians can approximate God's omniscient point of view by liberating themselves from their own place in history and surveying history as a unified whole. The aim of historical study is therefore a "feeling-with, co-knowledge of everything."[26] In striving for this kind of knowledge historians acquire a priest-like status:

> Immediacy to God is for the Lutheran, Ranke, the actual content of the Christian message. Re-establishing this immediacy that existed before the

Fall occurs not through the Church's means of grace alone. The historian participates in it insofar as he makes a fallen humanity in history the object of his research and recognizes this humanity in the immediacy to God that it has never entirely lost.[27]

For Gadamer, Ranke's "methodological naivety" lies in his failure to grasp the consequences of his own critique of Hegel. On the one hand Ranke objects to Hegel's derivation of the meaning of history from a speculative end-point in spirit's return to itself; on the other hand he locates the condition of the possiblity of historical understanding in an equally absolute point of view. Whereas Hegel assumed knowledge of the end of history directly, Ranke simply substitutes a God with such knowledge and locates the objectivity and legitimacy of historical work in its approximation to this suprahistorical position. Despite his criticism of Hegel's account of absolute knowledge, the structure of historical meaning thus remains teleological. The meaning of historical events is not an intrinsic essence, a meaning they have in and of themselves; it is rather a function of their relations to other events that come after them and indicate their significance. As Gadamer puts this point:

> That something succeeds or not is not decisive only for the meaning of this single act; it does not let it merely have a lasting effect or pass by without one. Its success or lack thereof rather lets a whole sequence of actions and events become meaningful or meaningless. The ontological structure of history is therefore itself teleological even if it is without *telos*.[28]

We can elaborate on this elliptical remark by looking at Arthur Danto's *Analytical Philosophy of History*.[29] Danto argues that historical "meaning" is necessarily retrospective, that it results from an understanding of the meanings events have in relation to other events that are seen to follow or fail to follow from them. Thus, the description of Petrarch's ascendency of Mount Ventoux as the opening of the Renaissance presupposes that the Renaissance has taken place and, indeed, that certain events have been seen as sufficiently related to one another to merit their common description as the Renaissance. The description of an event as the end of World War I is similarly retrospective; indeed, nothing can be defined as the end of World War I until the start of World War II and describing a series of events or actions as the start of World War II itself requires placing them in the context of other events and actions that follow. According to Danto, then, historical meaning involves a "retroactive realignment of the Past,"[30] that is, it is the outcome of a narrative structure imposed upon events from a position subsequent to them, in light of events that have been seen to come after them.

From this perspective, the confusion in Ranke's account of historical understanding becomes clear. Historical unity is not a fact about history, as he assumes, but the product of a retrospective narrative detailing the way in which events are interrelated. This means, first, that the meaning of an event or action is directly correlated with a particular historical perspective on it. In short, historical meaning is itself historically situated; it depends upon the perspective from which the events in question are seen. Second, then, the meaning of events will change with changes in historical perspective. The meaning of World War I, for example, changes depending on the historical "horizon" from which it is viewed: it can be described as the Great War or the war to end all wars at a certain point in history, but only until the start of World War II. Similarly, the events that comprise the start of World War II must have a different meaning before World War II becomes a recognizable entity than they do after it has achieved this identity in the consciousness of historical interpreters. The meaning of historical actions and events is contingent upon the vantage point from which they are perceived and historical understanding is necessarily perspectival and partial; it encompasses only that meaning events have from the position in history that the historian possesses. It follows that the suprahistorical, God-like and objective stance to which Ranke aspires is impossible. As Danto points out, we could have a complete knowledge of history only if we could know all the possible stories that could ever be written about a certain event or complex of events and all the points of view from which it could be discussed. History, however, has yet to attain the finality of a text; moreover, if and when it does there will be no perspective from which to write the final scene. History can never represent a whole for a historical consciousness and such consciousness will therefore always be limited. We will always understand historical events both from a wider perspective than our predecessors could possess and from a more narrow one than our heirs will acquire. By trying to avoid this conclusion while still rejecting Hegel, Ranke involves himself in a contradiction. Either, following Hegel, we assume knowledge of the end-point of history and hence attain a historical understanding that is not contingent upon our place in it. Or we deny knowledge of the end of history and therefore admit the inevitable partiality of our understanding. On Gadamer's view, to give up a Hegelian philosophy of history is also to concede that historical understanding will always reflect a specific historical horizon and that, for this reason, it will never be unconditioned or objective.

For Gadamer, Droysen's investigations into the foundations of historical understanding are important in as much as they avoid some of Ranke's naivety in this regard. Nevertheless the result is no less self-contradictory. The first significant aspect of Droysen's methodological reflections is his recognition that the historical meaning of an action or event goes beyond the agent's motives or intentions; indeed, Droysen criticizes a psychological interpretation of the meaning of events on the grounds that history never reflects the plans of human beings completely. As he writes: "Neither is what a person wants fully realized in a particular situation nor is what has developed the result of this person's strength of will or intelligence alone. It is neither the pure nor the complete expression of this personality."[31]

Gadamer makes a similar point in criticizing the account of historical understanding given by the English philosopher R. G. Collingwood.[32] On Collingwood's analysis historical understanding is a matter of discovering an agent's intentions by asking ourselves what problem he or she was trying to resolve with a given action.[33] For example, we figure out Nelson's intentions in the battle of Trafalgar by reconstructing the strategic problem he was trying to solve from his actions during the battle. Gadamer argues that this equation of action and intention presupposes that the battle proceeded in the precise way that Nelson planned and that, in general, the course of history conforms to its agent's intentions. But actions, as Droysen already suggested, often have unintended consequences, they react with the actions of others in unforeseen ways and are often the product of unpredictable events. To equate the meaning of an action with an agent's intentions is therefore simply to extrapolate a possible intention from the action, but the intention to which an action is thereby thought to correspond may not be anything like the intention the agent actually had. In Gadamer's words: "The interpreter of history always runs the risk of hypostatizing the context in which he recognizes a meaning as that meaning which acting and planning human beings really meant."[34]

A second significant aspect of Droysen's work for Gadamer is his emphasis on the degree to which historians are themselves subject to the historical situation in which they act or think; in his words, the individual in general belongs to the "moral forces" that rule history and is completely immersed in that which has already come to be, in the historical givenness of his people, his language, his religion, his state, of his register and system of signs . . . as well as in the givenness of all previously developed conceptions and interpretations that are the foundation of willing, acting and designing.[35]

Given this immersion in "ethical communities," there is no recourse to a theological solution to the problem of grounding the understanding of history. Historians cannot attain a omniscient perspective on history; their knowledge of it remains rather an "infinite task" in the sense that it is never complete. Such incompleteness, in fact, is the basis upon which Droysen distinguishes the historical from the natural sciences. Historians do not have the option of employing experiments to master their objects once and for all. "We simply investigate and can do nothing but investigate," according to Droysen.[36] The legitimacy of the historian's work therefore lies simply in the attempt to understand.[37]

Finally, Gadamer finds significant Droysen's recognition that the unity of history cannot be assumed as simply a fact about it. In his view, historical development rather reflects the attempt of human beings to give expression to "ethical ideas" that are only partially realized in the communities to which they belong. This attempt leads to the formation of new institutions and practices that themselves only partially represent "ethical ideas" and are therefore criticized anew. From this perspective, historical knowledge is a form of practical knowledge; it reflects not a disinterested, theoretical knowledge of objects but rather the active engagement of historical agents. To this extent, historical unity is the result of a process of "preservation" and "self-knowledge."[38]

In Gadamer's view, these aspects of Droysen's analysis indicate the superiority of his methodological reflections to those of Ranke. Droysen rather seems to presage Danto in locating historical meaning, not in the intentions of agents but in the retrospective consciousness of historically situated interpreters. Indeed, Droysen makes the additional point that historical understanding is not only historically situated but practically embedded in the projects of historical agents. We shall see that this is a significant point for Gadamer, one that in large part determines the importance Dilthey and Heidegger have for him. None the less, Droysen's own relation to his insights is somewhat ambivalent. In emphasizing the historical situatedness of understanding, its practical connection and the way in which historical meaning surpasses the intentions of historical agents Droysen seems to preclude a return to hermeneutic methods that rely on the hermeneutic circle of whole and part or on a divination of an agent's intentions. Still, Droysen's dependence on Schleiermacherian principles is apparent in his account of understanding and expression. Historical understanding in his view is the understanding of things "inner" by means of their outward expression and this involves the same emphasis on the creative act that we found in Schleiermacher's account of textual interpretation. As Droysen writes

> The possibility of understanding consists in the fact that the expressions that are present as historical material are original to us. . . . The sensuous spiritual nature of mankind manifests (*äussert*) every inner process to sensuous perception and in every outer expression (*Ausserung*) mirrors inner processes. In being perceived, the outer expression provokes the same inner processes by projecting itself into the inner of the perceiver.[39]

Here Gadamer argues that Droysen fails to hold fast to his own insights into the structure of historical understanding. Understanding consists in going behind an expression to re-experience the inner forces and motivations that provide the conditions of its genesis. In the end, history is to be studied as Schleiermacher studies a text, as the recreation and re-living of internal processes. Droysen therefore even returns to the notion of a communion with the authors or agents under study. On the one hand historians belong to ethical communities and these communities constitute the practical and historical embeddedness of their understanding of history. This embeddedness means that historians can only continue to investigate, that they never reach objective or unconditioned knowledge of their objects. On the other hand, precisely this participation in ethical communities forms the foundation upon which the historian's vision is able to transcend its historically determined finitude and re-attain the original context of an event or action. In this context, Droysen returns to a psychological version of the hermeneutic circle to overcome the temporal distance between historian and the object of study:

> The person who understands, because he is an "I," a totality in himself like the person whom he has to understand, completes this totality out of the individual expression and the individual expression out of the totality.[40]

From Gadamer's point of view, despite his recognition of the perspectival dimension of historical understanding and despite his critique of a historical intentionalism, Droysen thus ultimately continues the trend in hermeneutic theory begun by Schleiermacher. The focus of understanding is still the recreation of an original creation. When the creation in question is a historical expression, understanding it requires transcending the confines of the historian's perspective and re-experiencing the experience as it happened. The problem here, of course, is that if historical understanding is necessarily situated and if the meaning of an event therefore always goes beyond its agent's intentions, historical understanding cannot be described in these terms.

We can clarify this contradiction in Droysen's conception by looking at Danto's fictional account of an "Ideal Chronicler." Suppose there were a person or machine that knew everything that happened at the moment that it happened and could record it instantaneously. Such a Chronicler could not be wrong about what happened and therefore its account would not be subject to the revisions that ordinary historical accounts suffer by including false statements. Nevertheless, Danto argues, its account would remain incomplete. Given its absolute contemporaneity with the occurrence of events, the Ideal Chronicler would not be able to record in 1618 "the beginning of the Thirty Years War" nor in 1642, "the birth of the author of *Principia Mathematica* at Woolethorpe." But the Ideal Chronicler realizes just that sort of contemporaneous experience or re-experience that Droysen posits as the end of historical research. We have seen that historical understanding is retrospective in the sense that an understanding of subsequent events also determines the way in which prior events are grasped. Indeed, precisely this insight seemed to be the merit of both Droysen's rejection of an agent's intentions as the basis of attributions of historical meaning and his account of ethical communities. In calling for a "communion of souls," however, he seems to undercut this insight and to return to the Schleiermacherian notion of understanding as the recreation of an original creation. The problem here is that if historical meaning is contingent upon a historical horizon or perspective, then the historian cannnot seek to recreate the original course of an event without depriving it of the meaning it has from that historian's perspective. As Danto has put it: "We could only witness the past as 'it actually happened' if we somehow could forget just the sort of information which may have motivated us to make temporal journeys in reverse."[41]

It might be argued that Danto has overstated the case here. It may be that our historical understanding is historically situated so that we can never view historical actions as their agents did. But why should Schleiermacher's notion of recreating an original creation not still serve as

an ideal for historical investigations? Why should it not be at least a goal
of historical studies to understand how agents themselves saw the events
in which they were involved? This question is similar to the one I raised
with regard to Gadamer's criticism of Schleiermacher's literary hermeneutics. There the issue was the equation of understanding with a precise
specification of an author's intended meaning and I asked whether
Schleiermacher was not correct in assuming the necessity of understanding
an author's intentions before or in addition to understanding the validity
of his or her claims. With regard to Gadamer's and Danto's criticism of
equating an adequate understanding of the meaning of actions with a
comprehension of their agents' intentions, a similar question arises. In
this case, it could be argued that our *interest* in certain historical events is
motivated by a knowledge of their consequences, of which we and not
the agents themselves are aware. Nevertheless, as in literary interpretation, a *goal* of understanding may well be a discovery of the original
intentions behind the events.

An example used by another contemporary philosopher of history,
William Dray, to question positivistic accounts of historiography may
help to clarify this criticism.[42] Dray contrasts explanation in accordance
with laws with a "rational explanation" of "the reasonableness" of people
doing what they did given their beliefs and purposes. As an instance of
the latter he offers Trevelyan's explanation of why Louis XIV withdrew
pressure from Holland in 1688. According to Trevelyan Louis XIV
miscalculated what would happen if William of Orange invaded
England, thinking that it would leave him free to contend with Emperor
Leopold of Germany. This miscalculation, however, was one that Dray
thinks made sense or was rational "for a man in Louis's position with the
aims and beliefs he had."[43] Dray's point here is that an understanding of
the context of Louis XIV's decision lends insight into its rationality for
him. It thus reveals the limits of a positivistic approach to the study of
action, since the comprehensibility of the action depends not on a
knowledge of laws but rather on a contextual knowledge of the actor's
aims and beliefs. But the example also seems to exhibit the limits of
Danto's and Gadamer's account of historical understanding. One could
claim that our interest in Louis XIV's intention is aroused by our
knowledge of the consequences of his actions and thus by a retrospective
view. Still this view does not preclude taking it as a goal of our research
to reconstruct the situation as Louis XIV perceived it so that we
understand his own intentions in acting as he did.

The difficulty with this suggestion, however, becomes clear if one reexamines Gadamer's criticism of Collingwood. He suggests that it is not just our interest in an agent's intentions that is motivated by a knowledge of consequences, even our definition of these intentions is historically situated. Thus, just as we read Nelson's intentions off his actions during the battle of Trafalgar, we reconstruct Louis XIV's plan from the actions he took. But in order to equate an understanding of these actions with an understanding of his intentions we have to assume that he understood what he was doing at the time in exactly the same way as we understand it with hindsight. However, our understanding of the action represents a historically specific description of it and we must therefore select from the myriad intentions he may have had or expressed, emphasizing those that can be said to relate to the action as we understand it. Hence our understanding of his intentions is already interpretive. In identifying his original intention with our understanding of his action we risk just that hypostatization of intentions against which Gadamer warns. To claim that such a hypostatization is justified in at least this and similar cases is not to avoid the problem. We can perhaps reconstruct an intention Louis XIV had in the various different actions that he took; but there may be different ways of describing what he meant and how he meant it, just as there may be different ways of describing what he succeeded in doing. Even here, therefore, where we are interested in recreating an original intention, our very definition of the intention is contingent upon the way in which we understand subsequent events. The description of Louis XIV's intention as that of withdrawing pressure from Holland is already a description that depends on a certain historical point of view.

Gadamer's criticism of a historical intentionalism, then, is *not* that an agent's intentions ought not to be a subject of interest to the historian. His point is *rather* that we remain historically situated even where we are concerned with an agent's intentions, and our description of those intentions will therefore represent no more than one perspective on them. In imposing hermeneutic principles upon the study of history Ranke and Droysen ultimately ignore this implication of the historian's own immersion in history. Dilthey's merit for Gadamer lies in his partial acknowledgement of its importance. None the less, he finds the tension between a hermeneutic and a properly historical approach to historical understanding at its most intense in Dilthey's attempt to uncover the logic of the *Geisteswissenschaften*.

Hermeneutics and the Geisteswissenschaften

I noted earlier that Dilthey turned to hermeneutic theory to secure a basis upon which to distinguish the *Geisteswissenschaften* or human sciences from the natural sciences. His merit for Gadamer is that unlike the neo-Kantians, for instance, he recognized that this difference is a difference in modes of experience rather than objects of experience alone. In this recognition he approached an adequate understanding of history, according to Gadamer, but undermined his own insights in supposing that the legitimacy of the *Geisteswissenschaften* requires their methodological foundation. Gadamer describes the tension in Dilthey's work as one between life-philosophy (*Lebensphilosophie*) and Cartesian objectivism. In order to elucidate his position I shall first discuss the all-important concept of experience.

Since Husserl's work, at least, it has become usual to distinguish between two senses of experience differentiated in German by the terms *Erlebnis*, or lived experience, and *Erfahrung*, or scientific experience. We shall see that the first of these *Erlebnis*, and its verb form *erleben*, are already crucial for Dilthey's account of the foundations of the *Geisteswissenschaften*. (He credits Husserl with new insights in this regard.[44]) Gadamer further distinguishes between two senses of *Erfahrung* itself: the scientific sense, emphasizing the way in which experiences or experiments confirm one another, and a dialectical or historical sense that emphasizes negativity. The concept of experience established in the natural sciences focuses on the repeatability of procedures and results, on the confirmation that one experience is able to give to another. The concept of *Erfahrung* that interests Gadamer, however, is articulated by the notion of a "learning" experience, an experience that in a sense cannot be repeated and serves to negate our previous views. Indeed, what we learn through experience in ·this sense involves such a radical transformation of our views that we cannot go back to them to re-experience the experience of their negation. What we experience is the error or partiality of our previous views and we experience this in such a way that we are now too experienced or sophisticated to re-live the experience of believing in them. Gadamer calls this process a "reversal in consciousness" following Hegel's account of the dialectic in *The Phenomenology of Spirit*;[45] experience leads to the recognition that that which one previously took as the "truth" of the object under study (the "in itself") is precisely that: simply that which one took as its "truth" (the "in itself for us") and not its truth at all.[46]

This is the kind of experience that Gadamer thinks is embodied in historical understanding[47] and we can now redescribe the problem he identifies in the historical conceptions of Ranke and Droysen as follows: Against Hegel, they perceive a connection betweeen experience and understanding and therefore demand that history become an empirical as opposed to a speculative science. But if history is to be empirical or experiential, this means for them that it must conform to a natural scientific model. An empirical understanding is therefore one that repeats and confirms an original experience; empirically correct research results are those that other researchers, whatever their place in history can also repeat and confirm. This is the context in which Schleiermacher's hermeneutic principles are applied; first they provide for the reproduction of an original production and hence allow for empirical confirmation in the course of events themselves; second in so doing they offer a form of knowledge that can be confirmed by others and hence grant to historical understanding its scientific legitimacy.

As we saw, Gadamer criticized this application of hermeneutics to history for its failure to recognize the historicity of historical understanding; we can now see that it overlooks a crucial moment of experience itself. The point is that historical experience changes the meaning historical events can have for us. Such experience is dialectical in Hegel's sense in that both the object and our knowledge of it are transformed. Historical experience does not confirm the understanding of World War I as the Great War or the war to end all wars, to return to a previous example; with the experience of World War II, the understanding and therefore the meaning of World War I is rather itself transformed. To posit a recreation of the original experience of World War I as the goal of "objective" historical studies is thus to ignore the knowledge accrued in historical experience and to equate all experience with the repetitious experience central to the natural sciences.

In calling for a return to Kant after the breakdown of the Hegelian system, neo-Kantians followed the Historical School in overlooking the importance of this dialectical moment of experience. As already mentioned, Gadamer locates Dilthey's superiority to the neo-Kantians precisely in his recognition of the different concept of experience to which the *Geisteswissenschaften* refer: "For what supports the construction of the historical world are not facts taken out of experience that then enter into a value-relation. Its basis is rather the inner historicity that experience itself owns."[48] Gadamer, then, credits Dilthey with an insight into a form of *Erfahrung* obscured by the natural scientific emphasis on the repeatability of experimental results. The empirical character of the human sciences does not depend upon the repeatability of experience; rather such sciences are already implicated in the learning experiences of history. Historians cannot undergo or repeat the experiences of those they investigate because they have already inherited the knowledge the others acquired; they are in the position of "being experienced," of having greater historical sophistication than those that they study precisely because of the experiences the latter have had. It is for this reason, according to Gadamer, that Dilthey grounds the *Geisteswissenschaften* in life: "They only think further what is already thought in life experience."[49]

This is the point at which the concept of *Erlebnis* becomes important for Dilthey, and Gadamer stresses two uses he makes of it. In the first *Erlebnis* refers to what is directly given to individual consciousness and thus has a cognitive function. In this regard Dilthey distinguishes between *Erlebnisse* and the "constructions" of the natural sciences. The latter impose mathematical categories and physical laws on the natural world in order to form an objective account of it that is freed from "subjective-relative" conditions. In contrast, an *Erlebnis* reflects a "subjective" response to the world in which it is experienced as pleasurable or not, as having certain intuitively clear spatial and temporal relations and the like. *Erlebnisse* thus differ from the abstractions of natural science in presenting objects in their intuitive immediacy, as that which is "given" to consciousness and which therefore no longer contains anything "alien, objective or needful of clarification."[50] In this sense the concept serves as a critique of the "cold rationalism of the Enlightenment."[51] *Erlebnis* is supposed to signify the wholeness and intensity of human experiences against scientific abstraction; what is experienced in this sense contains the entire wealth of feelings and emotions that make an experience peculiarly one's own.

In the second place *Erlebnisse* for Dilthey are those experiences around which an individual life organizes itself, the crucial experiences that orient a person's self-conception and hence life-conduct. An *Erlebnis* in this sense is expressed in English in terms of "having an experience," in terms of going through a trauma or adventure that is, on the one hand, totally separate from the normal course of one's life and, on the other, peculiarly suited to revealing or changing the meaning of one's life as a whole. In this case, *Erlebnisse* form the center around which the meaning of a particular life-history unfolds and therefore constitute the basis upon which Dilthey applies the hermeneutic circle to life itself. On the one hand one conceives of one's experiences in the terms made available by the way in which one understands one's life as a whole — as experiences of obstacles or aids to the goals one has set, as experiences of support or rejection and so on. On the other hand the way in which one understands one's life as a whole is itself an interpretation of the various experiences one has had. Indeed, the way in which one anticipates the future depends upon the way in which one has understood experiences in one's past, just as the experiences one has reorient one's understanding of that past. Thus the understanding one has of one's life is constituted by certain central experiences that themselves gain and change their importance in consonance with the way in which one's life progresses and is understood. As Dilthey puts it,

> both, past and future, are related to experience in a series that forms itself into a whole through such relations. Every past, since its memory includes re-recognition, is structurally related as copy to a one-time experience. Future possibility is bound to the series by the circle of possibilities determined by the series . . . In this life course every single experience is related to a whole. This life-connection is not a sum or a collection of moments succeeding one another, but a unity constituted through relations that connect all the parts.[52]

This use of the concept of *Erlebnis* is compatible with the Hegelian sense of *Erfahrung* as a learning experience.[53] In Dilthey's conception understanding and experience spiral around one another: new experiences revise the way in which the past is understood and the future anticipated; at the same time, those experiences are interpreted in the context of an understanding of past and future. Gadamer thinks that this kind of "life-philosophy" is significant in so far as it locates self-understanding within the temporal structure of an individual life. On this analysis self-understanding is never complete but moves within a circle of experience, interpretation and revision. There can therefore be no "objective" self-understanding free from the "life-relations" (*Lebensbezüge*) in which one finds oneself. One cannot leap out of one's situation to gain impartial access to one's past. Self-understanding is rather related to the conduct of one's life and has an ineradicable practical dimension. The way in which one lives one's life and the way in which one understands it are mutually determining. This relationship is not a qualification on the self-knowledge an individual can acquire but rather its only possible definition.

According to Gadamer, the problem that ultimately led Dilthey away from this life-philosophy arose from his attempt to transfer this conception of self-knowledge from an individual life to the history of the species. The problem of historical knowledge is that of understanding not one's own experiences but the experiences of another person, another group or even a different culture. These experiences do not have the same relation to the conduct of one's own life and hence do not seem to involve the practical dimension that Dilthey suggests in that regard. As Gadamer puts it, "The problem of history is not how connection in general is experienceable (*erlebbar*) but how even such connections are supposed to be knowable that no one has experienced (*erlebt*) as such."[54] We have seen that the uses Dilthey makes of the concept of *Erlebnis* connect it to an on-going, always revisable but immediate and direct self-understanding and this is also the self-understanding that the *Geisteswissenschaften* are supposed to "think further." In what sense, however, are historical and social scientific understanding similar to the self-understanding of the individual? How are experience and understanding related when the experience and understanding do not belong to the same person and therefore do not have the foundational immediacy that Dilthey emphasizes? In short, how is the historical sophistication acquired through experience by one group transferred to another?

Gadamer suggests that Dilthey's attempts to answer this question brought him closer and closer to Hegel,[55] pointing out that in his later works Dilthey speaks of "*Geist*" or spirit in contexts where he earlier referred to "life." The concept of spirit resolves the problem of the distance between self-understanding and the experiences that are the object of social and historical knowledge by making these experiences the experiences of an over-arching consciousness or subject. Thus, Dilthey employs Hegel's concept of objective spirit to refer to the intersubjective, normative and institutional context in which individuals live their lives. An individual's life-history is now conceived of as taking place not only within the vertical dimension of the individual subject's life but within a horizontal dimension as well, incorporating the individual's social and cultural environment. Individuals, Dilthey explains, are involved with others in common practices; they partake of certain common assumptions and cultural modes of self-understanding; they understand and are understood by others. To this extent, the self-interpretations of individuals already reflect the experiences and self-interpretations of a larger common domain.

The individual experiences, lives and acts constantly in a common sphere and only within such does he understand. In the same way, everything that is understood bears within itself the mark of being familiar in terms of this common sphere. We live in this atmosphere; it surrounds us constantly. We are immersed in it. We are everywhere at home in the historical and understood world, we understand the meaning and significance of everything. We are ourselves intertwined in these communalities.[56]

Dilthey criticizes Hegel for transcending the historical forms of objective spirit and positing a suprahistorical knowledge in the forms of absolute spirit: art, religion and philosophy. Dilthey insists that all knowledge remains historical knowledge, grounded in "life," and that art, religion and philosophy are themselves simply expressions of life. Nevertheless, Gadamer insists that this criticism of Hegel should not be taken for more than it is. Dilthey's emphasis on historical knowledge is not to be taken as an objection to the notion of an absolute or unconditioned knowledge but is instead supposed itself to be absolute knowledge. In making this claim, Gadamer argues, Dilthey goes beyond the limits of life-philosophy and gives his grounding of the *Geisteswissenschaften* an objectivistic twist. Despite his analysis of the connection between experience and understanding Dilthey ultimately attempts to supersede the insights of experience and base the validity of historical knowledge on Cartesian foundations.

In essence Gadamer thinks that Dilthey is misled here by a fear of the relativistic implications of his own life-philosophy. At first Dilthey seems to found the legitimacy of historical understanding on what Gadamer sees as the knowledge immanent to experience. Knowledge of history is acquired in the same way as is self-knowledge – painfully, in a sense, or at least through experience and reflection upon it. In order to show the possibility of moving from the experiences of individuals to those of the species, Dilthey appeals to Hegel's notion of objective spirit, to the possibility of a common experience and species-wide possibilities of learning from it. Dilthey rejects Hegel's subsequent move from objective to absolute spirit, however, for historical consciousness is itself supposed to be capable of unconditioned certainty. But at this point the very relationship between experience and understanding in life that was meant to ground the *Geisteswissenschaften* seems adversely to affect their objectivity!

The immediate relation in which life and the *Geisteswissenschaften* stand to

one another leads in the *Geisteswissenschaften* to a conflict between the
tendencies of life and their scientific goal. Since historians, national
economists, jurists and sociologists of religion stand in life they want to
influence it. They subjugate historical persons, mass movements,
tendencies to their judgment, and this is conditioned by their individuality, the nation to which they belong, the time in which they live . . . At
the same time, however, in every science as such the claim to general
validity is contained. If there are to be *Geisteswissenschaften* in the strict
scientific sense they must set this goal in a more and more conscious and
critical way.[57]

On the one hand, then, Dilthey considers life the "fresh, fluid spring
of understanding"[58] while on the other he thinks that the objectivity of
understanding must be secured against life. On Gadamer's view, he
thereby neglects his own insight into the historicity or temporality
of experience and returns to the principles of traditional hermeneutics.
In the end, Dilthey follows the Historical School in conceiving
of the "social-historical world" as a text and the aim of understanding
as a "reproduction of an original production." He thus recurs to
Schleiermacher's conception of divination and empathy:

> Understanding is an inverse operation to the effective course of action. A
> perfect co-living is tied to understanding's continuing along the line of the
> occurrence itself. It moves forward, constantly progressing, with the course
> of life itself. In this way, the process of putting oneself in the situation
> (*Sichhineinversetzen*), of transposition broadens itself. Re-experiencing is
> creation along the line of the occurrence. Thus, we go forward with the
> history of time, with an event in a distant land or with something that
> happens in the soul of someone close to us.[59]

As Gadamer sees it, Dilthey's recourse to a theory of empathetic
identification stems from a failure to distinguish between two different
kinds of doubt: the doubt that arises in the course of life and a
methodologically sanctioned doubt. In life itself certain experiences can
cast doubt upon one's conceptions, prejudices and self-understanding.
Such doubts can lead to further reflection, revision in one's interpretation
of one's life or one's projects and then to further experiences and
revisions. This kind of doubt is thus part of the connection between
experience and understanding and part of the retrospective re-evaluation
of the meaning of one's life. In contrast, the methodological decision to
doubt all of one's experiences in advance — the strategy of Cartesian

doubt – does not have its roots in life but is rather directed "against life."[60] Gadamer suggests that such doubt is overly intellectual; it does not arise in response to the interpretive conflicts embedded in actual experiences but tries to resolve all conflict in advance. In this case, the goal is to achieve not a better understanding of oneself or the history of one's culture, but rather a definitive understanding, an understanding secured against the need for future revisions. The knowledge attained through this kind of doubt is thus to have nothing situational, contextual or partial left in it. In this regard, Gadamer thinks that Dilthey remains influenced by the same positivistic philosophy of science he criticizes and falls into the same trap that vitiated the insights of both Ranke and Droysen. Dilthey faulted Kant for ignoring the historicity of "reason"; yet ultimately he also assumes the possibility of transcending the historical situation to which one belongs to attain a purely objective, unconditioned knowledge of one's own life and the experiences of others. As Gadamer writes:

> For Dilthey, the consciousness of finitude did not mean that consciousness was made finite or limited in any way. It rather bears witness to the capacity of life to rise above all limitations in energy and activity. To this extent, it is precisely the potential infinity of spirit that is represented in it.[61]

Despite textual evidence for Gadamer's portrayal of a tension between life-philosophy and objectivism in Dilthey's hermeneutics, it is not clear that he has taken Dilthey's fear of relativism seriously enough.[62] For Gadamer, the historicity and practical embeddedness of social and historical understanding that Dilthey feared is rather to be seen as its essence. At this point, the question arises, however, as to whether the Cartesian doubt to which Dilthey recurs is not at least partially justified. For if experience and understanding are connected in life in the way that Dilthey describes, why assume that understanding is a form of knowledge at all? Can experience never be misleading? In any case, how does one know when one has appropriated legitimate lessons from one's experience or interpreted it correctly? Similar questions seem to arise in connection with historical or social scientific reflection: How can we be sure that our understanding of our history as a species is not fundamentally distorted? Are the historical and practical commitments of historians and social scientists not a problem for the reliability of their research results as Dilthey assumes? We are familiar enough with self-delusions in individuals' conceptions of themselves and part of the justification for positivistic forms of social science has always been the unreliability of a community's or group's description of itself. In both areas it has been considered necessary to go beyond agents' self-interpretations in order to grasp what they are actually doing in contrast to what they may think they are doing. To this extent Dilthey's attempt to extricate the *Geisteswissenschaften* from the basis in life on which he originally founds them seems justified, if in the end self-contradictory. His problem is that viewing the human sciences as a continuation or refinement of the self-understanding developed in experience leaves them prey to the same self-deceptions to which ordinary life is subject. Gadamer does not seem to think this situation is as problematic as Dilthey does, but the question is why not? Why does Gadamer find not only Dilthey's solution to the problem of practical life-commitments (in empathetic transposition) but the problem itself misguided? The question is whether the reflection that evolves out of history and experience is enough or whether some methodological assurance of its reliability is required. This is a question that a number of critics have raised against Gadamer's hermeneutics and we shall return to it later.

THE PHENOMENOLOGICAL TURN

We have seen that for Gadamer the deficiencies of Romantic hermeneutics derive from its attempt to use the principles of textual interpretation to ground social and historical studies. The difficulty here is that, as Schleiermacher elucidates them, these principles are too radically ahistorical to comprehend the historicity of understanding in the human sciences. Understanding in these sciences is connected to experience and thus has an inevitably temporal dimension; it is tied to the practical and historical horizon of interpreters and thus never attains finality. This point is one that Max Weber makes as well:

> The stream of immeasurable events flows unendingly towards eternity. The cultural problems which move men form themselves ever anew and in different colors, and the boundaries of that area in the infinite stream of concrete events which acquires meaning and significance for us . . . are constantly changing. . . . The points of departure of the cultural sciences remain changeable through the limitless future as long as a Chinese ossification of intellectual life does not render mankind incapable of setting new questions to the eternally inexhaustible flow of life.[63]

Of course, like Dilthey, Weber was interested in "objective" social science. For this reason Gadamer thinks that recognition of the significance of the historicity to which both Dilthey and Weber point is to be found not in their own work but in that of Martin Heidegger. In this regard, however, Husserl's phenomenology serves as an important point of transition. On Gadamer's view, it overcomes the latent positivism he is concerned to show in Dilthey's analysis of the logic of the *Geisteswissenschaften* and thereby leads into Heidegger's own investigations.

Gadamer points out that Dilthey's use of the concept of *Erlebnis* in his later work borrows from Husserl's distinction between *Erlebnis* and *Erfahrung*. For both *Erlebnisse* signal that which is immediately given to consciousness as a meaningful unity. To this extent the concept involves a criticism of an atomistic psychology according to which the consciousness of objects is built up out of more primary sense data or impressions. Dilthey and Husserl maintain, to the contrary, that primary experience is already structured or coherent, that what is present to consciousness are the "things themselves" in their "subjective modes of givenness," to use Husserl's language. We saw that Dilthey employed this notion of immediacy to consciousness to distinguish the *Geisteswissenschaften* from the natural sciences; the latter are directed "outward" toward the physical world and the "constructions" necessary to master its laws while the former are directed "inward" toward experience itself. None the less, Dilthey was concerned to show the equal validity of both orientations as forms of science. Husserl goes beyond Dilthey in this regard in using the concept of *Erlebnis* not to posit two equal forms of science but to trace the natural sciences back to the "life-world" from which they evolve. The "objective sciences" have their own basis in subjective modes of givenness and arise as projects of specific communities. In other words, the mathematical idealization of nature that Dilthey sees as a form of science correlative to the study of human experience rather remains dependent on human experience and serves merely as a means for facilitating the projects that emerge out of it. Thus, whereas Dilthey conceives of his task as the founding of a new form of objective science, Husserl attempts to illuminate the conditions of the possibility of objective science itself.

This is the point at which Husserl's conception of the life-world becomes important. The life-world is the horizon of subjective modes of givenness upon which the objectified world of the natural sciences is erected. It is the sensuous basis for the idealizations the objective sciences require and the ground of the interests and purposes that orient research in them. The objective sciences are thus conceived of as projects that arise from within the life-world, as forms of knowledge that reflect the concerns of specific communities and serve their needs. As Husserl writes with regard to all such projects:

> The life-world, for us who wakingly live in it, is always already there, existing in advance for us, the ground of all praxis whether theoretical or extratheoretical. The world is pregiven to us, the waking, somehow practically interested subjects, not occasionally but always and necessarily as the universal field of all actual and possible praxis, as horizon.[64]

In Gadamer's view, Husserl here articulates a fundamental insight into the historically and culturally situated character of all scientific efforts. As we have seen this insight is one that Ranke, Droysen and Dilthey all approached but undermined in their attempts to show the possible objectivity of social and historical knowledge. Thus, Ranke referred to the knowledge of God, and Droysen ultimately employed an ahistorical notion of communion with the objects of study, while Dilthey appealed to ahistorical conceptions of empathy and re-experience. In contrast, Husserl grounds the notion of scientific objectivity itself in the "fluid springs" of life that Dilthey acknowledged and then ignored. From this point of view the concept of scientific objectivity turns out to be itself a historical one; it is not a transcendent idea to which all forms of knowledge must adhere, but rather a standard suited to certain kinds of knowledge with certain purposes and goals.

In Husserl's later work, then, the objective sciences are seen to spring from the life-world; they are conceived of as forms of knowledge that participate in the concerns and views of specific communities and serve as one means of accomplishing their goals. But Husserl's critique of objectivism does not go far enough for Gadamer; having discovered the life-world Husserl then conceives of it as a problem for phenomenology. Phenomenology itself claims to be a *science* of the ways in which objects are given to consciousness – to be sure, not an "objective" science on the model of the natural sciences but, as Husserl always emphasizes, a "rigorous" science, none the less. In exploring modes of givenness, this science is to provide a map of the certain, intuitive knowledge of "essences" from which the objective sciences abstract. But Husserl remarks that in uncovering the abstraction upon which the objective sciences depend and in thereby revealing the life-world, phenomenology seems not to offer as much a map of "essences" as historical communities with all the variations in intuition that such communities possess. In other words, there is not one life-world but many. Thus, we seem to be able to arrive at "secure" facts only "within a certain range . . . in our experience and in the social group united with us in the community of life." The dilemma, then, is that either we focus on life-worlds, in which case we have to admit that "truths" that are fixed for "Negroes in the Congo, Chinese peasants etc." are by no means fixed for us; or we focus on "truths" that are "unconditionally valid" for all individuals, namely "spatial shape, motion, sense-quality and the like" and then "we are on our way to objective science." In short, Husserl concludes, "we have the embarrassment of wondering what else can be undertaken scientifically as something that can be established once and for all and for everyone."[65]

Husserl's solution to this dilemma is to see the different life-worlds as themselves varieties of a more basic universal structure. Phenomenological research is to penetrate below the different cultural life-worlds to an *eidos* "life-world" which is the product of an original, non-historical constitution of meaning, the product, to put it another way, of "transcendental subjectivity." In this solution, however, Gadamer finds a renewed tension between the claim of phenomenology to be a rigorous science and the recognition of the situational knowledge appropriate to Husserl's own insight into the life-world. Just as Dilthey calls for the emancipation of social-historical inquiry from the practical concerns of the social-historical world, Husserl appeals to the notion of transcendental subjectivity to surmount the variety of culturally and historically determined life-worlds. Our own experienced life-world turns out not to form the final ground of scientific objectivity but must itself be grounded in a non-relative, non-historical source, hence, in the constitutive activity of a transcendental ego. In Gadamer's view both strategies involve an "alienation" of "the actual content of the concept of life"[66] and it is therefore necessary to look beyond both to Heidegger's forceful conception of "being-in-the-world."

The importance of Heidegger's philosophy for Gadamer begins with its insistence on historicity, on a situatedness or "thrownness" in the world that cannot be overcome through scientific method or further reduced to a transcendental basis. In considering "being-in-the-world" fundamental, Heidegger places historicity at the foundation of the objective sciences and thus preserves the step that Husserl took beyond Dilthey. Scientific objectivity is no longer regarded as the measure of legitimate knowledge in general but as a methodological standard appropriate to certain projects within the life-world. At the same time, Heidegger suspends the search for ultimate cognitive foundations below the life-world and thus replaces Husserl's transcendental ego with being-in-the-world. But the significance of Heidegger's work for Gadamer goes beyond the move from transcendental subjectivity to being-in-the-world. In Heidegger's work, the hermeneutic account of understanding is itself transformed. The question of being that he raises in *Being and Time*[67] no longer refers to the question of how the objective world is constituted in consciousness, as it still does for Husserl; the focus is rather on the question of what human being is or, rather, how human life is itself a process and product of interpretation: "In *Being and Time* the real question was already not how being can be understood, but how understanding is being."[68] In order to bring out the difference this change in focus makes I shall briefly sketch aspects of Heidegger's account of understanding (*Verstehen*) that are relevant to the point.

In exhuming the so-called "question of being" Heidegger focuses on the being whose "being is an issue for it,"[69] in other words, on human beings and their understanding of their lives. The distinctive feature of *Dasein* or human life for Heidegger is that to which Dilthey already alluded, that in living human beings relate themselves interpretively to their lives, that they understand themselves in a continuous process of self-interpretation, experience and re-interpretation. For Heidegger, this circle of interpretation indicates that "being itself is time,"[70] as Gadamer puts it. The meaning of this claim is two-fold. In the first place, the way in which a human life understands itself is conditioned by time. The "being" that is an "issue" is not simply an entity like others to which various predicates can be attached but a life that exists as a temporal continuum. As we have seen, the past acquires its meaning in light of present experiences and anticipations while the meaning of the present and anticipation of the future are conditioned by the way in which the past has been understood. Heidegger therefore considers self-understanding to be "thrown projection." On the one hand, it involves projecting a future for oneself or projecting one's possibilities. On the other hand, these possiblities have already been determined to some extent by the way the future has already been projected in the past. One is "thrown" for Heidegger in the sense that one's self-understanding is never free in a Sartrian sense, one never has the possibility of doing anything at all. On the contrary, one's possibilities are already circumscribed by possibilities already abandoned or fulfilled, by the way one has projected oneself in the past.

This conception of understanding as "thrown projection" is crucial to Gadamer's own account of understanding in the human sciences since it gives Vico's statement that we understand history in so far as we are historical a new meaning. Dilthey referred to this claim in justifying his own return to Hegel: the scientific legitimacy of historical understanding is ultimately based on the possibility of re-experiencing the experiences of others, with whom one shares an essential "communality" within objective spirit. Dilthey writes: "The first condition of the possibility of the historical sciences lies in the fact that I am myself a historical being, that he who investigates history is the same as he who makes it."[71] We have seen that in Gadamer's view Dilthey's account of re-experience undermines his own insight into the structure of historical experience and Gadamer therefore reinterprets Vico's formula.[72] To claim that we can understand history because we are ourselves historical beings means now not that both we and the objects we study are located in a history common to us both; it means rather that we determine our history from a position within it. The way in which we anticipate the future defines the meaning the past can have for us, just as the way in which we have understood the past and the way in which our ancestors have projected the future determines our own range of possibilities. Thus, for Gadamer, Vico's formula entails that we understand history not simply because we make it but also because it has made us; we belong to it in the sense that we inherit its experience, project a future on the basis of the situation the past has created for us and act in light of our understanding of this past whether such understanding is explicit or not.

We shall return to Gadamer's use of the notion of "thrown projection" in examining his own philosophy. In his critique of the hermeneutic tradition, however, a second aspect of the claim that "being itself is time" is also significant. Heidegger's argument here is that self-interpretation is not merely conditioned by time, but required by it. His point is not simply that human beings interpret their lives and do so within a circle of anticipation and revision imposed by the temporal structure of life itself. His claim is that they *must* so interpret themselves, that they must live their lives in certain ways, determine some future and therewith the meaning of their past. As Heidegger states, human life always has the character of "mineness" (*Jemeinigkeit*): "its essence lies . . . in the fact that in each case it has its being to be and has it as its own."[73] In other words, human beings understand themselves in some way or other in simply living their lives, in acting out some future and in having acted in the past in one way or another. Understanding refers primarily to the necessary, practical relation one has to one's own life and is therefore nothing extraneous to, or optional for, human life at all. As Gadamer puts this point: "Prior to all differentiation of understanding in the different directions of pragmatic or theoretical interest, understanding is *Dasein*'s mode of being in so far as it is potentiality-for-being and possibility."[74]

Viewed from this perspective, understanding is not primarily a scientific understanding of entities but rather a practical understanding of one's life and possibilities. Heidegger finally succeeds in seeing the importance of the practical embeddedness of understanding to which Droysen initially pointed. Indeed, when Heidegger turns to an explicit analysis of understanding in *Being and Time* he defines it as "the existential being of *Dasein*'s own potentiality-for-being."[75] In fact, he insists that entities other than *Dasein* are understood in light of their relationship to *Dasein*, as equipment or "the ready-to-hand." Moreover, the "present-at-hand" or things understood scientifically, in their physical or chemical structure for instance, reflects a derivative form of understanding that involves abstracting from the ready-to-hand. Gadamer claims that historical understanding is an understanding of this primary sort as well; it is not a scientific understanding of the present-at-hand, not an objective understanding abstracted from the historical situation of understanding; rather it reflects an understanding of the ready-to-hand related to a practical and continuing understanding of oneself and the present.

Heidegger's importance for Gadamer is that, like Dilthey, he starts from the structure of self-understanding, from a practical self-relation and the question of how one understands oneself. Unlike Dilthey, however, he does not enter into the question of the possible objectivity of such understanding but rather looks at what it is. In Gadamer's view, this examination "bursts apart the whole subjectivism of modern philosophy."[76] For, although Heidegger begins with the question of the "being" of a specifically human self-understanding, his answer is that this being is time. All understanding is related to self-understanding and self-understanding is thrown projection; this means that it begins and ends outside the subject — in a past it did not create and a future over which it has no control.

The consequence of this position for the structure of historical understanding is to show that such understanding is itself inextricably historical. This means that it cannot transcend its historical situation, that the knowledge to which it attains is always partial and revisable and, most importantly, that this circumstance is not to be seen as a limitation on its objectivity. The notion of "objective" understanding is rather itself an illegitimate importation from the natural sciences via Schleiermacherian hermeneutics. On Gadamer's view an adequate account of the principle of understanding requires a break, then, with both the natural sciences and with the history of modern hermeneutics itself. If this hermeneutics is characterized by the turn from the truth-content of a claim to the intentions behind it and thus from the question of validity to the question of method, the turn must be reversed.

2

Hermeneutics and authorial intention

Chapter 1 raised at least two questions that have not yet been answered. Historical understanding is situated in history and, in Gadamer's view, this means that it cannot be conceived of as an objective knowledge of an agent's intentions. In the first place the meaning of actions and events always goes beyond those intentions. Actions have unintended consequences, and even where no such unintended consequences occur immediately historical actions always become part of a nexus of events and reactions that go beyond the possible intentions or motivations of their agents. In the second place historians are also themselves part of history. They may be both more sophisticated than the subjects they study, in so far as they inherit the historical experience of these subjects, and more parochial than their own descendants who may be able to put events within a larger perspective. Because historical understanding is both historically and practically embedded it is always perspectival, involving an understanding of events and actions in light of their relations to those subsequent events and actions in which, at any point in history, historians take an interest.

The two questions I raised in regard to this analysis were, first, how it applies to textual understanding and, second, whether it does not lead to the kind of practically motivated misinterpretation of history that Dilthey feared. I shall explore the second question more fully in chapter 3. This chapter will focus on Gadamer's answer to the first question: namely, whether textual understanding is perspectival in the way that history is. We have seen that there are good grounds for arguing that historical meaning supersedes an agent's intentions – that, for example, our understanding of World War I goes beyond the self-understanding of those involved in it such that our account of the meaning of World War I will change with the start of World War II. But how does this account of understanding apply to texts? Why should our understanding of a text change because of our historical experience? Why should it be contingent on our place in history or our practical concerns at all? Is it not possible with regard to textual understanding at least to identify an understanding of meaning with an understanding of intentions? Are texts not creative products in Schleiermacher's sense and does understanding them not therefore amount to recreating the creative process that engendered them? If a text is not to be understood in light of its author's intentions then how is it to be understood?

These questions are similar to those E. D. Hirsch has raised in his attempt to defend a Schleiermacherian notion of textual understanding. In this chapter I shall therefore look briefly at his work in order to illuminate Gadamer's contrasting position. Of course, the Schleiermacherian equation of textual understanding with an understanding of an author's original intentions has been under attack for many years from such different perspectives as the New Criticism, reader-response theory and deconstruction. Gadamer's hermeneutics agrees with these alternative perspectives in some respects and differs in others.[1] My aim in this chapter, however, is not to display similarities and differences in recent developments in literary theory but rather to examine the cogency of Gadamer's own view. Hence, I shall take up only one aspect of Hirsch's argument which is particularly instructive for assessing Gadamer's analysis and I shall then turn to Gadamer's account of textual understanding and aesthetic experience in general. In so doing, I shall also specify more concretely what Gadamer means in opposing the understanding of truth to that of intentions.

HIRSCH'S INTENTIONALISM

Many critics have pointed to the ambiguity in Hirsch's identification of textual meaning with an author's intentions: while Hirsch directs his argument against the anti-intentionalism he associates with the New Criticism, he also seems to agree with the New Criticism in rejecting an overtly psychologistic conception of intentional meaning.[2] In equating textual meaning with an author's intention, Hirsch does not follow Schleiermacher in identifying that meaning with the mental acts and experiences that occurred in the author's mind at the time the text was written. He rather appeals to the phenomenological concept of "intentionality" to formulate a notion of a "verbal meaning" that is the self-identical object of various mental acts. Verbal meaning, in other words, is the meaning the author intends through certain mental acts, not those acts themselves. But Hirsch does not think that authors can intend whatever they like with their intentional acts; they are, rather, constrained in what their words can mean by the linguistic conventions of their culture. His preliminary definition of verbal meaning is thus "whatever someone has willed to convey by a particular sequence of linguistic signs and which can be conveyed by means of those linguistic signs."[3]

This preliminary definition of verbal meaning needs to be further clarified to deal with meanings of which an author may not have been consciously aware but that are still part of a correct interpretation of his or her intention. Hence, after discussing the notion of type Hirsch makes the following claim: an author's meaning can include more than that of which the author is explicitly aware because the author's intended meaning specifies a certain type of thing as opposed to a particular mental content. Thus, for example, if I say "Nothing pleases me so much as the Third Symphony of Beethoven," I mean that nothing of a certain type or nothing aesthetic pleases me as much. I exclude such pleasures as swimming but also include certain aesthetic pleasures that I am not consciously considering such as a viewing of Brueghel's *Hay Gathering*.[4] Verbal meaning is therefore a "willed type" that both prevents interpreters from reading into a text or statement any meaning they desire but also may encompass more than that upon which the author has directly focused.

This definition of verbal meaning has been criticized for many reasons. Although Hirsch's use of phenomenology distinguishes his account of meaning from a psychologistic conception, in delineating the consequences of his account for literary criticism, Hirsch often seems to vacillate between the two.[5] Moreover, since he also distinguishes between the "subjectivity of the author" and the "speaking subject" and claims that only the latter is relevant to textual meaning, it is unclear how far he differs from the New Critics he attacks.[6] None the less, the peculiarity in Hirsch's analysis of verbal meaning that concerns us involves his conception of its "shareability." We have seen that Hirsch no longer defines meaning as a private act but claims rather that it is embodied in language and limited by linguistic conventions. Verbal meaning is therefore accessible to other speaking subjects and can be shared by them. Hirsch argues further, however, that if verbal meaning is to be shareable it must be "determinate"; that is, it must be self-

identical and unchanging otherwise it would be impossible for other
subjects to reproduce for themselves the meaning an author intends.
Hence, if I say "close the door," on Hirsch's view, I can communicate
this order only because "door" has a single, public meaning that the
people I am addressing can recreate for themselves through their own
intentional acts.

This is an odd conception of the shareability of meaning as one of
Hirsch's own examples illuminates. Hirsch imagines a poet who intends
a poem to convey a sense of desolation but manages to communicate to
some readers only that the sea is wet and to others simply that twilight is
approaching. Although Hirsch grants the distinction stressed by New
Critics between an author's intentions and his or her success in
articulating them, he none the less maintains that in this case the sense
of desolation is the only "universally valid meaning of the poem."[7]
Verbal meaning, then, is linked to an author's intention irrespective of
his or her success in communicating it. Hirsch has two reasons for this
position. First, he argues that wet seas and approaching twilights are
often or typically used to represent a sense of desolation. Hence, the poet
could have meant a sense of desolation because he or she conformed to
prevailing linguistic conventions in trying to convey the sense by
referring to phenomena of this kind. Second, as we have seen, Hirsch
argues that if the meaning of a poem is to be shareable, it must be
determinate. If verbal meaning is intrinsically public and available, a
poem cannot have two different meanings for two different groups of
readers. In Hirsch's view, this means that the correct interpretation of
the poem's meaning must be one that grasps a single meaning with
which everyone can agree. But the only standard on which all readers
will agree in attempting to determine the correct interpretation "is the
old-fashioned ideal of rightly understanding what the author meant."[8]
Hirsch admits that if the poem in his example conveyed to everyone
simply the sense that twilight was approaching "such unanimity would
make a very strong case for the practical irrelevance of the author's
intention."[9] Nevertheless, he doubts whether such unanimity ever occurs
and claims that interpreters must rather defer to the author's intentions
since this is probably the only standard that can motivate consensus. In
this regard, he suggests that whereas no interpreter will be likely to give
up a favored interpretation for some other reader's interpretation, all at
least ought to be ready to defer to the author's.

This argument renders Hirsch's emphasis on the shareability of verbal
meaning somewhat dubious. He argues that the sense of desolation in the

example above has to be the meaning of the poem because meaning has to be determinate in order to be shared and no determinate meaning other than that tied to an author's intention is likely to gain unanimous assent. Yet, in Hirsch's own example the sense of desolation is in fact shared by no one. Presumably we know that this sense is the poem's meaning because we are gifted at guessing or the poet tells us the original intention but such guessing or telling seems to suggest a very impoverished account of the shareability of verbal meaning. In what way do we share the sense of desolation if we have to be told or guess that this was the poem's meaning? For Hirsch, the shareability of verbal meaning appears to refer simply to two circumstances: first, that the words of a text can be used to convey the sense that an author wants to convey and, second, that interpreters can discover that this is in fact the sense he or she wants to convey. But it seems that they need not discover this fact about the author by comprehending the meaning of his or her text. All that is required for the shareability of verbal meaning is that somehow they *do* discover what the author intended and read the text in terms of this intention. The intention need not be immediately discernible in the text. Thus, despite his critique of psychologism, Hirsch sees the communication of meaning as a process of somehow uncovering the meanings another person has intended and in this regard, he even agrees with Schleiermacher that some form of divination or "genial guess" may be needed.[10]

The narrowness of this definition of the shareability of verbal meaning is also indicated by the example of Beethoven's symphony to which I have already referred. Hirsch writes:

> The hyperbolic uses of "nothing" to stand for "no work of art" is a common sort of linguistic extension and can constitute verbal meaning in any context in which it is communicable. My friend could have understood me. He misunderstands for the sake of the example.[11]

Here by "a common sort of linguistic extension" Hirsch means that I can mean what I intend to mean given prevailing linguistic conventions and you could have shared my meaning although you did not. But what sense of sharing is this? How does it clarify the problem of textual interpretation to claim that "my friend could have understood me" if he did not? My friend knows what I intended and perhaps he can even see how I thought my words would convey the meaning I intended. But he does not "share" my meaning; he simply recognizes that this is what I intended and only recognizes this after I have explained myself more fully.

For Hirsch, then, an author's meaning is what he or she consciously or unconsciously intends as part of a willed type; by its "shareability" he means that an interpreter can unearth what an author "willed" and by such hermeneutic methods as genial guesses and subsequent comparisons with prevailing linguistic usage he means to signal appropriate processes of disinternment. To this extent, Hirsch's account of the shareability of verbal meaning conforms to the minimalist and relatively monological view of traditional hermeneutics: one shares an author's meaning when one intuits it, re-experiences the author's intentions within oneself or simply knows what the original intention was. If one shares a common linguistic context with an author then sharing verbal meaning will also be fairly easy. One will know, for instance, that "nothing" can mean "no work of art" and one will be able simply to move from the meanings typical of the linguistic practice of the culture to the author's probable intention. Where a common linguistic context and hence knowledge of typical meanings does not exist, understanding will be more difficult. In this case, one will have to reconstruct the relevant cultural, historical and biographical situation before one can know or share what the author meant.

It seems to me that nothing separates Gadamer and Hirsch so much as their views on sharing verbal meaning. As I shall explain below, for Gadamer, if the meaning of a text is shared then such sharing involves more than either a knowledge of what an author's intentions were or a capacity to reconstruct them; it means rather that readers share the text's understanding of its subject-matter. The interpreter does not know merely that a poet intended to convey a sense of desolation, for instance; if the poem is about desolation, this means that in reading the poem, the reader comes to understand precisely the way in which twilight and wet seas *can be* desolate. Where interpreter and writer already share a linguistic context, agreement on the subject-matter of a text may be easier or come about more quickly. Nevertheless, hermeneutic understanding does not depend upon a previously shared idiom but rather serves to create one. Moreover, where reader and writer do not share a linguistic context, the hermeneutic process is not exhausted in reconstructing the linguistic conventions that the author assumes. Rather, understanding the meaning of a text involves constructing a common language and thereby coming to an understanding of the text's "truth."

This position reflects the importance to Gadamer of the assumptions of pre-Romantic hermeneutics to which I referred in chapter 1. The view separates him not only from Hirsch but from so-called "reception" theorists and reader-response critics as well. For, if textual meaning cannot be located in the author's intentions, neither can it be identified with a reader's — even an informed or ideal reader's — experience.[12] Rather, when a text is understood its meaning cannot be attributed to either writer or reader. The meaning of the text is a shared language, shared in the sense that it is no one person's possession but is rather a common view of a subject-matter. Gadamer begins to defend this position by means of a phenomenological account of game-playing and an appropriation of Aristotle's account of mimesis. In what follows I shall look at each in turn.

THE STRUCTURE OF GAME-PLAYING

Gadamer's remarks on the similarity between playing games and reading books or experiencing art works in general are largely suggestive rather than conclusive.[13] In this section I shall therefore simply indicate what these suggestions are and then turn elsewhere to elicit Gadamer's arguments for them. He begins by examining a familiar aspect of both game-playing and aesthetic experience: namely, the way in which in reading a book, viewing a painting or playing a game one is transported out of one's ordinary existence. Games and works of art both have an essential priority over the individuals that experience or play them. In playing a game, players enter a new and total environment. Indeed, it is often necessary to enter a space — a gym or playing field — set aside for the game. In entering this space the players put aside their own concerns and desires and submit to the purposes of the game itself. Its goals and requirements take over and dictate actions and strategies to the players. The subject of action in a game is therefore not really the person playing it; the person's actions and aspirations are rather reactions to tasks the game itself imposes and hence it is the action of 'the game, or what Gadamer refers to as the to-and-fro movement internal to it, that is the decisive factor in any game-playing. As he writes:

> The appeal of the game, the fascination it exerts, consists in the fact that it becomes master of the player. Even when games are concerned in which one tries to fulfill tasks one has set oneself, it is the risk, the question of

whether it "works," "succeeds," or "succeeds again" that exercises the game's attraction. The actual subject of the game (precisely those experiences make this clear in which there is only a single player) is not the player but the game itself.[14]

This analysis of involvement in games has an obvious application to the experience of texts and works of art in so far as we are used to thinking of art works as encompassing and, indeed, overwhelming readers and spectators. Reading a book, watching a play or examining a painting could thus be considered to have the same character of entry into a new domain as does playing a game. In each case, players, viewers or readers are transported out of their own lives into another reality with its own overriding concerns and purposes. But this account of the experience of art does not differentiate Gadamer's analysis from many others. For Schiller and post-Kantian aesthetics, for example, art is a beautiful illusion, a dream that suffuses and overcomes its viewers. Spectators are therefore lifted into a separate domain in the same way as are the players of a game; once again, they leave their own concerns behind and are engrossed in those of the work of art itself.

A crucial difference between this position and Gadamer's own, however, is indicated by his emphasis on the normative authority of a game. Playing a game involves not only entering a different reality but, more importantly, submitting to its norms and requirements. Games comprise a set of rules and principles to which participants must adhere and which at least partially determine those participants' own goals and aspirations. The game thus has authority over its players and even specifies a range of appropriate attitudes and responses. Gadamer's suggestion is that art has a similar normative authority. Readers and spectators do not simply enter a new sphere; the books they read and the plays and paintings they view rather have authority over and make a claim on them. For this reason art cannot be thought of as a dream or illusion; Gadamer emphasizes rather its bindingness on its viewers. Art is not something from which they awake into the mundanity of their ordinary existence but instead something that presents a challenge to that existence.

Of course an intentionalist such as Hirsch could endorse this analysis of aesthetic experience. He could admit that reading a book or seeing a play involves entering not simply a separate domain but a normatively binding one. At the same time, he could simply deny that this experience has any significance for the criteria of valid textual understanding. Standards for determining textual meaning would still have to rely on the discovery of an author's intentions; in fact these intentions would constitute precisely the authority that dictated the range of appropriate responses on the part of the readers or viewers. On Gadamer's analysis, the mistake here, however, is analogous to that made by post-Kantian aesthetics. If this aesthetic theory disregards the bindingness of works of art on readers and viewers, the Hirschean misses its source. A work of art has normative authority not because it compels its audience to discover its author's intentions but rather because it raises a claim to truth. We shall have to explore Gadamer's argument for this point later. At this point, it is necessary to introduce a second important characteristic of playing games since this indicates the direction in which Gadamer's argument will proceed.

We have seen that games have a priority over their players since their norms and purposes dominate their players. At the same time, however, a game is not simply that which is codified in a book of rules or reflected in a set of strategies; it is rather that which is played. Thus, despite the dominance of the game over those that play it, their playing it remains essential to it. For this reason, Gadamer calls games "self-representations."[15] On the one hand, in playing a game players represent it in the sense that their actions and responses reflect its principles. On the other hand, games have to be represented in the actions and concerns of players. The peculiarity of games is thus that, on the one hand they have authority over their participants, determining their goals and aspirations for the duration of the game, while on the other they exist in a concrete sense only through the participation of their players.[16] A game both determines the actions of its players and is nothing other than these actions themselves.

The important point that Gadamer elicits from this self-representative feature of games is that the players of a game are, in a sense, also its creators. The rules of the game are not created by the players; hence the particular confluence of actions that constitute any specific instance of the game do not create its structure. Yet, outside particular instances of the game it has no concrete shape or existence. On the one hand, then, a game determines the range of appropriate actions and attitudes on the part of its players; on the other it really exists only in particular actions and attitudes. This phenomenon means that while any playing of a game is that game, in a sense it only is that game because players play it. The players thus "create" the particular instance of the game although, at the same time, they could not create or play it if it did not already exist.

Gadamer explains the implications of this relationship between autonomy and dependence in discussing the celebration of festivals:

> The festival is only there in so far as it is celebrated. But this in no way says that it is of a subjective character and has its being only in the subjectivity of those celebrating. Rather one celebrates the festival because it is there.[17]

If works of art and games are similar in regard to their character as self-representations, this similarity suggests that works of art will take on a concrete existence only in being viewed or read. Thus, although works of art will have the same normative priority over viewers and readers that games have over players, viewers and readers will also be as essential to works of art as players are to games.

Gadamer draws a second consequence from this analysis. If a game takes on a concrete existence only in being played, then clearly its concrete existence is capable of changing. Indeed, games are rarely played the same way twice. Instead, they involve different particular actions, the use of different strategies, an encounter with different circumstances and reactions and finally different results. Thus, although a game remains the same game in some sense it can also be entirely different each time it is played. If the same holds true of a work of art it will also remain self-identical while constantly changing. Indeed, at issue, according to Gadamer are entities that are "only in being different."[18]

Both suggestions above indicate problems with a Hirschean intentionalism. First, if works of art exist in a concrete form only in being viewed or read it will be difficult to identify their meaning with the author's intentions alone. Rather, just as the content of a game is concretized in the actions and attitudes of their players, the content or meaning of works of art will be concretized in the actions and attitudes of their audience. Second, if such concretization involves a constant transformation of the phenomenon in question, as it does in the case of games, the meaning of a work of art will not be determinate, as Hirsch maintains but will rather change with the circumstances of its instantiation. In fact, Gadamer suggests that both games and art works involve a relation of the general to the particular which he eventually attempts to elucidate by exploring Aristotle's account of practical reasoning, as we shall see in chapter 3. At this point in his discussion, however, he concentrates on the way in which games become works of art.

Gadamer's initial remarks on works of art confuse rather than illuminate the similarity between involvement in games and aesthetic experience. He begins his analysis with drama since, in his view, a play can be viewed as simply a game of make-believe that is presented to an audience. We shall see that this presentation is not unimportant. But, in moving from games to plays, Gadamer focuses first, not on the audience, but on the actors. Actors have the same relation to the drama that players do to a game. In the first place, a drama has priority over the actors in the same sense as a game has priority over its participants since, again, the range of proper responses and actions is dictated by the play not the actors. A play has a power over them that requires that they give up their own purposes and indeed their identity as long as they act in it. In the second place, however, the play has concrete "existence" not as a series of words in a script but rather as represented by its actors. It follows that its actors are also its creators in the same sense as the players are creators of a game. Actors do not make up the play; neither do players make up the game. None the less the drama must be presented and can only be presented through the concrete actions of concrete individuals.

Clearly, this same relationship between autonomy and dependence holds at least for all the performing arts. Once again, although a musical piece or dance exists in some sense whether or not it is performed, it takes on a concrete existence only in being performed. As Gadamer puts this point "A drama exists really only when it is played and certainly music must resound."[19] Nevertheless it is not yet clear what significance this analysis of the performing arts has for Gadamer's argument. Gadamer claims to be delineating relationships that are relevant to the experience of art in general, thus to the understanding of texts, paintings and other forms of art that do not need to be performed. And in these cases it is not clear why anything more than the work itself and thus any creator other than the original author or artist is required for the work to have concrete existence.

Furthermore, even if Gadamer wants to restrict his analysis to the relationship between performing artists and the work they perform, it is not clear that he draws the correct conclusions. He suggests that since performers are essential to the representation of a work they can change its meaning just as players can change the specific content of a game. In *Truth and Method* he therefore directs a great deal of attention toward the way in which each performance of a work of art highlights different aspects of the work. No production of a play, dance recital or performance of a musical piece is the same as any other. Indeed, the idea of a canonical production to be simply repeated ad nauseam is antithetical to the nature of the performing arts in general. Each performance rather involves different actions, different emphases and nuances and hence will present a different result. But a Hirschean might argue that despite the essentiality of performers to the presentation of certain works of art, the meaning presented is still bound to its author's intentions and hence that the performers cannot be considered creators of the work in a sense that would allow them to change its meaning. Indeed, this is the most obvious way of explaining the primacy of a work over its performers, director, choreographer or the like: the latter must adhere to the author's intentions and meaning not their own. Thus, even though the work takes on a concrete form only through the activity of its performers and even though they create it in this sense, an intentionalist might still claim that what they at least ought to create is what the author or artist intended for them to create.[20] Thus far, then, Gadamer's remarks leave at least two questions unanswered: First, what is the relevance to aesthetic experience in general of the relationship between the performers of a work and the work? Second, how does this relationship affect the status of an author's intentions?

Gadamer begins to address both questions in his comments on the consequence of opening a game to an audience in the transition to drama. As he describes it, this consequence is that the game now has a clearly separable and identifiable content. Games can also be played in front of an audience and there is a sense in which players in a game can also watch it, serving temporarily at least, as its audience. But when a game's presentation to an audience is its *raison d'être* and when this audience is only an audience, the game becomes a performance. The game appears to the audience as a self-contained whole; indeed, it undergoes what Gadamer terms a "transformation into structure (*Gebilde*)".[21] The audience is that to which the whole of the work of art appears as something closed in itself and something separable from their daily lives.

This analysis constitutes Gadamer's answer to the first question raised above as to the relevance of his emphasis on the performing arts to the analysis of aesthetic experience in general. The reflections above indicate that the possibility of a game's having meaning and thus becoming a work of art depends upon its presentation to an audience. The conditions of the "concrete existence" of the performing arts are thus the conditions of art in general; it must somehow be presented to an audience – either by being performed or by being read or seen. To be sure, a book exists whether it is ever read or not just as a piece of music exists whether it is ever performed or not; nevertheless, just as "music must resound" the book must be read as part of its "self-representation." In other words, it must be represented to an audience for whom it is an independent structure and therefore meaningful. What distinguishes works of art that must be performed from those that can be experienced directly by an audience is thus simply that the former must undergo two processess of concretization. The work is concretely realized first in its performance and second in the experience of its audience. But in both cases the audience turns out to be as essential to it as its orginal creator. The answer to the second question raised above follows: since the very possibility of its possessing meaning requires its presentation to an audience, the meaning of a work of art cannot be identified with its author's intentions alone.

Still, this argument does not yet suffice as a critique of Hirsch's identification of textual understanding with an understanding of an author's intentions. Gadamer has shown that an audience is essential to the possibility of a work of art's possessing *a* meaning since it is only with its presentation to an audience that a game appears as a whole and therefore takes on a surveyable content. But the argument does not yet show that the audience is essential to what *the* meaning of the work of art is. It may be, for example, that a reader is necessary if a book is to have a meaning or at least that a reader is crucial to there being a meaning that is surveyed or grasped. None the less, Hirscheans could still claim that readers at least ought to try to grasp that meaning which the aut..or intended. Gadamer does not fully clarify the part the audience plays in the meaning of a work until the end of his discussion of mimesis and we shall see that even there it raises certain problems. Still, a crucial part of his argument against any Hirschean-like intentionalism lies in another aspect of the transition from games to drama. Important in this regard is not only that the game takes on a meaning for an audience but that meaning is representational.

One kind of argument that might be used against Hirsch's position is that his notion of intentions is too restricted, that he neglects the dimension of authorial intention which means to create a separate world. Ronald Dworkin puts this position quite well in his comparison of legal and literary interpretation:

> We can perhaps isolate the full set of interpretive beliefs an author has at a particular moment (say at the moment he sends final galleys to the printer) and solemnly declare that these beliefs in their full concreteness fix what the novel is or means . . . But even if we (wrongly) call this particular set

of beliefs "intentions" we are, in choosing them, ignoring another kind of level of intention which is the intention to create a work whose nature or meaning is not fixed in this way because it is a work of art. That is why the author's intention school, as I understand it, makes the value of a work of art turn on a narrow and constrained view of the intentions of the author.[22]

Dworkin cites John Fowles in support of this position: "Only one reason is shared by all of us [novelists]: we wish to create worlds as real as, but other than, the world that is. Or was. That is why we cannot plan . . . We also know that a genuinely created world must be independent of its creator."[23]

Gadamer's view seems at first glance similar to these. We have seen that he emphasizes the primacy of games over players in so far as games encompass their players, substituting their goals for the players' own and functioning as a kind of different reality into which they enter. When the game becomes a play or any other kind of presentation, it is this reality that is offered to the audience as a self-contained, meaningful structure. The audience is thus presented with a structure that is supposed to signify or represent a world in its own right, independent of any single individual's beliefs or intentions with regard to it. Art represents a world, as Fowles puts it, and reducing its meaning to an expression of an author's creativity disregards this degree of its autonomy.

But Gadamer goes further than either Dworkin or Fowles. The point here is an extension of one I noted earlier, that games constitute not only a separate domain but also a normative authority which the players have to accept. With the transformation of games into dramatical present-ations, this normative authority becomes binding on an audience. What was once a structure that dominated its players is now a structure that encompasses both players and audience; hence, the claim that a game exerts over those who play it is transferred to the audience; it forms an all-encompassing reality with rules and demands not only on players and actors but on the audience as well. Art presents a challenge to the way the audience lives its life, a challenge to live it differently. It does not simply introduce a new imaginary domain as Fowles asserts; instead it presents a reality with consequences for the world its audience inhabits. Art, on Gadamer's view, turns out to be an attempt to represent truth. Reducing its meaning to an expression of its author's creativity reflects both a failure to recognize its autonomy and, more importantly, an unjustifiable restriction on the knowledge it contains.

The results of Gadamer's suggestions thus far, then, are that the possibility of aesthetic meaning depends upon the presence of an audience and that what this audience experiences is a claim to truth. The experience of meaning cannot be restricted to experiencing or re-experiencing an author's or artist's intended meaning because it is primarily an understanding of the truth-content of the work itself. To this extent, aesthetic experience is similar to a knowledge of Euclidean geometry: just as this knowledge cannot be reduced to a knowledge of Euclid's intentions, the experience of a work of art must be seen as more than an experience of the artist's motivations. Gadamer turns to Aristotle's theory of mimesis to clarify this position. We shall see that if this analysis precludes a Hirschean account of textual understanding, it leads to problems of its own.

MIMESIS

Gadamer admits that the mimetic idea that art imitates reality appears old-fashioned in light of post-Aristotelian developments in aesthetic theory. In particular he points to the "aesthetics of genius" that followed Kant and stressed the freedom and spontaneity of expression that we have already noted with regard to Schleiermacher's hermeneutics. The concept of mimesis appears outmoded from other perspectives as well, in particular from the point of view of an aesthetic sophistication that focuses on the logical dissimilarity between a representation and its original.[24] This position denies that any representation can mimic reality "as it is" or that reality is anything apart from standard systems of representation. What appears as realism in art, then, is not a matter of a direct imitation of the way the world is but rather refers to the use of certain culturally specific conventions.   Of course, it is clear from the Gadamerian account of historical understanding that we have already examined that this is a position to which Gadamer, apart from his defense of mimetic theory, would otherwise seem quite close. In his analysis of historical understanding, he suggested the impossibility of any "objective" or neutral knowledge of historical events and claimed that our understanding is rather always interpretive and retrospective; it is rooted in both the greater breadth of our experience in comparison to the events we study and the narrowness of our perspective in comparison to future points of view. With regard to aesthetic understanding as well, then, we would expect Gadamer to dispense with the notion of an "innocent eye" that could see the world "as it really is" and hence to dispense with the theory of mimesis altogether. Gadamer does in fact suggest that art is just as interpretive as history. Indeed, on his view, both art and history present the world not as it is "absolutely" but rather as it appears from a certain point of view. He defends the concept of mimesis none the less. Perspectival and interpretive as it is, art is also representational and it is for this reason that its meaning cannot be reduced to an expression of creativity alone. In what follows I shall attempt to make sense out of this position.

Gadamer's view that art is mimetic comprises three interrelated claims. First he attempts to forestall the objection that Fowles, say, might raise: namely, that the world his novels create is a fictional one, not representative of anything outside itself. In claiming that art is representational, however, Gadamer is not claiming that it necessarily constitutes a report or depiction of actual events. He insists that modern painting remains mimetic even where it avoids conventional representations of objects as Cubism does, for example. In this case, what the paintings might be said to represent is the fragmentation of the modern world and the destruction of the integrity of the object that occurs with its production for consumption.[25] In connection with this position, Gadamer tries to show, second, that mimetic theories need not depend on the notion of a reality "in itself" that art exactly reproduces. Here, he distinguishes between a copy of reality and "the appearance of what is there."[26] His point is that, although art represents an aspect of the world or reality, this aspect is not one that is apparent outside the painting or representation. Works of art are not reproductions of a reality that can be identified independently of the work of art and used to judge the adequacy of its representation; rather, the features of the objects works of art represent — their fragmentation, lack of substance or whatever — are illuminated only by means of the representation itself; certain events or features are exaggerated, the importance of others minimized and the like. Hence the representation does not provide a mirror of reality that exactly reflects it; rather, on Gadamer's view, artistic representation shows the "truth" of "reality." As he puts it, "'Reality' is defined as what is untransformed and art as the raising up of this reality into its truth."[27]

By "truth" here Gadamer means that an aspect of human experience has been separated out from others, given an emphasis of its own and thus illuminated for all. To this extent, his conception has affinities with Heidegger's account of truth as *aletheia* or disclosure; it marks an uncovering of some aspect of the world, our lives, a text or the like that was previously occluded. Gadamer attempts to clarify this conception by exploring the premises behind a dramatical presentation of a series of events. In themselves, he claims, the meaning of these events is not clear since they are always part of an as-yet-undetermined future. In itself World War I, for example, is simply a set of different battles, individual tragedies, claims to national victories and the like, the meaning of which, as we have seen, depends upon both the future course of history and the practical concerns of the historians who are part of it. As depicted artistically, however, the consequences and ramifications of the events depicted are entirely contained within the boundaries of the play and the meaning of these events therefore takes on a certain structure and closure. Nothing is left undecided; instead the events are crystallized out of all their various and infinite historical relationships and revealed, as Gadamer writes, "in the heightened truth" of their "being."[28] Artistic representation is thus a representation of truth in the sense that it releases its subject matter from its contingency. There is no future set of events within the play or work of art that can affect the meaning of the events it portrays and there is thus nothing more to be added. When one views a work of art one has the whole of what it represents in front of one; hence, in principle, the whole truth of what it represents is available to one as well. As Gadamer puts this point: "The being of all play is always realization, sheer fulfillment, *energeia* which has its *telos* within itself."[29]

Gadamer might therefore agree with the anonymous quotation with which Nelson Goodman begins *Languages of Art*: "Art is not a copy of the real world. One of the damn things is enough."[30] Nevertheless, he does not draw the conclusions that Goodman draws from this position. On Gadamer's view, the applicability of a mimetic theory of art does not depend upon art's constituting a copy of reality. Through mimesis art rather reveals the truth of reality, a truth it precisely does not possess on its own. Hence works of art do not capture reality as it "really" is. They rather extricate their subject-matter from that which is considered to be inessential to it and simultaneously reveal that which is most significant. MacIntyre offers a way of making sense out of Gadamer's position here by distinguishing between external and internal represen-tations.[31] External representations are merely reproductions of their objects or copies, the purpose of which is to refer their viewers back to the original they reproduce. Passport photographs are instances of this kind of representation; they have no independence from that which they depict but simply supply a means of identifying or referring back to it. As such they constitute what Gadamer calls "signs."[32] Artistic or internal representations, on the contrary, do not refer back to an original in the sense that they could be evaluated with regard to their faithfulness to it. Instead that which is depicted comes to light only through the depiction itself. In other words, it is through the artistic representation itself that we can comprehend the artistic subject-matter. We therefore see what the work of art has taught us to see, but this means that we cannot verify the representation by comparing it to the original because we already see the original in its light.

MacIntyre offers Rembrandt's *The Nightwatch* as a case of this kind of representation. The portrait cannot be condemned as a faulty reproduction or copy; those miffed at Rembrandt's portrait of them were confusing the two types of representation, on MacIntyre's view, and viewing the painting as if it were a passport photograph. The value of the painting lies not in the way in which Rembrandt presents a mirror image of his subjects, but rather in the way in which he distinguishes features of his subjects' appearance that do not have the prominence or self-evidence that the painting gives them outside of the painting itself. The painting illuminates aspects of its subjects that were not previously apparent but that, once revealed, can be seen to divulge something essential about those subjects. Hence, as MacIntyre writes, "Rembrandt teaches us to see in the human face what we could not – and perhaps did not want to – see before."[33]

This explanation of Gadamer's point leads to the third claim encompassed by his defense of mimesis. Here he argues that art and aesthetic experience are forms of knowledge. One learns to see the object represented in terms of the truth that the representation reveals about it. Hence we learn to see the sea as a Turner seascape teaches us to see it just as Rembrandt's work teaches us the depths of character a human face can reveal. In so far as works of art are mimetic they are therefore not only representational but pedagogical. In picking out certain features of their objects they teach their viewers or readers more of their objects than that audience previously understood. Gadamer connects this cognitive function of art to Plato's account of anamnesis. On the one hand, we learn from a work of art; thus, by focusing on light, Impressionist paintings let us see objects and light in a new way. On the other, we recognize this new way as something familiar, as something we knew or should have known. *The Nightwatch,* for instance, shows us something we could not see without it; yet having seen it, we recognize it as a crucial aspect of what we always saw. Gadamer sees this relation between newness and familiarity as part of the meaning of recognition in general and as the most important part of the experience of art. He writes:

> What recognition is according to its deepest essence is . . . not understood
> if one sees in it only that there something that one already knows is known
> again. The joy of recognition is rather that more is known than only the
> known. In recognition what we know emerges, as if by illumination, from
> all the contingency and variability of circumstances that condition it and is
> grasped in its essence.[34]

On the basis of this cognitive or educational function of art, Gadamer
wants to reverse what he sees as the "subjectivization" of aesthetics that
he thinks began with Kant.[35] The experience of art turns out to be not at
all equivalent to the experience of a dream or a beautiful illusion;
instead, it is at least capable of being a learning experience in the
Hegelian sense we examined in chapter 1. In other words the experience
can be one in which we recognize the truth of the representation, discard
our previous understanding of the subject-matter and incorporate our
new understanding into our lives. We may not have previously
understood the fragmentation of the object and may not have noticed the
play of light on the sea. But, on Gadamer's view, this is precisely the
pedagogical point of art: it presents its objects in such a way that the
understanding of its audience can be enhanced and it may even be moved
to change its life. Indeed, on Gadamer's view, unless the audience
attempts to guard itself from the confrontation with their own lives that
art provokes, the experience of art is one in which the audience is
necessarily taken up into the work, experiences it as authoritative and
learns to view its own world in light of the work of art. Aesthetic
experience is thus itself a form of knowledge. The example he considers
is tragic drama.

We saw in connection with Gadamer's analysis of game-playing that
he emphasizes the involvement of the players in the self-representation of
the game. That is, although players are subject to the norms of the
game, the game is subject to the necessity that it be played. He then
suggested that the audience is essential to a drama in a similar way. This
suggestion he finds confirmed by Aristotle's including in the definition of
tragic drama its effect on the spectator. In this context, Gadamer
considers the usual translations of *eleos* and *phobus* as pity and fear
respectively (*Mitleid* and *Furcht* in German), too psychologically oriented
to indicate the actual involvement of the audience in the tragedy.
Instead, he substitutes *jammer* and *schauder* which might best be

translated as "to moan in distress" and "to shudder in fright." The point here is that talk of the pity that the fate of the tragic hero elicits from us or the fear of tragic possibilities that is evoked in us is much too distanced a reaction to express the actual power of the events portrayed in the drama. The events are events that overwhelm the spectators. They are not events that happen simply to the hero; neither are they events that we recognize as merely possibilities for us. The fate of the hero is rather our fate as well and in tragic drama we recognize that we too are subject to forces and causal connections that are more powerful than we are. The involvement of the spectator in the drama is thus a total one; the claim made by the drama is one that it exerts not only over its actors and fictional characters but over its audience as well.

Gadamer's interpretation of the Aristotelian account of catharsis or the purification that results from *eleos* and *phobus* follows from this analysis. On his view, it does not involve awaking from an illusion; rather, we are purified precisely in so far as we affirm the reality of the play as a reality for us. That is, while our first reaction to the fate of the hero is one of denial, a rejection of any acknowledgement that the fate of the hero could have happened to anyone, much less to ourselves, in catharsis this denial is replaced with acceptance. Gadamer makes clear that this acceptance is not an acceptance of the justice of the hero's punishment. Instead, what is affirmed is the disproportionality between crime and punishment and it is just this disproportionality that we recognize as binding on us.

> It is a true commonality that is experienced in such an excess of tragic harm. The spectator recognizes himself and his own finite being in the face of the power of fate . . . The "so it is" is a form of self-knowledge on the part of the spectator, who returns with insight from the blindness in which he, as everyone, lives.[36]

The spectators are thus transformed by the tragic drama. Not only the tragic hero but the spectators as well experience the tenuousness of their own purposes and aspirations in view of natural and historical causalities stronger than they. Gadamer argues that the inclusion of the audience in the events of the tragic drama holds for all aesthetic experience. The reader or viewer is not only drawn into the movement of a play, narrative or painting but learns from and is transformed by its representation of "reality." This effect is one that Hans Robert Jauss affirms in discussing the scandal occasioned by the publication of Flaubert's *Madame Bovary*.

As he puts it, Flaubert's style – a simple report of the events as opposed to the more conventional confessional form – "was able to jolt the reader out of the self-evident character of his moral judgment and turned a predecided question of public morals back into an open problem."[37] Here too, then, the audience is drawn into a domain that has authority over it and that can even require it to change. Gadamer writes:

> The familiarity with which the work of art touches us is at the same time and in an enigmatic way a collapse of the customary. It is not only the "This is you" that the art work discloses in a joyous and terrible shock. It also says to us "You must change your life."[38]

This discussion of mimesis and tragic drama thus confirms the anti-Hirschean suggestion that Gadamer made in his analysis of the logic of playing games. Like games, works of art have a normative authority over their spectators and make claims on them. The account of mimesis indicates that in regard to works of art this is a claim to truth. The work of art presents reality to its spectators in the "heightened truth of its being." Hence they are not only drawn into the work of art and do not only accept its problems and purposes as their own; in addition they are able to see the truth it represents and hence to learn from it. Aesthetic experience is thus primarily an understanding of truth. What is understood in the experience of art is not simply or primarily the author's vision but the validity of the claim the work makes, not what the artist sees but how the content of the work may require its spectators to confront and change their lives.

But, at the same time as Gadamer's position appears to indicate the narrowness of a Hirschean focus on understanding the intentions behind a work of art it also seems to substantiate Hirsch's further point that meaning is "determinate." In comparing aesthetic experience to the playing of games Gadamer suggests not only that the audience is a condition of the possibility of meaning in a work of art but that this meaning can therefore change with the audience and their understanding of it. Now, however, we have seen that what is understood in relation to works of art is their truth. Indeed, Gadamer's talk of "essences," "heightened truth" and the like makes it sound, at least, as if his rehabilitation of mimesis relies on a substantialist metaphysics, as Hans Robert Jauss has insisted.[39] But if this is the case it is entirely unclear why an understanding of such truth should change. In fact, Gadamer's own example of the effect of Greek tragedy appears to show that the understanding of the truth-content of the dramas does not change. We rather recognize the same subservience to fate that the plays portray. In contrast, we do not experience the same shock at Madame Bovary's actions as the public did at the time that the novel was published. None the less, it could be argued that we still understand the novel in the same way — as a representation of the ambiguity of moral experience. The question, then, is why Gadamer insists that meaning is not determinate if, as he suggests, understanding is primarily an understanding of truth. Certainly, if understanding Euclidean geometry is a case of such understanding, it is not clear how such knowledge changes. Of course, we now place Euclidean geometry in the context of other geometries but what we understand when we understand its propositions surely remains the same. That is, we understand that two of the angles of an isosceles triangle are equal within Euclidean space and the like. Why, then, should what we understand when we understand a work of art change? Do we not still understand the character of the individuals in *The Nightwatch* in the way that the original public did and if we do not in what sense does the painting represent the truth about them?

Gadamer's defense of a mimetic theory of art raises another question: namely, how understanding differs from a simple acquiescence to an artwork's point of view. We have seen that the defense of mimesis is not as naive as it may initially appear, at least in so far as Gadamer does not suggest that art mirrors "reality" as it "actually" is. His remarks are rather meant to suggest the way in which works of art can illuminate important aspects of our world or ourselves. The conclusion, in other words, is that art is mimetic because it separates its subject-matter from the myriad relationships in which it is involved and presents it to viewers or readers in such a way that they can learn something essential about it. But if this argument precludes a Hirschean intentionalism by denying the possibility of reducing the knowledge contained in art to an expression of its author's intentions, it also seems to bring the experience of a work of art perilously close to a simple acceptance of that work's point of view. If works of art are supposed to illuminate or represent some truth about their subject-matter and if this truth is one from which the audience is supposed to learn as the theory of mimesis insists, the question arises as to why. Why should we learn from the vision depicted in *The Nightwatch*, for example, or why should we accept the authority of Greek tragedy's depiction of fate? On Gadamer's analysis, the paradigmatic aesthetic experience is supposed to be one of recognition. We recognize the representation as a distillation of that which is crucial to its object. But this means that the experience of art is not simply a learning experience; it is a learning experience in which one learns *to accept* the work's depiction of its subject-matter. But if this acceptance is what Gadamer means by sharing verbal meaning, then one is forced to wonder whether Hirsch's analysis of shareability as simply the capacity to *reconstruct* an author's intentions is not, at least, less dangerous.

This second question I am raising involves the terms of Gadamer's analysis. He denies that works of art present the world "as it is," apart from any representation. Artistic representations rather "invent" their objects in so far as the recognition of their subject-matter is dependent upon the representation itself. Furthermore, a successful aesthetic experience involves acknowledgement of the work of art's representation. This analysis thus seems to preclude the possibility of disagreeing with artistic representations. We cannot compare them to a reality independent of them; neither can we dismiss them as a reflection of their authors' personal visions alone, for, in a manner similar to a game, they become the reality that has authority over us. But clearly there are certain artistic representations that portray their objects in a way that is supposed to be true or illuminating but ought none the less to be rejected. The Nazi attempt to depict Jews as rats is an obvious example and the question, then, is how one differentiates between this case and Rembrandt's *Nightwatch*. Were those whom Rembrandt's painting portrayed perhaps justified in considering it slanderous or did it indeed reveal something true about them? What about pornographic depictions of women? We can learn from such portrayals and some feminists would say that far too many people do. The question is whether we *should* learn from them and *what* we are learning. Is there some criterion to which we can appeal to differentiate between representations from which we ought to learn and those that we ought to reject? Or is Gadamer's view that all art is a representation of truth that can educate us?

In the remainder of this chapter I want to examine Gadamer's answers to these questions and indicate a problem to which those answers seem to me to give rise. I shall begin with his remarks on the indeterminacy of aesthetic meaning.

UNDERSTANDING AS PARTICIPATION

I noted earlier that Gadamer emphasizes the variability in dramatic productions of the same play. In a manner similar to a game a play can be represented in different ways. One director will emphasize the comic elements of *Waiting for Godot* while another will stress its horrific features. One production of *Othello* will understand the central problem that leads to his killing of Desdemona as a lack of familiarity with the necessary customs and mores while a different production will simply stress his jealousy. On Gadamer's view, such variation is part of a play's character of self-representation. The play must be represented in a concrete production in order to "exist" but this means that it is subject to the different emphases and interpretations that different actors and directors give to it.

A Hirschean might well deny that such differences can legitimately affect the meaning of a play since that meaning is a product of its author's intentions. I suggested above that Gadamer's own mimetic account of art as a representation of truth makes it equally unclear how such differences can affect the truth represented. For him a work of art is supposed to illuminate the essence of its subject-matter; but if art is representational in this sense, then it seems that at least part of Hirsch's analysis remains correct. Even if meaning is to be identified with the truth-content of a work rather than with its author's intentions, meaning still seems to be determinate, as Hirsch insists. And if this is the case why should one director's understanding of a play differ from that of another? If a work of art illuminates the truth of its subject-matter, must not every audience understand it the same way if they understand it at all?

Gadamer's answer to this question rests on a distinctive feature of his claim that understanding is primarily an understanding of truth. On his view, the idea of a canonical production of a given play and hence the idea that there should be only one correct way of understanding it ignores the claim that the play makes on its audience. As he writes:

A correctness striven for in this way would not do justice to the true binding character of a work, which imposes itself on each interpreter in a special and immediate way and prevents him from making things easy by simply imitating a model.[40]

In effect, Gadamer's position here is that, precisely *because* the understanding of a work of art is an understanding of its truth, it must be differently understood. A work of art makes a claim on those that view, read, hear or perform it; indeed, as we have seen, it claims to represent the truth of its subject-matter in a manner that may require members of an audience to change their lives. As such, however, the truth of a work of art must be relevant to the lives it can affect. As Gadamer puts it in *Truth and Method*, "No text and no book speaks if it does not speak the language that reaches the other person."[41] Aesthetic experience is a learning experience in which a reader or viewer understands the significance of a work of art for his or her life. In understanding a work of art, an audience understands the truth-claim it imposes on them from the perspective of their own concerns and problems. Hence, differences in the production of a play are not unessential to its meaning but rather have a significance based on each reader's, director's or viewer's apprehension of the play's truth. Gadamer therefore concludes:

> Interpretation is probably in a certain sense recreation. This recreation however does not follow a preceding creative act; it rather follows the figure of the created work that each person has to bring to representation in accord with the meaning he finds in it.[42]

This explanation indicates how little Gadamer's view depends upon a substantialist metaphysics. On his account, works of art are representational in as much as they bring "truth" to light and reveal the "essence" of their subject-matter to an audience. If this essence is an essence for an audience, however, it is not eternally the same but is rather relative to the audience that perceives it. Gadamer therefore refers to the consistently contemporary character of great works of art in so far as they raise a claim to truth that their viewers must redeem in connection with their own circumstances. The truth of works of art is a contingent one: what they reveal is dependent on the lives, circumstances and views of the audience to whom they reveal it. Indeed, for Gadamer the point of hermeneutics is precisely to destroy "the phantom of a truth severed from the standpoint of the knower."[43] Thus we are not all educated by Greek tragedy in the same way, for the way in which it can educate us depends upon what we already know. To an audience that still takes the idea of gods and furies somewhat seriously, the tragic fate depicted necessarily means something different than it does to an audience that has inherited modern science. It is not just that tragic fate has a particular poignancy for us, given our faith in science. Rather, tragic drama teaches us to recognize the tenuousness of scientific advance in the light of events for which we cannot prepare. One might argue that the same kind of change occurs in our understanding of the axioms of Euclidean geometry:

because we are aware of alternative geometries we are also aware that parallel lines can intersect and so on. Hence, just as what we learn from art differs drastically with the conditions of our life, the relativization of Euclidean propositions to Euclidean space turns out to be decisive for our understanding even of their internal content.

This conclusion corresponds to the results of our investigation of historical understanding in chapter 1.[44] Just as the understanding of World War I changes with the advent of World War II, our understanding of Greek tragedy acquires new dimensions in light of our new situation. The conclusion also confirms the final suggestion Gadamer made in analyzing the structure of game-playing. Just as the content of a game can change with each instance of its being played, the meaning and truth to be found in works of art can change with the situations in terms of which their validity has to be clarified. Thus we understand Greek tragedy from the viewpoint of its meaning for scientific enlightenment, *Madame Bovary* in light of our familiarity with neutral description, adultery and so on. The point here is that while works of art have normative authority over those that read them or view them and so on, in the sense that understanding is primarily an understanding of truth, none the less, the content of this normative authority or, in other words, the content of the claim works of art impose on their audience, cannot be specified outside of the particular situations in which the works are seen, read etc. Therefore, the content has no "determinate meaning" in Hirsch's sense. For Gadamer, this constitutes the very meaning of a claim:

> A claim is something lasting. Its justification (or alleged justification) is primary. It is precisely because the claim lasts that it can be made to obtain at any time. The claim exists against someone and must therefore be made to obtain against him. None the less, the concept of a claim apparently contains the idea that it is not itself a fixed demand, the fulfillment of which is clearly agreed upon, but rather the ground of such fulfillment. A claim is the legal foundation for an undetermined demand.[45]

Hirsch has responded to Gadamer's argument here by insisting that, in thus violating the principle of the determinacy of meaning, Gadamer overlooks a crucial distinction between understanding the meaning of a text and understanding its significance. On his view, understanding the meaning of a text remains understanding "that which the author meant by his particular linguistic symbols" and is therefore always the same.

Since Flaubert could have intended only one meaning with the neutral
description in *Madame Bovary*, the only valid interpretation is the one
that correctly apprehends this meaning. On this account, differences in
interpretation do not stem from any leeway inherent to the process of
understanding but rather reflect differences in the *significance* a work may
have for different interpreters at different times or indeed for one
interpreter at different times. An interpreter's situation and concerns are
thus relevant to textual interpretation but only with regard to the
significance a text is thought to have for different issues and different
problems. In Hirsch's view, its relation to different concerns and issues
does not show that it can be legitimately *understood* in different ways as
well.[46]

It is important to note here that Gadamer's position does not merely
overlook a distinction between understanding meaning and understanding significance; it *denies* one. On his view, we understand the meaning
of a text, work of art or historical event *only in relation to our own situation*
and therefore in light of our own concerns. In other words we understand
it only in light of its significance. Thus, our understanding of Mark
Twain's *Huckleberry Finn* may differ from Twain's understanding of it or
the understanding of it by his immediate public. Because of our
heightened awareness of racial stereotyping we may find the portrait of
Jim more problematic than people did at the time that the book
appeared and this may affect our understanding of the content of the
book as a whole. Alternatively, because of a new awareness of homosexual
issues, we may see the relationship between Jim and Huck in a way that
would have been inconceivable at an earlier time and this perspective on
the text may allow us to understand it in a different way than our
predecessors. Understanding is primarily an understanding of the claim a
work of art imposes on us and this means that we understand a work in
its relevance to our own situation. That situation does not affect simply
the significance of a work but rather enters into the interpretation of
meaning itself, into what is shocking, what is unclear and into what the
work "really" says.

On this analysis, then, the understanding of a work of art involves
participation in its meaning. The audience of a work of art is not as
much a mere receiver of information as a catalyst of content. It follows
that the audience does not simply acquiesce to the viewpoint of a work of
art in coming to understand it, as the defense of mimesis suggests. The
audience rather participates in the meaning and truth the work of art
has. This is what Gadamer means in suggesting that the meaning of a

work of art is shared by creator and audience. Aesthetic experience, like historical understanding, involves a mediation of meaning with one's own situation, or what Gadamer calls a "fusion of horizons."[47] By this he means the integration of one's understanding of a text or historical event with its relevance to one's own circumstances in such a way that an "original" or "intended" meaning cannot be differentiated from the meaning of the text or event for oneself. This fusion is part of all hermeneutic understanding, on Gadamer's view, and, as we shall see, it separates hermeneutic forms of knowledge from what he considers non-hermeneutic forms such as the natural sciences. Hermeneutic sciences have no object that is independent of themselves. The meaning an object has it has as a fusion of the interpreter's perspective and the object. For this reason, Gadamer finds something suspect in the attempt to restore the authenticity of works of art by placing them in their original settings; on his view this attempt to retrieve an original meaning simply obscures any meaning works of art have as fusions of horizons. Understanding does not involve re-experiencing an original understanding but rather the capacity to listen to a work of art and allow it to speak to one in one's present circumstances. As Gadamer writes with regard to historical understanding:

> A really historical thought must also think its own historicity. Only then will it not chase the phantom of a historical object that is the object of progressive research but rather learn to recognize in the object the other of itself and hence the one as the other. The true historical object is no object but the unity of the one and the other, a relation in which the reality of history, as the reality of historical understanding consists.[48]

If Gadamer's argument here suggests the limits of Hirsch's criticism it also suggests another objection that might be raised against his position: namely, that despite his remarks on the normative authority of a work of art he risks identifying the meaning of a work of art with whatever an audience happens to find in it. If readers necessarily see the claims of a work of art in the context of their own situation and interpret it in this light, this seems to imply that their interpretation is entirely arbitrary. That is, it may be that we understand *Huckleberry Finn* in light of its portrait of Jim and understand that portrait in light of our sensitivity to certain issues. But are some issues to which we could relate it not more appropriate than others? Is it necessarily the case that because we understand *Huckleberry Finn* in the terms in which we understand it we

also understand it adequately? Could our understanding not be a
distortion precisely because we read it in terms of contemporary issues
that are inappropriate to it? Gadamer's own treatment of Greek tragedy
might be a case in point; here one might raise a different criticism from
the one I raised earlier. Could it not be the case that in viewing Greek
tragedy from a Heideggerian perspective – as a challenge to our faith in
science, or at least as an indication of a universal human subservience to
fate – Gadamer obscures what may be more essential to it: namely, its
peculiarly Greek aspects? Even if one argues that we must necessarily
understand even these aspects in light of our own situation, the problem
seems to remain. How do we decide what the appropriate facets of our
situation are for understanding a work of art? Can we equate an adequate
understanding with any relation we assume between the work and our
circumstances? On this view, does understanding not become an entirely
subjective affair?

Arthur Danto draws this conclusion with regard to historical
understanding, claiming that it always includes "an inexpungeable
subjective factor" and, indeed, an "element of sheer arbitrariness."[49]
Stanley Fish seems to take much the same position in regard to textual
understanding, while Harold Bloom makes an even stronger point. On
Bloom's view, the understanding one poet has of another poet's poetry is
not only utterly subjective; it is also a more or less conscious
misunderstanding for the sake of the first poet's own poetry. Bloom
therefore argues that all interpretation is misinterpretation and all
criticism "prose poetry."[50] Hirsch and, more recently, P. D. Juhl have
interpreted Gadamer's position in a similar light. Hirsch paraphrases
Gadamer's position as follows: "The fact that our interpretations are
always governed by our prejudices is really the best guarantee that texts
will have significance for us."[51] Juhl likewise claims that for Gadamer "A
statement about the meaning of a work is a statement about a particular
critic's subjective understanding, about his personal perspective, about
his own *Vorurteile*."[52] We shall examine Gadamer's account of prejudice
in the next chapter. Here, I simply want to point out that if Hirsch and
Juhl have interpreted Gadamer correctly, his rehabilitation of a mimetic
theory of art seems to have undergone a peculiar metamorphosis.

It will be recalled that in his discussion of mimesis Gadamer objected
to the "subjectivization" of aesthetic experience on the grounds that it
overlooked the cognitive potential of works of art. On this view, works
of art are representations that reveal the essence or truth of their subject-
matter and can therefore enhance the understanding of their audiences. I

argued earlier that this conception of art seems to identify aesthetic experience with a simple acceptance of the view of reality represented by a given work of art and that it offers no criterion for discriminating works of art that can enhance our understanding from those that we ought categorically to reject. In trying to make sense of the way in which the understanding of works of art can change, however, Gadamer suggests that the view of reality accepted in aesthetic experience is contingent upon the interpreter's own situation. In other words, the truth than an audience sees in a work of art is one that is relative to their own concerns. Hence, as I already noted, the audience does not simply submit to the view of reality contained in a work of art but rather participates in what its truth is. Thus whereas in the account of mimesis Gadamer stresses the way in which an audience can be educated by a work of art, in his discussion of changes in aesthetic understanding he emphasizes the opposite. Here aesthetic experience is not a question of seeing our lives or an object in terms the work of art offers. We rather bring the work of art into our world and interpret it from the point of view of our own concerns.

As I pointed out, this latter analysis of aesthetic experience is consistent with Gadamer's analysis of historical understanding. None the less it seems to undermine the original point of his defense of mimesis. If the truth represented by art is simply its truth for us, in what sense can we speak of truth at all? What happens to the normative authority of the work if its content is simply relative to our situation? Does this account of aesthetic experience not countenance opportunistic misappropriations of works of art, bending their content to fit the needs of the present? In light of this question a talk Gadamer gave on Herder in Paris in 1941 is particularly unsettling. Herder, he states, was the

> visionary of a new fundamental force in the public sphere: this is the life of the folk. He perceives the reality first in the voice of the people in songs; he recognizes the supportive and nurturing power of the mother tongue; he traces in this the imprinting force of history that fuses with the natural conditions of blood, climate, landscape and so on. Thus, through him the word "folk" achieves in Germany a new depth and a new power entirely remote from that political catchword, a world apart from the political slogans of "democracy."

Gadamer notes that Herder's emphasis on the folk and the unity of the people remained quite distant from a focus on establishing laws and forming civil governments, and he ends his talk by suggesting that this specifically political immaturity on the part of Herder and Germany as a whole may be "the precondition for the fact that, in an altered present, the German concept of folk, in contrast to the democratic slogans of the West, demonstrates the force for a new political and social order."[53]

It would be ahistorical to overlook the political context in which Gadamer made these remarks, a context in which they may have been quite moderate, in fact. In his autobiographical reflections, translated as *Philosophical Apprenticeships*, however, Gadamer himself seems aware of the kind of interpretation to which the remarks might be subjected. There he insists that they had a purely academic intention and expresses hope that at least some of those in the audience at the time understood them in this way.[54] But this hope reflects precisely the problem to which Gadamer's account of understanding gives rise. Why should his listeners have been able to penetrate to his academic intention given the tenor of the times? How can Gadamer even appeal to his intentions given his account of textual meaning? The influence of the situation on one's understanding of texts and the like is, he claims, not only unavoidable but potentially enlightening. How, then, do his remarks themselves escape the verdict of historical hindsight? Whether moderate for the time or not, to speak of Herder in terms of a contrast between the German concept of "folk" and the Western stress on democracy seems to us already to reflect a problematic political influence. There are two questions here: Do we distort Gadamer's meaning by interpreting it in light of a historically developed sensitivity that he could not have shared? Or, conversely, did the political circumstances in which he spoke lead him to distort Herder's meaning to comply with Nazi ideology? In short, can hermeneutics distinguish between distortion and situated interpretation or must it ultimately sanction the subjectivism to which the emphasis on "situatedness" seems to lead? In order to answer this question we must turn to Gadamer's systematic analysis of hermeneutic understanding in general.

3

Hermeneutics and the problem of subjectivism

In Chapter 1 I noted that Gadamer's hermeneutics starts from the claim that understanding another's meaning involves primarily coming to an agreement (*Verständigung*) with him or her about a subject-matter (*Sache*). Despite its naivety, the pre-Romantic hermeneutics of such theorists as Spinoza and Chladenius came closer to recognizing this crucial feature of understanding than did the Romantic analysis. For the pre-Romantics such texts as the Bible were assumed to be true; understanding them involved comprehending their truth or, in other words, coming to agree with them about the truth-content of their claims. In contrast, for the Romantics understanding a text involved comprehending it as the expression of its author's creativity. Texts, works of art and the like were thus no longer considered claims to truth but rather seen as the concrete embodiment of creative genius. The validity of an interpretation was thought to depend upon the extent to which the interpreter could retrace the path of genius by isolating the creator's intentions. We saw that the Historical School and Dilthey adopted this conception of hermeneutic understanding for the study of historical action and that it still influences such contemporary literary critics as E. D. Hirsch.

Gadamer has two objections to this shift in hermeneutics from an understanding of truth to an understanding of creative genius. First, as his analysis of mimesis suggests, it neglects the representational feature of works of art. Works of art contain claims to truth; a focus on the creative intentions behind them therefore misses the point. Second, the shift in hermeneutics overlooks the "situatedness" of understanding, or the way in which it is oriented by the concerns or vantage point of the interpreter. I do not understand Petrarch's ascent of Mount Ventoux in the way that he understood it, nor in the way that his contemporaries viewed it. Rather, for me it is connected to certain other events of which neither Petrarch nor his contemporaries could have had knowledge. Even where my concern is an agent's intentions, my understanding of these intentions is itself a situated one. Thus I understand Louis XIV's intention as one of withdrawing pressure from Holland by reading it into those actions, statements and so on of which I am aware and in which I take an interest. From a different vantage point his intention might be described very differently. The same holds for textual and aesthetic understanding. My understanding of Shakespeare's *Hamlet* may be connected to my understanding of psychological issues and existentialist themes. These may not be issues or themes that motivated Shakespeare himself; neither are they ones of which his public was necessarily aware or ones that will necessarily always orient the understanding of the play. Nevertheless these issues and themes help determine both the meaning the play can have for me and, indeed, the way in which I understand Shakespeare's intentions. As Gadamer writes:

> The real meaning of a text, the way in which it speaks to the interpreter does not depend on contingencies that the author and his original public represent. At least, it is not exhausted by them. It is also always codetermined by the historical situation of the interpreter. The meaning of a text goes beyond its author not only occasionally but always.[1]

On Gadamer's view, this rootedness of aesthetic, textual and historical understanding in an interpreter's situation cannot be avoided either by the theological and empathetic solutions offered by the Historical School or by the Cartesian strategy that Dilthey adopts. Such understanding is rather always dependent on both the historical circumstances in terms of which interpreters perceive their objects and the concerns interpreters bring to them. I argued in chapter 2 that this position seems to have subjectivistic consequences. Although works of art illuminate truth, on Gadamer's view, such truth is not determinate. Rather, if works of art are true they must be true for specific communities of interpreters and thus must speak to their concerns. In understanding a work of art we therefore do not understand its truth as an unchanging representation of what a given object "really" is; we rather understand its truth for us or from our point of view. Similarly, in understanding an historical event or social practice we do not arrive at a determination of its "objective" meaning. We rather see it only in terms of our own historical point of view. On these grounds, however, hermeneutic understanding threatens to become indistinguishable from subjectivistic and, indeed, opportunistic interpretation. We do not achieve knowledge about the texts, works or actions with which we are concerned; we simply connect them to our own circumstances. This result is the one that worried Dilthey; the question it raises is whether any individual circumstances constitute as valid an orientation to a given subject-matter as any other. Is there a difference between a situated perspective that illuminates the meaning of an object and one that distorts it? Or is it the case that, because any understanding is a situated one, all have the same status?

An examination of Gadamer's analysis of prejudice and tradition is essential to answering these questions. I shall then turn to three other features of Gadamer's hermeneutics: (a) his notion of an anticipation of completeness; (b) his analysis of the applicative moment of understanding; and (c) his account of its dialogic structure.

THE REHABILITATION OF PREJUDICE AND TRADITION

Gadamer holds the Enlightenment responsible for both the negative connotations of the notion of prejudice and the negative implications of a recourse to the authority of tradition. In the perspective of the Enlightenment prejudices arise from two sources: first from a reliance on traditional views and refusal to employ one's own reason and second from an over-hasty, unmethodical use of that reason where it is employed. In achieving an adequate understanding of a subject-matter, reason and method are allied with one another against prejudice and authority. In opposition to this view, Gadamer argues that prejudice and tradition are essential to understanding. His "rehabilitation" of their status comprises three steps, the first two of which focus exclusively on prejudice.

The first step involves an adaptation of Husserl's insight that any understanding of an object is an understanding of that object *as* something. In other words, all understanding involves projecting a meaning upon one's perceptions that is not strictly contained in the perceptions themselves. Thus, on the basis of an experience of one dimension of a three-dimensional object I take the object to be three-dimensional. I never see all sides of the object at once. None the less, I still see or, as Husserl puts it, intend each side *as* a side. In this context it is important for Husserl that I do not first have an experience or sense-impression and then understand it in a certain way. Rather, I simply anticipate the three-dimensionality of the object in my perception of it and thus see what I see as a dimension of something three-dimensional.[2]

Gadamer argues that Husserl never did justice to the interpretive element that this kind of anticipatory perception involves.[3] However, if the perception of an object involves an intentional act of meaning-giving, as Husserl claimed, and if this means that consciousness is to be seen not as a *tabula rasa* but as an active determiner of meaning, then the very perception of objects involves projections of meaning, or interpretations. This means, moreover, that the content of a perception is never entirely grounded in pure givenness or evidence; it is rather always "prejudiced" by vantage point, anticipations and the like. As Gadamer writes:

> There is no doubt that seeing as an articulated reading of that which is there looks away, as it were, from much that is there so that for sight it is simply no longer there. Equally, however, it is also led by its anticipations to read in what is absolutely not there. . . .Pure seeing and pure hearing are dogmatic abstractions that artificially reduce the phenomenon. Perception includes meaning.[4]

Gadamer's position here is similar to the analysis of the hermeneutic circle in textual understanding that we examined in chapter 1. The claim there was that understanding a text always involves a projection of its meaning on the basis of a partial experience of it. Thus, for example, on the basis of its title and author I may assume that a certain book is a detective novel. This assumption goes beyond the evidence as yet available to me but I must project some meaning in reading the book in order to understand it at all. Of course, I can always retract my initial anticipation of the point or genre of the book. I may find, for instance, that my assumption that the book before me is a detective novel is placed in question by what appear to be long digressions or irrelevancies. In this connection, Gadamer points out against the Enlightenment that prejudice (*Vorurteil*) literally means simply pre-judgment (*Vor-urteil*) or, in other words, a judgment made before all the evidence has been adequately assessed. A prejudice can therefore be either confirmed by further reading and experience or refuted. To assume that all prejudices are illegitimate and misleading as the Enlightenment does is, in Gadamer's view, simply a "prejudice against prejudice."[5]

But Gadamer's "rehabilitation of prejudice" goes well beyond this point. Its second step refers to ideas that we have already discussed both in chapter 1, in connection with the structure of historical understanding, and in chapter 2, in connection with the possibility of changes in the understanding of works of art. Here Gadamer follows Heidegger rather than Husserl and argues that interpretive projections of meaning are rooted in the situation of the interpreter. If, for example, I understand *Huckleberry Finn* in terms of the issue of racial stereotyping this is not an issue that is "objectively" related to the book or eternally inherent in its meaning. It is rather an issue in terms of which I can understand its meaning although others may understand it in other ways. This situated determination of meaning reflects that which Heidegger refers to as the fore-structure of understanding. His point is that even before I begin consciously to interpret a text or grasp the meaning of an object, I have already placed it within a certain context (*Vorhabe*), approached it from a certain perspective (*Vorsicht*) and conceived of it in a certain way (*Vorgriff*). There is no neutral vantage point from which to survey the "real" meaning of a text or object; even a scientific approach to an object places it within a certain context and takes a certain attitude towards it. The meaning of any object, then, is co-determined by one's own circumstances or "life-relations" (Dilthey) and expectations. For this reason, Gadamer notes not only the connection between prejudice and prejudgment that I cited above but also the contrast between prejudice (*Vor-urteil*) and judgment (*Urteil*). Against the Enlightenment he argues that no understanding is objective in a Cartesian sense; all understanding rather involves projections of meaning that arise out of one's own situation and go beyond the observable "facts." For Heidegger, this means that we are "thrown" and Gadamer claims:

> Heidegger correctly insisted that what he called thrownness and what projection is belong together. Thus, likewise there is no understanding and no interpretation in which the totality of this existential structure is not functioning – even if the intention of the knower is none other than to read "what is there" and to infer from sources "how it actually was."[6]

These first two steps in the rehabilitation of prejudice obviously raise the spectre of subjectivism. If I necessarily understand a text in a "prejudiced" way or, in other words, if I necessarily project a meaning upon it that surpasses the available "evidence" and has its roots in my situation, then what distinguishes understanding from purely subjective interpretation? Is there any difference between personal prejudice and adequate understanding or is all understanding a matter of an individual point of view? We have seen that on certain readings of Gadamer's point, those of Hirsch and Juhl in particular, the answer to this last question is a simple "no." It is the third step of Gadamer's rehabilitation of prejudice and tradition that clarifies how far his analysis is from at least the form of subjectivism these critics attribute to him.

I have already noted that Gadamer follows Heidegger in anchoring understanding in the concerns of the interpreting subject or, as Heidegger puts it, in a structure of practical involvements. More emphatically than Heidegger, however, Gadamer locates this structure of involvements in history. This means that the issues we bring to the process of interpretation are not our preoccupation alone but rather refer to issues and concerns that have developed within the historical tradition to which we belong. Our understanding of Shakespeare's work, for example, is one that has developed historically. At least initially we understand it in the way our predecessors understood it; that is, we bring certain assumptions to the work, assumptions that it will deal with certain perenially human problems, that it will use language beautifully and, in general, that it will meet a high standard of excellence. Indeed, where a work attributed to Shakespeare does not meet this standard, such as the "Shall I die?" sonnet, we doubt that it is really Shakespeare's work. The point here is that the situation of "thrownness" from which we understand a work of art or historical event is not itself an unconditioned or arbitrary one; rather, our understanding stems from the way in which the event or work has previously been understood and is thus rooted in the growth of a historical and interpretive tradition. To take another example: We not only make certain assumptions about Shakespeare's work, we have certain prejudices as to what constitutes a work of art in general, prejudices that determine what we will consider in aesthetic terms and how we approach it. These prejudices are not our personal property alone, however, nor are the standards they involve the product of our own decision. Our aesthetic ideas rather arise from historical developments in painting, sculpture, art criticism and the like. Certainly, we can reassess these developments; they can be made to incorporate different forms of art and new aesthetic sensibilities. None the less, the way this incorporation progresses is itself oriented by the tradition from which it deviates: the shock quality of much contemporary art, for instance, is contingent upon the traditional expectations it obstructs. This art is therefore part of the tradition since it depends upon the assumptions of the tradition for its effect. Prejudices thus condition our understanding both in what is accepted immediately because it is familiar and in what is disturbing because it is new. In both cases, what one generation believes and assumes is grounded in — as a continuation of or reaction to — what a previous generation has formulated and suspected.

This analysis of the relation between understanding, prejudice and tradition indicates the superficiality of Hirsch's and Juhl's interpretation of Gadamer's point. On Gadamer's view, the knowledge that an individual or community has of a particular object domain is not that individual's or community's product alone but that of history. A statement about the meaning of a work of art is thus not a statement about individual perspectives or the personal prejudices of a group of interpreters, as Juhl claims; it is instead one that represents their inheritance. Indeed, part of Gadamer's point is how little interpreters and their personal points of view matter, for even where interpreters attempt to break with tradition and approach their subject-matter without preconceptions, the tradition retains its normative force. I indicated above how this is true for traditional aesthetic norms; Gadamer refers to the historicist attack on the concept of the classical as another example.

He notes that this concept has always had two meanings: it refers both to the artistic style of a certain historical period of Ancient Greece and to a normative ideal of beauty and perfection. Despite historicist attempts to eliminate this second meaning, its normative force is still evident in such things as the idea of a classical education and the question of whether Homer is classical. The notion of a classical education means not only that certain books have been read but also that these are the books that ought to have been read and that the person so educated has been well educated. Similarly, to ask whether Homeric epics are classical is to ask not so much when they were written as whether they conform to the normative ideal that the classical represents. In spite of historicism, then, the second sense of the classical retains its power and continues to guide our aesthetic understanding. As Gadamer writes: "The classical is that which resists historical critique because its historical dominion, the binding power of its validity that it preserves and hands down already precedes historical reflection and sustains itself through it."[7]

At work here is what Gadamer calls "effective history" (*Wirkungs-geschichte*) by which he means the operative force of the tradition over those that belong to it, so that even in rejecting or reacting to it they remain conditioned by it. Their rejection is either less radical than they claim, as in the historicist reduction of the idea of the classical to a stylistic concept, or it is no rejection at all but rather an affirmation by way of negation as in the case of contemporary art. In either case, the interpreter remains subject to the hold of effective history, to the way in which the object has already been understood in the tradition to which he or she belongs. For this reason, the act of understanding is no longer to be conceived of as a subjective act but rather as an aspect of effective history. As Gadamer puts the point, "Effective-historical consciousness is inevitably more being (*Sein*) than consciousness (*Bewusstsein*)."[8] Moreover:

> Long before we understand ourselves in retrospective reflection, we understand ourselves in self-evident ways in the family, society and state in which we live. The focus of subjectivity is a distorting mirror. The self-reflection of the individual is only a flicker in the closed circuits of historical life.[9]

In Gadamer's view, these considerations apply not only to our understanding of texts and works of art but also to our understanding of such concepts as rationality and objectivity themselves. Our ideas as to what constitutes an objective judgment or rational decision are themselves ideas of a particular tradition. What we count as an objective, unconditioned determination of a given object-domain is itself conditioned by our tradition or, more precisely, by what in our tradition counts as objective and unconditioned. In this regard Gadamer holds that the error of the Enlightenment is to have assumed a wholly ahistorical idea of reason and hence to have contrasted reason and method on the one hand, to prejudice and tradition on the other. To see that any understanding of a subject-matter is necessarily prejudiced, however, is to see that the idea of reason itself refers to that which has come to be taken as rational within a particular tradition. Our idea of reason is itself grounded in the tradition and the contraposition of reason and tradition makes no sense.

While the idea of reason itself is informed by prejudices, this is not to say that it is informed by a purely subjective point of view. As we have seen, my projections of meaning refer rather to concerns and assumptions that are part of the historical experience of the community to which I belong and thus precede my own approach to my object-domain. Indeed, on Gadamer's view this historical experience limits the potential arbitrariness of my understanding for, in so far as my understanding of a given object is rooted in a whole history of interpretations of that object, I am protected from an entirely idiosyncratic interpretation of it. In fact, from the point of view of a consciousness of effective history, it is the Enlightenment's appeal to reason and not the rehabilitation of the role of prejudice and tradition in understanding that is arbitrary and subjectivistic. This Enlightenment appeal assumes the possibility of an interpreter's determining the meaning of an object in an autonomous and unconditioned way, as an individual subject, with the use of his or her reason alone. But insight into effective history reveals not only the extent to which all knowledge is historically mediated but also the extent to which the force and influence of prejudice and tradition constrain the willfulness of a purely "subjective" interpretation. Gadamer therefore draws different conclusions from his analysis of the situated character of understanding than do Danto, Fish and Bloom: "The naive belief in the objectivity of historical method was a delusion. But what replaces it is not a simple relativism. Indeed, it is not chance and not arbitrary who we ourselves are and what we can hear from the past."[10]

But even if it is not a matter of "chance" as to who we are and how we understand the things with which we are concerned, it is not clear that Gadamer has resolved the problem of subjectivism with which we began this chapter. We have seen that he locates the personal attitudes of interpreters in history and thus undermines both an Enlightenment conception of objectivity and an individualistic subjectivism. But even if my understanding of a given subject-matter is conditioned by the tradition to which I belong, can that tradition not give rise to two or more very different approaches to the issues? And, if this is the case, how do we decide between them? Our tradition contains very different interpretations of Shakespeare's plays, modern art and even the meaning of such ideals as freedom and democracy. All of these can be seen to be rooted in an effective history of interpretation; none the less they can also contradict one another, often in radical ways. Is allegiance to one or another of these interpretations a matter of the prejudices one happens to have and, if so, how does the rootedness of prejudice in tradition restrict the subjectivism of understanding? Do not our interpretations of texts, works of art and, indeed, the values of the tradition to which we belong still remain arbitrary in so far as they refer simply to prejudices — historically rooted prejudices, to be sure, but prejudices all the same? The question I raised at the beginning of this chapter remains: Is there any way of distinguishing between a historically situated understanding that illuminates the meaning of a text or issue and one that obscures it?[11]

In the third section of *Truth and Method*, Gadamer focuses on the linguistic character of understanding to show that, despite our situatedness, understanding is nevertheless possible. Here Gadamer is concerned to counter suggestions that because we are prejudiced or, otherwise put, because we speak a certain language and employ certain categories we are cut off from other languages, other cultures and even our own past, and thus can only misunderstand them. On Gadamer's view this kind of argument makes sense only if one accepts the notion of a determinate meaning or meaning in itself, a notion he rejects. Understanding is always interpretation and meaning is always a "fusion" of the "horizons" of the interpretation and the object. It follows that one's historical and linguistic situation presents no barrier to understanding but is rather the horizon or perspective from which understanding first becomes possible. As we have seen, one has to have some way of approaching the object; one has to place it within some context. One's language is thus not a limit to understanding but the orientation that permits it in the first place.[12] But this analysis does not resolve the problem of subjectivism with which we are concerned. For even if understanding can be shown to be possible, indeed, even if linguistically constituted prejudices turn out to form the condition of its possibility, the question remains as to how it actually is to be achieved. All languages may be equally suited to illuminating their objects; prejudices, in general, may serve as our orientation to meaning and, hence, as the basis for the possibility of understanding. But certainly a language can admit of diverse ways of understanding a given object. The question is whether all of these are correct or equally adequate and, if they are not, how an interpreter can decide between them.

This is not a question that Gadamer ignores. Rather, he notes the necessity Heidegger discusses of "securing our scientific theme by deriving our fore-having (*Vorhabe*), fore-sight (*Vorsicht*) and fore-conception (*Vorgriff*) from the things themselves."[13] In addition, he claims that the "really critical question of hermeneutics" is that of separating "the true prejudices by which we understand from the false ones by which we misunderstand."[14] None the less it is not clear that his response is entirely successful. In order to understand and assess it we shall have to examine his idea of an anticipation or preconception of completeness (*der Vorgriff der Vollkommenheit*) and then consider his analyses of the applicative moment and dialogic structure of understanding.

THE ANTICIPATION OF COMPLETENESS

Gadamer introduces the idea of anticipating completeness or perfection (*Vollkommenheit*) as a counterforce to the potential arbitrariness and idiosyncracy of textual interpretation. As the remarks cited above indicate, he does not think that the extent to which all understanding is prejudiced and historically conditioned precludes the possibility of assessing the adequacy of prejudices or revising them in light of "the things themselves" or of a "better" understanding of the subject-matter at issue. Of course, such revision and assessment can no longer appeal either to an Enlightenment conception of unprejudiced reason or to the idea of an unconditioned perception of "the things themselves." The question then is how we can test the adequacy of our prejudices to "the things themselves," given that the way we understand "the things themselves" is itself determined by our historical prejudices. In order to answer this question Gadamer returns to the hermeneutic circle of whole and part, to which both Schleiermacher and Dilthey pointed.[15]

As we have seen, their conception of the hermeneutic circle is based both on the insight that one must anticipate or project meaning in order to understand a text and on the claim that this initial projection can be corrected in one's further reading. Gadamer points out that the presumption here is that the text forms a unity, an internally consistent whole, and that one can use the regulative ideal of unity to assess the adequacy of one's interpretations of its various parts. To return to a previous example: one may assume that a certain book is a detective novel and understand certain psychological portraits it contains in this light, as giving clues to the identity of the criminal or adding to the suspense. As one reads more of the book, however, one may find that the "clues" do not lead anywhere or that no suspense is added. Hence one's initial assumption as to the point of these studies may need to be revised. But in this case the revision is guided by the criterion of unity, by the need to integrate the psychological portraits more completely with the text as a whole. The condition of the possibility of revising initial projections of textual meaning is thus a presumption of the text's own internal unity. The text must be approached as an internally consistent whole because it is this assumption of self-consistency that provides a standard for keeping or discarding individual interpretations of the text's parts. Conversely, if one denies that a given text is internally coherent from the start, one has no way of knowing whether its inconsistency is the fault of the text or one's understanding of it. For this reason hermeneutic efforts are directed at finding an interpretation that can both make sense out of the individual parts of a text and integrate them into a consistent whole.

Deconstructionist critics have recently disputed the value of this methodological commitment to a text's unity by suggesting that this commitment leads one to overlook tensions and contradictions inherent to the text. Deconstructionists thus focus on the inconsistencies in a text, on the gaps between intention and meaning, content and rhetoric and the like.[16] From a hermeneutic perspective, however, it might be argued that the conviction of coherence is necessary even if one is concerned with textual self-contradictions, since contradictions are contradictions only within, or of, a presumed general meaning. The presumption of unity thus does not preclude the discovery of points at which the text "deconstructs" itself; instead it is essential to it. Be this as it may, Gadamer himself partially concurs with the deconstructionist assessment of the presumption of unity. He suggests, however, that its value is limited not because it is unnecessary or metaphysically misleading, but rather because it does not suffice to resolve the problem with which Schleiermacherian hermeneutics begins: namely, that of misunderstanding.

It is not hard to see how Gadamer might come to this conclusion. If one focuses simply on the unity or self-consistency of a text, it is conceivable that one might still be unable to see through an initial, inappropriate projection of meaning. That is, one could construct a conception of a work that both made sense of its parts and integrated them into a whole but was still a distortion of, or limitation on, the meaning of a text. Indeed, as Hirsch points out, such distortion would seem to be the normal case. Calling initial projections of meaning "genre ideas," he writes, "It is very difficult to relinquish one's own genre idea since that idea seems so totally adequate to the text. After all, since the text is largely constituted by the hypothesis how could the hypothesis fail to seem inevitable and certain?"[17] The problem here is that if one begins to understand the individual parts of a text in light of an assumption as to the meaning of its whole, it is not clear how these parts, so understood, can lead one to revise one's understanding of the whole. Conversely, if one projects a meaning of the whole on the basis of an interpretation of the way in which individual parts cohere with one another, how can the understanding of the whole, so projected, lead one to change one's understanding of the parts? Why, in other words, is the hermeneutic circle not simply a vicious one in which one's understanding of the individual parts of a text confirms one's assumption as to the meaning of the whole and vice versa? Based on his analysis of the role of prejudices in understanding, Gadamer puts this question as follows:

> Here the question arises . . . how is one supposed to find his way out of the boundaries of his own fore-meanings? Certainly there can be no general assumption that what is said to us in a text will fit perfectly with my own opinions and expectations. On the contrary, what someone says to me,

whether in a conversation, letter, book or whatever, stands first under the presupposition that it is his, not my, opinion which is expressed and which I have to appropriate without necessarily sharing. This condition does not make understanding easier, but harder since the fore-meanings that condition my understanding can remain entirely unnoticed. If they motivate misunderstanding, how is misunderstanding in general to be perceived with regard to a text where there is nothing else to contradict?[18]

Hirsch points to conflicting interpretations of Wordsworth's "A Slumber Did my Spirit Seal" as an example of the predicament to which the prejudiced character of textual interpretation leads.[19] Here different initial assumptions as to the poem's meaning seem to have led to two contradictory ways of integrating its last lines. Thus, Cleanth Brooks interprets the poem as an expression of inconsolable grief at Lucy's death and emphasizes the negative lines ("No motion has she now, no force; She neither hears nor sees") as well as the lifelessness contained in the image of being "Rolled round in earth's diurnal course."[20] F. W. Bateson, in contrast, sees the poem as an affirmation of a pantheistic immortality and emphasizes the similarity between the dead Lucy and the "rocks, and stones, and trees" of the last line.[21] Both interpretations are equally well rooted in traditions of Wordsworth scholarship and seem equally well able to make sense out of the poem. The question that arises, then, is whether it is possible to choose between them in any way other than a purely arbitrary one.

Hirsch, of course, follows Schleiermacher and Dilthey in arguing that one can choose between these conflicting interpretations by moving outside the text and referring to the poet's intentions as gleaned from a knowledge of his life, typical concerns, beliefs and the like. Hirsch also claims that this procedure confirms Bateson's reading of the poem since extra-textual evidence indicates that Wordsworth was a pantheist at the time that he wrote the poem. Now, Hirsch admits that this interpretation remains only probable because "we shall never be certain what any writer means"[22] but he does not seem to perceive any other problems with his solution. The problem that concerns us here, however, is that the solution fails to clarify how the kind of extra-textual evidence to which he appeals is supposed to aid purely textual interpretation since one also needs an interpretation of this evidence and of its relation to the text. In other words, the extra-textual evidence to which Hirsch points can be itself considered from the point of view of the hermeneutic circle. If the problem of textual interpretation involves separating an adequate understanding of the meaning of a text from possibly misguided assumptions about it, then this problem also affects the extra-textual evidence to which Hirsch points. This, too, will have to be interpreted, integrated with other textual and extra-textual evidence and formed into a unified whole. If there is more than one way of doing this, then the solution Hirsch proposes simply remits the problem to a different level. The problem itself remains the same: how can one get at the meaning of a text if one's initial projections of meaning dictate one's understanding of that which is supposed to be the textual or extra-textual evidence for one's view?[23]

We have seen that the viciousness of the hermeneutic circle may not always be avoided by relying on criteria of coherence alone. But neither can it be avoided by trying to move outside the circle and referring to psychological or biographical data external to the poem or text itself. Gadamer's own response to the problem is the anticipation or preconception of completeness. He suggests that the self-confirming character of initial assumptions of meaning can be avoided only if one attends not to the author's probable intentions but to the "substantive accuracy of what the other says."[24] In other words, one has to assume that a text is possibly true and that it therefore has something to teach or say to one. The argument here is structurally the same as the argument for assuming unity: only this assumption provides a standard for retaining or discarding self-consistent interpretations of a text's meaning. Thus, if an interpretation of a text along the lines of the hermeneutic circle makes the text take a position that appears obviously false, this, for Gadamer, serves primarily to indicate the possible inadequacy of the interpretation. In every case one has to test one's assumptions of meaning in light of what Gadamer sees as an openness to the otherness or to the distinctness of the text and to the possible challenge the text presents to one's own views. Conversely, if one abandons the criterion of truth from the start, one will have no way of deciding whether the implausibility of the text derives from its intrinsic failures or one's own inability to understand it. It follows that one will be unable to either revise or confirm one's own projections of its meaning. As Gadamer writes: "The anticipation of completeness thus contains not only the formal element that a text should completely express its meaning but also that what it says is the complete truth."[25]

With regard to the problem of avoiding arbitrary or idiosyncratic interpretations of a text, this claim suggests that one has to assume that a text has something to teach one and is a better authority on the subject-matter at issue than oneself. Given the logical confines of the hermeneutic circle, a relative independence from the effects of one's own initial prejudices is possible only under the assumption that the text has the authority to challenge those prejudices. I have to assume that the text says something new, different and truer or more complete than what I previously believed about both it and the subject-matter it addresses; otherwise I can only confirm my original, possibly uneducated, views about both. For this reason Gadamer states that "the hermeneutic task turns of itself into a substantive (*sachliche*) inquiry and is always already codetermined by this."[26] I assume that Wordsworth's poem can teach me something about death and am therefore sensitive to possible differences between its views and my own assumptions or the assumptions that I have inherited from the tradition. Such sensitivity to differences allows certain elements of the poem − for instance, the immortality implied in not feeling "the touch of earthly years" − to appear in high relief. This illumination allows me to see the validity of Bateson's interpretation of the poem. More importantly, it leaves me free to question not only my own initial assumptions about Wordsworth's poem but my own inherited beliefs about death. Gadamer describes this approach as a process of putting one's prejudices at play, of allowing them to be confronted by the claims of a text. As he writes:

> Whoever wants to understand will not be able to yield to the contingency of his own assumptions and thereby fail to hear the text's opinions as consistently and stubbornly as possible. . . . Whoever wants to understand a text is rather prepared to let it say something to him. Hence a hermeneutically schooled consciousness must be sensitive to the otherness of the text from the beginning.[27]

For Gadamer, then, the possibility of distinguishing between arbitrary prejudices that distort meaning and those that illuminate it depends on an openness to the possible truth of the object under study. It is essential to grant to the text one is studying a certain normative authority, for it is only by doing so that one can test the adequacy of one's views about either the text or the issues on which it focuses. Deconstructionists, of course, dispute not only the original claim of the hermeneutic tradition that understanding requires a presumption in favor of the coherence of the text to be understood; they also dispute Gadamer's emendation of this claim to include a presumption in favor of the truth of the text. In a discussion of Gadamer's hermeneutics Jacques Derrida thus suggests that the anticipation of completeness or a "good will" towards the text in so far as one is committed to grasping its truth simply harks back to an outmoded metaphysical conception about "truth." On his view, the encounter with a text is characterized far more by a "rupture" in understanding and far more by insight into the way in which the text subverts its own truth-claim than by a harmonious process of coming to see the truth in what another has said.[28]

From our point of view, Derrida's criticism of a "good will" toward the text is important not so much because of the notion of "rupture" that he substitutes for it but because it does highlight an apparent problem with the idea of anticipating completeness.[29] The question that arises in this regard is whether Gadamer resolves the problem of misinterpretation by using the object of study itself as a standard of truth. This question reposes one of the questions I raised in connection with the revival of a mimetic theory of art: namely, if works of art are representations of reality that must be understood as such, how does aesthetic knowledge differ from a simple agreement with the views of a work? On Gadamer's mimetic view, as we saw, the experience of art is an experience of truth and may require a transformation in Hegelian fashion of one's previous beliefs. Similarly, according to the idea of anticipating completeness, I must assume the truth of my object as the condition of testing my prejudices with regard to it and discarding those that foster opportunistic or subjectivistic misunderstanding. But if I must assume truth in this way, we seem to be right back at the problem posed by the analysis of mimesis: an adequate hermeneutic understanding seems again to involve a willingness to accept the greater authority of one's object or, as Gadamer puts it, to "accept with agreement;" the question now is how understanding differs from a simple submission to the views of another. The anticipation of completeness allows us to examine our previous assumptions about a text or object and the subject-matter with which it deals. But if we discard these assumptions in light of the views we ascribe to our object, what guarantees that the new views we adopt are any less arbitrary, idiosyncratic or misleading than the prejudices we discard? In other words, what assures us that the truth we find in the object is a truth we ought to substantiate or affirm?

In examining this question, it is important to recall the distinction between two senses of understanding made in chapter 1. For Gadamer the primary sense of understanding is the substantive one: one understands the meaning of a text when one can see its truth, just as one understands Euclidean geometry when one understands its truth (even if this is relativized to allow for other forms of geometry). But Gadamer admits that this kind of understanding is not always possible, that there are texts the claims of which can no longer appear plausible at all. On his view, then, the attempt to understand the truth of a work of art or the challenge it presents to one's own views has to *guide* the process of interpretation – otherwise there is no way of evaluating one's own or someone else's understanding of the work's meaning, since there is no way of distinguishing between the false claims a work may make and a complete misunderstanding of them. Still, this attempt to understand in the primary sense of understanding truth can fail and when it does one may have to be content with a genetic understanding of the conditions under which the claims could appear to be true.[30] Hence, Gadamer's point is not that one always adopts the views of one's object in understanding it at all. His argument is rather that an *openness* to the *possible* truth of the object is the condition of understanding, that one must at least provisionally concede authority to one's object, even if this concession may ultimately be rescinded. In reply to Derrida's suggestion that textual understanding involves an act of deconstruction or subversion, Gadamer therefore claims that "the literary text, the linguistic work of art, meets us not only as a barrier but is also accepted with an agreement that is the beginning of a long, sometimes of an often repeated attempt to understand."[31] Just as in the case of presuming coherence, it is only by presuming truth that what may appear first as a "rupture" in the text can be seen to require not only a new textual interpretation but a new understanding of the subject-matter at issue. From this perspective, to begin with the deconstructionist assumption that claims to truth are rarely warranted and in fact undermine themselves is to sacrifice a clear opportunity not simply to understand but, moreover, to learn.

Nevertheless, it is not clear that this caveat to the anticipation of completeness suffices to resolve the problem to which I have pointed. Gadamer does allow that an openness to the possible truth of one's object will not always bear the fruit of understanding and that there are texts, works of art and the like the claims of which one must ultimately reject (or explain historically or psychologically). Now the question is, which ones? When is one supposed to give up the attempt to learn from one's object? According to the anticipation of completeness, the apparent falsity of a text or work is supposed only to lead to greater efforts to be educated by it. Is there not a danger here that, if we do not simply misinterpret works so that they comply with our own beliefs, we will end up learning from truth-claims we ought long ago to have dismissed? Gadamer's own hermeneutic analyses of Plato, Hegel and others are for the most part exemplary models of the knowledge to be won by adopting his premises.[32] At the same time, however, his attitude toward the hermeneutic tradition analyzed in chapter 1 seems to be an example of the insights to be won through critical distance. The question, then, is how and when such critical distance is justified. If we have to assume the normative authority and possible truth of a work in order to allow for an adequate understanding of it, how *can* we possibly learn to criticize it? When do we give up the attempt to learn from *Mein Kampf*, for example? From a hermeneutic perspective, it would seem that it has to be regarded as a possible interpretation of the subject-matter with which it deals and hence an interpretation to which we must remain open.

It seems to me that this question about *Mein Kampf* gains considerable force when it is placed in the context of Gadamer's remarks on tradition. We have seen that the potential arbitrariness of hermeneutic understanding is limited by at least two conditions: by both its foundation in an interpretive tradition and by the necessity that it provisionally accept the truth, indeed, the normative authority of its object. Our interpretations are not our interpretations alone but have historical roots; moreover, we can test their adequacy by comparing them to the truth of the object with which we are concerned. But what is the object of hermeneutic understanding? In chapter 2, I suggested that the human sciences differ from the natural sciences in that the objects they study – texts, works of art, social norms and the like – are not independent objects at all but "fusions of horizons." This means that they are themselves already the result of interpretations by a tradition. The text that is handed down to us is a fusion of previous opinions about it, a harmony of voices, as Gadamer often puts it, to which we add our own. But this means that object of hermeneutic understanding is already a fusion of the interpretations of a tradition and our encounter with it is an encounter with the tradition. If this encounter entails according to the object the normative authority claimed by the idea of anticipating completeness, then normative authority is accorded to the tradition itself. From this point of view Gadamer seems to have replaced the allegiance to personal prejudices that his critics attribute to him with an allegiance to the past. The tradition is not only the source of the old interpretations that we test in anticipating completeness; our new interpretations are themselves readings of the tradition's authority.

It could be argued that this conclusion presents a new form of subjectivism. We have seen that on Gadamer's view our interpretations can no longer be described as personal idiosyncracies; neither are we without a means of distinguishing understanding from the kind of misunderstanding that refuses to take seriously either the coherence or the truth of a text or other aspect of the tradition. Still, in discarding our initial assumptions about a text or subject-matter in light of the truth we find in the object, we seem simply to be replacing certain unexamined prejudices, themselves conditioned by the tradition to which we belong, with other views explicitly adopted from the tradition. But what guarantees that the views we explicitly adopt from the tradition are any less arbitrary than the prejudices that we previously held in an unreflective way? If the learning that occurs through the anticipation of completeness reflects simply the acceptance "with agreement" of an aspect or interpretation of the tradition other than that to which we previously held why assume that it involves learning at all? We seem to be able to revise the prejudices we have inherited from the tradition only by assuming the validity of other prejudices the tradition contains. This kind of subjectivism thus approaches the kind of conservative defense of tradition that many critics have, in fact, associated with Gadamer's work. In order to explore the extent to which this reading is warranted we must turn to his account of the applicative moment of understanding.

UNDERSTANDING AND APPLICATION

The idea of anticipating completeness has raised the question of whether Gadamer does not avoid the subjectivism that issues from endorsing any understanding of a text or subject-matter whatsoever by recurring to a different form of subjectivism that simply affirms the interpretations of the tradition to which one happens to belong. If we must assume the truth of a text or tradition in order to gain a standard for discriminating between different accounts of it, how can we ever learn to reject the truth we have assumed? It may be, as Gadamer argues, that because of our historicity we can never transcend the prejudices of the tradition to which we belong and evaluate them according to independent critieria of reason. Still, does the fact that we are conditioned by our tradition also mean that in our attempts to understand the phenomena with which we are concerned we must also "accept" that tradition "with agreement"? Does all hermeneutic understanding involve acceptance of the interpreted claims of its tradition and, if so, how does it avoid becoming simply a kind of apology for it?

One answer Gadamer provides to this question follows the same strategy he used to answer the similar question about mimesis. There Gadamer showed that an understanding of the way in which a work of art is representational is always an understanding of the way it is representational for me or for my situation. He makes a similar move in providing an answer to the question about understanding in general, claiming that the views of a tradition are not simply adopted but modified in accordance with changed historical circumstances. In elucidating this position, Gadamer makes use of Aristotle's criticism of Plato's account of ethical knowledge.

As is well known, Aristotle argues against Plato that ethical understanding is a form of knowledge distinct from metaphysics. To Plato's theoretical knowledge of the Form of the Good, Aristotle contrasts an understanding of "the good for man" that has to be concretized in practical situations. The peculiarity of ethical knowledge is thus that, on the one hand, "the actor must see the concrete situation in light of what is demanded of him in general;"[33] that is, agents must understand given situations in light of the general norms that are relevant to them. On the other hand, an intellectual or theoretical understanding of these norms is useless since one has to know in addition how to apply them. That is, one has to know not only that one ought to be good to others, for example; one has also to know how to be good to a particular person given who he or she is and the particular situation in which he or she is involved. On Gadamer's analysis of Aristotle's point, then, ethical knowledge is a matter more of practical than theoretical knowledge, of knowing how rather than knowing that.[34] He insists, however, that it is a kind of knowing how very different from technical know-how and his further analysis of Aristotle is therefore concerned to show the difference between these two forms of applied knowledge.

Ethical and technical knowledge differ first with regard to the relation of knowledge to its application. Aristotle claims that one becomes virtuous by performing virtuous acts and in this regard the structure of ethical knowledge appears to be identical to the case of technical expertise. In both cases one learns through practice: one becomes a good dentist by filling teeth and a good person by performing virtuous acts. Nevertheless, the two forms of knowledge are importantly different. By filling teeth one gains a certain proficiency; one learns how to be faster and more efficient; one becomes less tentative and more secure in one's knowledge. Still, what one knows when one knows how to fill teeth does not fundamentally change. It always involves knowing how to plug up a cavity with some kind of metal. In contrast, the elements involved in knowing how to act courageously, for example, may change radically. Courage may involve a willingness to die but also a refusal to die, standing up for one's rights as well as yielding to others. Thus, whereas the actions to be performed are always more or less dictated by the task set for technical knowledge (plugging up a cavity), the actions that the virtue of courage involves are not so given but rather depend to a far greater extent on individual circumstances. Particular problems encountered in filling teeth may require variations in the procedure one follows. Variations in the act of being courageous, however, are not simply questions of procedure. They rather affect the knowledge of what courage is. Gadamer puts this point as follows:

> The image that the person has of what he ought to do, thus, for example, his concepts of right and wrong, of decency, courage, honor, solidarity and so on . . . are guiding images in a certain sense, to be sure. But still a fundamental difference is recognizable from the guiding image that the blueprint of an object to be produced represents for the artisan. What is right, for example, is not fully determinable independently of the situation that demands the right from me, whereas the *eidos* of that which an artisan wants to produce is certainly fully determined, namely by the use for which it is intended.[35]

A first peculiarity of ethical knowledge is thus that the concrete situation that requires it affects it to a far greater degree than it affects technical knowledge. The principles or models to which practical knowledge looks are never applicable as they stand but must *always* be modified to suit individual circumstances. Ethical knowledge is a matter of understanding how a general norm is to be given concrete content — or what its meaning is — with regard to a particular situation. Technical knowledge is a matter of fulfilling a general norm or paradigm as best one can given one's material and tools. The difference between this kind of technical ability and practical knowledge is that the latter affects the norm and paradigm in question. It is not just a matter of fulfilling the norm of courage as best one can but rather of filling in what that norm actually means.

This first difference between technical and ethical understanding already suggests a second difference. Technical knowledge is knowledge of the means to an end. One has a clear picture of that which one wants to produce and needs simply to calculate the most efficient way of producing or at least approximating it. In contrast, although Aristotle claims that ethical knowledge is knowledge of the means, ends considered as means to further ends are clearly part of ethical deliberation as well. The final end of such deliberation is "the good life" in general but, in itself, this notion has no clear content. It is not a life of which we have a concrete image and to which various means can lead. Rather, the means one chooses to attain the good life itself affects what one takes that life to be, just as what one understands by courage, honor or the good life in general will affect the means one chooses to achieve any of these. The relationship between means and ends, then, is a reciprocal one. Ethical knowledge is a matter of weighing various options against a general normative framework that is itself clarified through the options one chooses. For this reason it can never involve simply the application of a formula but rather requires reflection. As Gadamer writes, "The knowledge that guides action is demanded by the concrete situation in which we have to choose the thing to be done and cannot be spared the task of deliberation and decision by any learned or mastered technique."[36]

Gadamer notes a third peculiarity of ethical knowledge that concerns the knowledge of what others, as opposed to oneself, ought to do. In this case, virtuous people are not those who simply impose their knowledge on others or dogmatically apply their own experiences to the situations of others. They are rather those who want what is good for the other person involved, not that which might be good for themselves, and are therefore open to differences in experience and situation. Here as elsewhere, then, ethical knowledge involves an ability to apply general principles to different concrete situations. In contrast to the case of the application of technical knowledge, ethical knowledge is not unaffected by its mode of application, nor can the desired result be determined in advance of the situation. What is required is both a general understanding of the relevant ethical norms and a sensitivity to relevant differences in circumstance.

If this analysis of ethical knowledge is extended to the case of hermeneutic understanding, the primary effect is to underscore a point made in chapter 2. There I mentioned that playing a game raises the issue of the relation between general and particular since a game embodies a set of rules that must be applied in different ways under different circumstances. In order for a game to exist it has to be played; this means that it must be represented by different players in different actions with potentially different results and Gadamer therefore describes games as entities that exist "only in being different."[37] We have seen the same relation between general and particular in ethical knowledge. In this context, in fact, Gadamer almost echoes his earlier statement: "The agent is concerned with a kind of thing that is not always the way it is but can also be otherwise."[38] Both games and ethical principles must be represented by players and agents who act in light of norms and rules but who also act differently in different situations. Ethical knowledge and knowledge of how to play a game are thus both concretized only in the application of a general normative understanding to specific circumstances. Gadamer now suggests that the same holds for textual understanding and for hermeneutic understanding in general. The interpreter "may not look away from himself and the concrete situation in which he finds himself. He must relate the text to this situation if he wants to understand at all."[39]

This point thus reiterates the point we have already discussed in some depth that hermeneutic understanding is situated and contextual. The meaning a text has it has for me in my concrete circumstances, just as the meaning an ethical norm has it has for me in a concrete situation of action. For this reason, Gadamer denies that there is any essential difference between dogmatic and exegetical hermeneutics. With regard to legal hermeneutics, for example, the judge and legal historian must both perform the same task. If, as a legal historian, I want to know what the law against killing innocent life means I must understand it in terms of possible applications. Does it preclude abortion, murder in self-defense or mercy-killing, or must it be interpreted in such a way as to allow for these? In attempting simply to understand the law against murder, then, I must perform the same action as the judge: I must learn how to apply the law to different concrete situations so that, at the same time, I uphold the spirit of the law. By the same token, if one wants simply to know what the American Constitution says about unlawful searches one still has to understand this in light of its applications. One's understanding will therefore always go beyond that of the original framers of the Constitution because one will always have to be concerned with possible applications of which they could have had no knowledge. The case of wire-tapping is a good example. Here, what one understands an illegal search to be will be affected by the decision as to whether such phenomena as wire-tapping are cases of it or not. We thus do not have a purely exegetical knowledge of the meaning of an unlawful search which we can then apply to the case of wire-tapping; rather, our knowledge of what an unlawful search is already involves application. The same holds for textual understanding in general. As we have seen, the question of whether or not *Huckleberry Finn* is racist is a question posed from a contemporary point of view. None the less, one cannot read *Huckleberry Finn* and then apply its content to this question; the question rather conditions the content one finds in it. Both ethical knowledge and hermeneutic understanding, then, involve application and this means that they are themselves affected by varying situations and concerns. As Gadamer writes, "We understand differently if we understand at all."[40]

This reiteration of the situated character of understanding partially resolves the problem to which I pointed in the last section, namely that on Gadamer's account hermeneutic understanding seems to involve a simple acquiescence to the views of its object. It is now clear that if we must anticipate the truth of our object it still remains a truth for us, one that must make sense to us in our concrete circumstances. Hence, we do not simply adopt the views of our object or the tradition; rather, the way we understand their truth already involves application to our situation and hence modification in line with our circumstances. For Aristotle, ethical knowledge begins with a proper upbringing and the appropriation of a general normative framework. Indeed, although he does not appeal to the Form of the Good he does appeal to clearly formulated ethical norms. Nevertheless, as we have seen, the point he makes against Plato is that ethical matters do not admit of categorical resolutions, that although ethical action requires a general normative understanding, the norms to which it appeals cannot be applied in the same way in all instances but must be modified in accordance with the demands of the situation. On Gadamer's analysis, hermeneutic interpretation in general achieves a similar "concretization of the universal."[41] In this case, it is important that a tradition of interpretation presents normative parameters for the hermeneutic understanding of meaning. For instance, whether we are familiar with the literature on Shakespeare's work or not we approach his work in a way influenced by a tradition of Shakespeare interpretation so that we assume its excellence, importance and so on. But, just as we cannot apply ethical norms categorically we cannot adhere to a tradition of interpretation dogmatically. Rather, in approaching Shakespeare from the perspective of changed historical circumstances, we necessarily modify and extend the traditional way in which the excellence and importance of his work has been understood. Similarly, in trying to understand the meaning of the prohibition against killing innocent life or of the views of the Constitution on illegal searches, we must at least provisionally accept their general "truth" or validity; at the same time, the way in which we interpret this truth or validity is necessarily concretized and transformed in connection with concrete issues. In each case, a hermeneutic understanding of meaning thus both assumes the truth of its object and modifies it. Indeed, for Gadamer the tradition in general takes on the function that ethical norms have for Aristotle: that of providing a "guiding image" for interpretation. Such a guiding image orients our understanding; none the less, we cannot apply it dogmatically; neither does it categorically decide the meaning of the object under study. Rather, it presents a framework for interpretation that is itself modified in accordance with the concrete circumstances of the interpretation itself.

This applicative moment of understanding is already implied, in fact, by Gadamer's account of the anticipation of completeness itself. In this regard, at least one of his remarks contradicts the interpretation I have thus far suggested. Gadamer claims that "the understanding of the reader is always . . . guided by the transcendental expectations of meaning that stem from the relation of what is meant to the truth" and means by this that "we understand . . . transmitted texts on the basis of expectations of meaning that are created by our own previous relation to the subject matter."[42] I have argued that Gadamer's analysis of the anticipation of completeness stresses the challenge the object of interpretation can present to our prejudices about it. Here, however, Gadamer seems instead to suggest that in assuming the possible truth of the text we assume that it conforms to our own previous understanding of truth or, in other words, to our prejudices. By an openness to the truth of the text, he thus means a willingness to believe that it can say something that makes sense to us, that coheres with our own understanding and hence appears rational or plausible to us. If this were the whole story Gadamer's analysis would appear to favor interpretations like Brooks's interpretation of Wordsworth's poem since it allows the poem to present a reaction to death that is much closer to *our* ordinary way of conceiving of it. In the very next sentence Gadamer reverses himself again however, writing "And just as we believe the news of a correspondent because he was there or somehow knows better, we are fundamentally open to the possibility that a transmitted text knows better than our own fore-meanings want to admit.[42]

Here, openness to the possible truth of a text or someone's claims seems again to involve an openness to the possible challenge these present to one's prejudices. The appparent conflict here is an indication of the complexity of Gadamer's position. On the one hand he is concerned to demonstrate the challenge that a text can offer to our present views and thus the way in which it allows us to test the arbitrariness and subjectivism of our initial interpretations. On the other hand he needs to make it clear that this challenge is not an ahistorical one. The way in which a text or any object of understanding challenges our beliefs is contingent on both the way we interpret the object and on just what our beliefs are; in other words, it is contingent upon our situation and our understanding of truth therefore involves application whether we are conscious of such application or not.

This extension of Aristotle's account of the situated and contextual character of ethical knowledge to hermeneutic knowledge in general seems to lead again to the same subjectivistic consequences that emerged from the account of the truth of art. Gadamer insists that application has nothing to do with "making free with the text" and that the judge who must understand and apply a law is "wholly committed" to its meaning.[42] Still, the emphasis in his analysis of application is on the contextuality of interpretation or, in other words, on the way in which interpretations will necessarily and legitimately differ depending on the different concerns and issues in terms of which the objects of interpretation are understood. But if we must apply ethical norms, texts or the interpretations of the tradition in order to understand them, what prevents us from seeing them in the light of arbitrary prejudices or even distorting them for individual purposes? How do we avoid "making free with the text?" If our ethical understanding has the structure Aristotle attributes to it may it not too easily become opportunistic, so that we interpret norms in a way that allows us to do what we want? By the same token, if our understanding of texts or other aspects of a tradition involves their application to our own historical situation do we not risk re-interpreting their claims for our own historical uses?

In his criticism of Gadamer's account of application Emilio Betti answers these questions in the affirmative, claiming that Gadamer's analysis "open[s] door and gate to subjective arbitrariness and threaten[s] to cloud or distort and, be it only unconsciously, to disfigure historical truth."[43] Indeed, we appear to have answered the subjectivism implied in the anticipation of completeness – namely, that we simply substitute alternative prejudices for our own – by reverting to the kind of subjectivism it was supposed to resolve: namely, that of arguing for the adequacy of any interpretation whatsoever in so far as all are situated and contextual. In fact one might argue that Gadamer's hermeneutics exhibits a peculiar oscillation. To the original charge that his hermeneutics permits subjective arbitrariness in interpretation he replies by pointing to the need to anticipate the truth or completeness of the object in question. To the charge that this solution simply reflects a prejudice in favor of the truth of the object he replies by pointing to the way in which understanding involves application and hence to the way in which interpretations of the truth of the object change in accordance with historical circumstances. To this extent his hermeneutics appears to founder on a dilemma: on the one hand, it can avoid opportunism in interpretation only by becoming what one might call "conservative" and accepting the truth of the object; conversely it can avoid this conservatism only by becoming opportunistic and failing to provide any criteria for discriminating between understanding and misunderstanding.

Gadamer claims that all interpretation is prejudiced. For this reason it will no longer be possible to appeal to guarantees of "objective" understanding such as an author's intentions, the perspective of God or scientific method since, as should be clear at this point, the understanding of all of these is itself a situated and therefore prejudiced one. At the same time he denies that the situatedness of interpretation makes it completely a matter of subjective opinion. An adequate understanding of an object is rather a question of appropriating a tradition of interpretation as a general normative framework and the tradition is thus supposed to provide some kind of normative limit to the free range of interpretation. But as we have seen, since the tradition cannot be applied dogmatically or restrict the number and variety of historically situated, adequate interpretations, it remains unclear what these limits on interpretation are. We must assume the truth of our object in order to attain distance from our prejudices; at the same time this assumption cannot lead to a literal or rote reiteration of the claims of the object, for if those claims are to be true they must apply to our particular circumstances. Thus, we must both grant normative authority to the object and apply this normative authority so that it makes sense for our situation. But what are the standards here? How do we know when we have applied a tradition of interpretation in an appropriate way so that although we modify its claims we do not interpret them opportunistically? I want now to turn to Gadamer's analysis of the dialogic structure of understanding to see if that provides any answer to this question.

THE DIALOGIC STRUCTURE OF UNDERSTANDING

For Gadamer, the dialogic structure of understanding follows from the tension noted above between the idea of anticipating completeness and the account of application. The conflict here between presuming the truth of the claims of one's object and adapting them — even if unconsciously — according to the prejudices of one's time and place constitutes understanding as a kind of discussion between different points of view. The conditions of conversation ought, therefore, to clarify those of understanding.

On Gadamer's account, a genuine conversation is one in which each partner to the conversation is concerned entirely with the subject-matter (*die Sache*) and with arriving at the truth with regard to it. In the first instance, this presupposes what Gadamer refers to as the *docta ignorantia*. Genuine conversation is based upon a recognition of our own fallibility, on a recognition that we are finite and historical creatures and thus we do not have absolute knowledge in Hegel's sense. The knowledge we do have is akin to that of Socrates: a knowledge that we do not know and hence an openness to the possible truth of other views. In the second instance, then, each participant in a genuine conversation must be concerned with discovering the real strength of every other participant's position. The participants cannot try simply to out-argue or outwit each other; neither can they try to reduce the views of others to the conditions of their genesis. At issue is not the intention behind a person's saying what that person says but its possible truth. Each participant must thus be taken seriously as an equal dialogue partner, as someone who despite heritage, quirks of expression or the like is equally capable of illuminating the subject-matter. As Gadamer writes:

> Thus, it is part of any genuine conversation that one submits to the other, allows his viewpoint really to count and gets inside the other far enough to understand not him, to be sure, as this individuality but rather what he says. That which has to be grasped is the substantive validity of his opinion so that we can be united with one another on the subject-matter.[44]

Gadamer's reference to a unity on the subject-matter here is important. The unity with which he is concerned is not the result either of one partner's imposing his or her views on another or of one partner's simple acquiescence to the views of another. Rather, if individuals or groups come sincerely to a shared understanding of a subject-matter, the understanding they share is not the original property of one or the other but represents a new understanding of the subject-matter at issue. Gadamer's model here is that of a Socratic dialogue in which the position to which Socrates and his interlocutors come at the end represents a significant advance over the position each maintained at the beginning. Each begins with certain views and assumptions but in confronting opposing views and assumptions has to reconsider and develop his or her own. The process, then, is one of integration and appropriation. This does not mean either that the participants give up their positions or that they use those of others simply to buttress their own. Rather it means that each participant takes account of the other opinions, attempts to show what is wrong and right with them as well as with his or her own position and thereby formulates, in concert with the others, a view that each recognizes to be closer to the truth than any of the original positions. As Gadamer writes:

> Coming to an understanding in conversation presupposes that the partners are ready for it and that they try to allow for the validity of what is alien and contrary to themselves. If this happens on a reciprocal basis and each of the partners, while holding to his own ground simultaneously weighs the counter-arguments, they can ultimately achieve a common language and a common judgment in an imperceptible and non-arbitrary transfer of viewpoints. (We call this an exchange of opinions.)[45]

And even more forcefully:

> What steps out in its truth is the *Logos*, which is neither mine nor yours and which therefore so far supersedes the subjective opinions of the discussion partners that even the leader of the discussion always remains the ignorant one.[46]

The successful conclusion of a dialogue thus reflects a shared understanding and one that, moreover, reflects a transformation of the initial positions of all the discussion partners. Gadamer argues that the same kind of shared understanding and transformation also marks the successful conclusion of the hermeneutic dialogue with aspects of one's own or another tradition. His analysis here is helpful in countering both the conservative thrust of the anticipation of completeness and the subjectivistic implications of the account of application. Genuine understanding, on his view, derives not from an imposition of one's own prejudices or needs on the object to be understood as the notion of application sometimes seems to suggest; neither does it result in the abject acceptance of the views of that object, as the idea of anticipating completeness seems to imply. We have seen that the condition of true understanding is the same as that of genuine conversation: a recognition of one's own lack of knowledge and willingness to learn. Moreover, regardless of the conscious motivations of interpreters, what is understood is not the intentions of historical actors or creative artists but a meaning that is always determined in relationship to issues or topics with which we are concerned. In the same way as conversation, then, genuine understanding involves the attempt to uncover the light an object or interlocutor sheds on the concerns in terms of which we understand them. The focus of understanding, like that of dialogue, is the "truth" of the subject-matter at issue; this requires taking seriously the claims of one's text (in the broadest sense), defining and testing one's own prejudices against these claims and coming with the text to a new understanding of the subject-matter at issue. Understanding thus represents a new unity of judgment or, as Gadamer puts the point, understanding (*Verstehen*) is equivalent to reaching an understanding or consensus (*Verstandigüng*) and this takes us back to the claim with which I began this chapter: "Understanding is primarily agreement."

But what kind of agreement is this? Surely the mere fact that conversation often issues in a new unity of judgment cannot itself show that successful understanding involves the same kind of agreement on a subject-matter. Can we not understand a text or tradition without coming to an agreement with it over issues? If we adhere to the Socratic model Gadamer follows then it becomes clear that understanding does not involve simply acquiescing with someone else's opinion on a given subject-matter or submitting to a traditional authority. Still, it does seem to involve integrating the tradition or opinions of others into one's search for the "truth," treating them as equal partners in dialogue and attempting to come to some kind of position that both they and we can support. But why should we look for this kind of consensus? We have already encountered the problem that arises here. It may be, as Gadamer argues, that in any interpretive effort we already share profound assumptions and views with others within our tradition, that even in our attempts to disengage ourselves from this tradition we are oriented by it. By why should agreement with the tradition be the goal of understanding or the criterion of successful understanding? Why must understanding be associated with achieving a common judgment about an issue? Can we not seek to define ourselves and our opinion in opposition to the tradition?

To some extent, these questions miss the point of Gadamer's identification of understanding and agreement, for Gadamer explicitly equates the consensus that results from hermeneutic understanding with the "fusion of horizons."[47] As noted earlier, what Gadamer means by this "fusion of horizons" is the integration of our historically determined concerns with the object of understanding in such a way that this integration determines the content of the object for us. In equating successful hermeneutic understanding with dialogic consensus, then, Gadamer means merely to depict the kind of mediation between past and present or between the alien and familiar that is part of any sincere attempt to understand. On this reading, hermeneutic *Verständigung* can include disagreement: we simply agree to disagree. Although we cannot break out of the tradition to which we belong, we can break with it on any given issue by emphasizing other elements of the tradition, showing the way in which the older opinion has to be modified in light of the way the evidence now looks to us and so on. In this case our agreement with the tradition consists in the fact that we can justify our new opinion only by coming to terms with its counter-position and understanding in just what way we do disagree with it. Hence, the possibility of distinguishing our own position on a given subject-matter from that of a text or of the tradition as a whole is not precluded. Gadamer's point is rather that a reasoned account of an aspect of the tradition involves appropriating it, integrating it within our own understanding of the subject-matter at issue in the sense that we can see strands of agreement and disagreement and use these to come to a "better" position. In short, Gadamer's point is a Hegelian one: coming to understand a "text" involves appropriating it, integrating it within one's own understanding of the subject-matter in an awareness of both its insights and its mistakes with regard to *die Sache*. In the consensus or synthesis that results the truth of one's own position and that of the object are both preserved in a new stage of the tradition and cancelled as adequate positions on their own.

On Gadamer's view this account of hermeneutic understanding signals another difference from the natural sciences. For the latter, the opinions and discoveries of the past are significant only as precursors to present scientific views, as earlier stages or detours on the way to a "correct" explanation of a phenomenon. For hermeneutic forms of knowledge, however, the past is not only a precursor to present inquiries. It is a tradition of which account must be taken, a partner in dialogue the positions of which matter even as they are revised and integrated within a new understanding. As Gadamer puts this point with regard to historical research:

> What fills our historical consciousness is always a variety of voices in which the past echoes. . . . Modern historical research is itself not only research but the mediation of tradition. We do not see it only under the law of progress or of secured results; in it, as well, we have historical experiences, as it were, since each time in it a new voice is heard in which the past echoes.[48]

Gadamer's point in equating hermeneutic understanding with dialogue, then, is that the former is a learning experience. In attempting to understand a text or other aspect of the tradition, we both bring that object into our world, illuminate the meaning it has for us, and transform our own previous perspective. Hermeneutics involves mediation or, in other words, a capacity to see the significance of a truth-claim for our own situation. This means both that our situation circumscribes the meaning an object can have for us and that its truth provokes us to reconsider that situation and move to a new understanding of it. In describing understanding as a form of dialogue, then, Gadamer is not suggesting that the successful outcome of a process of understanding favors either the initial claims of the interpreter or those of the object. Rather, just as the conclusion of a genuine conversation is not the sole property of either one of the dialogue-partners, the outcome of *Verstehen* is neither our own property, the result of the dominance of our prejudices, nor the property of the tradition, the result of its dominance. Instead, just as in conversation, the result is a unity or agreement that goes beyond the original positions of the various participants; indeed, the consensus that emerges in understanding represents a new view and hence a new stage of the tradition.

This account of the Hegelian sense in which Gadamer means the equation of understanding and agreement notwithstanding, the question may be raised as to whether a more substantive form of acquiescence to the tradition is not concealed here. Gadamer's reference to the Socratic dialogues is a case in point. As he himself notes, in contrast to the relatively free exchange of opinions that characterizes the early dialogues and the beginning sections of *The Republic*, for instance, the later dialogues and later sections of *The Republic* are monopolized by a Socrates whose opinion the other participants in the dialogue simply accept.

In my view this latter image of consensus as acquiescence rather than as Hegelian synthesis is reflected in Gadamer's analysis of the concept of the classical. Earlier I indicated that the concept of the classical serves him as a paradigm for the normative hold of a tradition. As we saw, the concept includes both the artistic style of a certain period in history and a general ideal of beauty. Despite historicist efforts to reduce the concept to the former definition alone, the ideals asssociated with it are preserved in such notions as that of a classical education and in the question of whether certain forms of art are "classical" regardless of the period of their creation. In this way, the legacy of the classical continues to exert a force, whether it is acknowledged or not, and thus provides a clear instance of what Gadamer calls effective history. But in his analysis of the concept of the classical Gadamer makes another point as well. The classical is not simply a notion that orients our aesthetic responses, it is also a concept that reveals truth. As he puts it, it is "a special way of being historical, the historical achievement of preservation that, in a continually renewed proof lets something true exist."[49]

Here the Hegelian sense of preservation that includes both the integration of what has been preserved and its modification as part of a more sophisticated and differentiated position seems to give way to a notion of preservation that emphasizes continuation. Hermeneutic understanding seems no longer to have the character of mediation or self-education; nor does it result in a transformation of both one's own prejudices and those of the object. Instead hermeneutics becomes simply that which rescues the truths of the past from oblivion and allows their validity to be seen. The point of a hermeneutics of the classical is to demonstrate the continuing truth of classical texts. Hermeneutic consensus then refers not to the integration of the object under study into a better understanding of the subject-matter but rather to the capacity to see that object's superiority.[50]

In the final pages of *Truth and Method*, Gadamer refers back to his analysis of games and makes the following claim:

> When we understand a text, its meaningfulness charms us just as the beautiful charms us. It brings itself to validity and has always already charmed us before we come to ourselves, so to speak, and are able to test the claim to meaning that emerges from it. What confronts us in the experience of the beautiful and in understanding the meaning of the tradition really has something of the truth of a game. In understanding, we are drawn into a happening of truth and come, as it were, too late if we want to know what we should believe.[51]

Here, again, Gadamer seems to move from the Hegelian sense of agreement to a sense that involves just that acceptance of tradition which threatened to emerge from the analysis of both mimesis and the anticipation of completeness. We are drawn into the tradition as we are drawn into games and works of art; it is the normative authority that makes a claim on us, that pulls us out of our own concerns and imposes its norms upon us. Indeed, this "enchantment" occurs before we can come to ourselves and assess the claim the tradition makes upon us.[52] In this perspective, then, agreement entails a simple submission to the tradition. We adopt the tradition's view of the truth and, moreover, "come too late" if we attempt to justify or question it for we have always already adopted it.

But Gadamer's analysis of the conditions of understanding do not, in general, support this claim. As we have seen, we always agree with the tradition in the sense that we are part of it and oriented by it. But we also modify the tradition in seeking the truth of the subject-matter with which we and it are concerned, mediating its truth-claims with our changed historical circumstances and even assessing its values in light of other norms and principles that we have inherited from it. We need not agree with it in the substantive sense that we embrace its views but simply in the sense that those views are an integral part of out own self-understanding whether we agree with them substantively or not. In my view, Gadamer fails adequately to distinguish these two senses of agreement, one of which entails a concrete unity of judgment and the other reflective and critical integration. In reducing the second sense of agreement to the first, moreover, he slips from an investigation of the conditions of understanding to the basically conservative thesis according to which we are not only members of a tradition but also its ideological supporters. The suspicion that this thesis lies at the heart of Gadamer's position has motivated much of the criticism of his work. In chapter 4 I shall examine the objections of Jürgen Habermas and Karl-Otto Apel since these seem to me to raise, if not resolve, the important issues.

4

Hermeneutics and the critique
of ideology

On the interpretation I have offered, the hermeneutic understanding of meaning need succumb neither to conservativism nor to subjectivism. The apparently conservative resonance of some of Gadamer's remarks results from his idea of the necessity of anticipating the truth of the object of interpretation; their subjectivistic overtones emanate from his claim that all understanding involves application and hence modification in light of new perspectives or changed historical circumstances. In elucidating the dialogic structure of understanding, however, Gadamer shows that it involves neither adopting the prejudices of one's text or text-analogue nor imposing one's own upon it. Understanding rather involves a transformation of the initial positions of both "text" and interpreter in a "fusion of horizons" or consensus over meaning that reveals new dimensions of *die Sache* and issues in a new stage of the tradition of interpretation.

But this notion of consensus has raised another problem with Gadamer's account of hermeneutics. As we saw, for the most part he seems to mean by a consensus over meaning a purely formal agreement: we reach an understanding with our object and appropriate it into our own self-understanding when we have learned from it and taken account of its views in formulating and refining our position. This kind of consensus represents a "fusion of horizons" in a two-fold sense: on the one hand we understand the object from the point of view of our assumptions and situation; on the other, our final perspective reflects the education we have received through our encounter with the object. Such fusion, then, does not entail any concrete agreement. It means merely that we have learned to integrate a certain point of view and have thereby advanced to a new understanding of the issues in question. Nevertheless Gadamer at times seems to suggest that the consensus with the object or the tradition is substantive in that it issues in just such a concrete agreement. In these contexts, the "fusion of horizons" is taken to mean that there is no longer any difference between our position and that of the object; understanding involves finding a way to agree about *die Sache* and hence ignoring the possible necessity of criticizing the text or text-analogue under study. It is this inattention to the role of critical reflection that disturbs Habermas and Apel. I therefore want to pursue the matter further by examining their objections to Gadamer and his replies.

HABERMAS'S REVIEW OF *TRUTH AND METHOD*

Habermas's first discussion of Gadamer's work occurs in *Zur Logik der Sozialwissenschaften*, in which he locates the value of hermeneutics in its contribution to debates over the logic of the social sciences. In this context, the merit of hermeneutics lies in the alternative it offers to both positivistic and neo-Wittgensteinian approaches. As Habermas characterizes them, positivistic approaches focus on the need for a neutral "observation language" that can lift social analysis above subjective impressions and descriptions and thereby secure for it the same objectivity that is found in the natural sciences. As against this, hermeneutics stresses the situatedness of all understanding; indeed, Gadamer maintains that the structure of prejudice he describes obtains not only for historical and textual interpretation but for the natural and social sciences as well. Forms of scientific knowledge themselves constitute traditions; they develop certain norms and methods, rely on certain criteria of verification and falsification and make certain assumptions about their own development. To this extent all understanding or observation of an object-domain involves a pre-judgment in terms of a particular interpretive "paradigm" or set of prejudices. Hence, not only are our interpretations of history or texts rooted in our situation and tradition, even those "methodologically based" judgments of meaning that we take to be most objective are prejudiced in particular ways. It follows that there can be no observation of "facts" or confirmation of theoretical hypotheses that is neutral or objective in the sense for which positivism searches since there is no observation or confirmation that is not conditioned by a tradition.

Of course, this hermeneutic insight into the situated aspect of scientific analysis has been echoed by Anglo-American philosophers coming out of the empiricist tradition. In the philosophy of the natural sciences, Willard van Orman Quine, Thomas Kuhn and Paul Feyerabend, for instance, have all stressed the dependence of observation on theory and the conventional character of the confirmation and rejection of theories. In the domain of the social sciences, as well, neo-Wittgensteinian critics of positivism have argued against the possibility of an "objective," "value-free" explanation of events or social practices. Such theorists as Alasdair MacIntyre, Peter Winch and Charles Taylor emphasize instead the situated character of social scientific understanding, inasmuch as it constitutes what Winch, following Wittgenstein, calls a "language game" and what Taylor refers to as a semantic field.[1] Their common point is that the direction of research within a given field, the standards by which research hypotheses are confirmed and rejected and the criteria for the relevance of data all refer to a normative framework of assumptions, conventions and purposes. Social scientific knowledge can therefore no longer be considered value-free in any strict sense, since it is conditioned by this normative framework – or by what Gadamer sees more historically as a tradition and its prejudices.

MacIntyre, Winch and Taylor also stress a second feature of social scientific knowledge, however, one that renders its logic considerably more complex than that of the natural sciences. Against the original positivistic claims concerning the scientificity and objectivity of social scientific inquiry, they point not only to the language game that constitutes a given social science at a particular time but also to the language game or semantic field that constitutes its object-domain. The social sciences have the structure of what Anthony Giddens has called a "double hermeneutic."[2] Not only are they constituted within a tradition or language game; the symbolically structured objects and events they study are themselves constituted by their location within complexes of beliefs and practices, values and norms – in short, within language games or traditions. This means, as I have suggested before, that the "meaning" of an event or social practice is itself bound to a symbolic framework, to a group's assumptions, purposes and expectations. Hence it is not accessible to empirical observation alone but must be understood, at least in part, in terms of the language game to which it belongs. But this means that positivism's hope for a universal object language in social science remains utopian in two senses. It requires both detaching theory from the hermeneutic situation in which it is formulated and separating actions, norms of action and the like from the language games that give them their sense.

Despite what Habermas sees as the importance of Winch's work in

clarifying this structure of social inquiry, he maintains that Winch
ultimately fails to makes sense of the conditions of the possibility of
understanding. Winch follows a fundamentally Wittgensteinian strategy
and conceives of the possibility of understanding a language game other
than one's own primarily in terms of a resocialization within it; one has
to learn the new language of value and practice from the ground up, as it
were, by virtual participation, as a member, in the activities of a given
group. But the problem, on Habermas's account, is that it remains
unclear what language game the participating social scientist is playing.
Does Winch suppose, as Dilthey does, that social scientists can simply
leave their native languages behind them in learning a new one? Or, as
in Gadamer's hermeneutics, are the two languages or sets of prejudices
brought into relationship with one another and, if so, how? Habermas
writes:

> Wittgenstein conceives of the task as an analysis of similarities or family
> relationships. The language analyst must see common things and
> differentiate differences. But if this enterprise is no longer to be turned into
> therapy, a systematic viewpoint for comparison is required. The language
> analyst in the role of the comparing interpreter must always already
> presuppose a concept of a language game in general and a concrete pre-
> understanding in which different languages converge.[3]

It is because Gadamer emphasizes precisely this convergence and
mediation between languages that Habermas finds his work so important
for delineating the structure of social inquiry. As we have seen, Gadamer
equates understanding with consensus in dialogue and thus makes the
double hermeneutic to which Giddens points the centerpiece of
interpretation in general. Understanding, whether of others within one's
own culture or of members of an alien culture, involves achieving
consensus on meaning or, in other words, placing two sets of prejudices
into a relationship with one another.

Habermas examines the logic of this kind of understanding by
focusing on Gadamer's reflections on translation. For Habermas's
purposes, Gadamer's most valuable insight here is the recognition that
translation involves neither resocializing oneself nor finding a set of rules
through which to reduce one language to another. It involves, rather,
learning to say in one's own language what is said in another. Translation
does not require producing a correlate in one's own language for each
word that is expressed in the other but being able to say in one's own

words what one finds in the words of someone else. To this extent translation is not in principle different from the achievement of understanding through dialogue. On the one hand, one has to make sense of someone else's position and can do so only through the lens of one's own understanding in terms that make sense to oneself. On the other hand, making sense of someone else's position leads to an expansion and refinement of one's own. It is for this reason that Habermas stresses that the relationship into which two languages or sets of prejudices are brought is a *productive* one. As he quotes Gadamer: "The hermeneutic problem is thus not a problem of the correct mastery of language but one of coming to an understanding in an appropriate way of what happens in the medium of language."[4]

For Habermas, then, hermeneutics has its place in the context of ordinary language where consensus is always possible but where it is not simply given with the unambiguous meanings of a formalized language. Hermeneutic understanding is necessary where meaning remains ambiguous, where a potential consensus is disturbed and where coming to an understanding therefore requires sorting out difficulties, using one's own language or point of view to get clear on another and extending one's own language to see the point of what is said in another. By conceiving of hermeneutic understanding along these lines, Gadamer is able to clarify the conditions of social scientific knowledge in Habermas's view. It does not require a universal object language, as positivism assumes; neither is it dependent on the social scientist's ability to take a "free-floating" position in order to participate in any language game, as Winch suggests. Rather it involves "a productive achievement to which language always empowers those who have mastered its grammatical rules: to assimilate what is foreign and thereby further to develop one's own linguistic system."[5] In Gadamerian terminology, one's own language forms the horizon of one's relation to other languages and thereby incorporates an openness to other worlds.

In spite of their contribution to the philosophy of the social sciences, Gadamer's reflections on language, translation and understanding raise a problem for Habermas. While Gadamer is correct to see understanding as a consensus on meaning, Habermas argues that he overlooks the possibility that such consensus may be "systematically distorted." Habermas is concerned in this regard with the influence of ideology. Suppose the consensus that forms the tradition at any given time is not the product of an uninhibited discussion and not the expression of mutual understanding but the result of force and coercion? For Gadamer, understanding is primarily an understanding of truth and relies upon an effort to see the truth in what someone else says. In focusing on truth, however, does he ignore the ideological function certain perspectives may have in maintaining a repressive status quo and uneven distribution of power? The example of the traditional consensus on women's needs and interests may help clarify the problem here. One could argue that too many women took the possible truth of this consensus too seriously for too long since it served to mask a hierarchical power structure. In approaching traditional views of women hermeneutically, in trying to make sense out of them on their own grounds and incorporate their truth into their own lives, women did so at their own expense. In effect, the claim Habermas makes against Gadamer is that some recognition of the connection between the views of women and the power relations they help sustain is necessary for a rational response to them. Because hermeneutics focuses on the *truth* of claims, however, it is not capable of such a recognition. Indeed, hermeneutics represents a "linguistic idealism:" it assumes that traditions are self-contained, that nothing outside them affects their direction or influences the discussion that goes on within them. In so doing it ignores the fact that they may also reflect the constraint of social and economic factors "outside" them. As Habermas puts the point:

> An interpretive sociology that hypostatizes language to the subject of forms of life and of tradition ties itself to the idealist presupposition that linguistically articulated consciousness determines the material practice of life. But the objective framework of social action is not exhausted by the dimension of intersubjectively intended and symbolically transmitted meaning. The linguistic infrastructure of society is part of a complex that, however symbolically mediated, is also constituted by the constraint of reality – by the constraint of outer nature that enters into procedures for technical mastery and by the constraint of inner nature reflected in the repressive character of social power relations.[6]

In a later essay, he also cites Albrecht Wellmer's remarks with approval:

> The Enlightenment knew what hermeneutics forgets – that the dialogue which, according to Gadamer, we "are" is also a context of power and precisely for this reason no dialogue. . . . The universal claim of the hermeneutic approach [can only] be sustained if one assumes that the context of the tradition as the locus of possible truth and factual agreement is, at the same time, the locus of factual untruth and continuing force.[7]

We have seen that Gadamer is himself aware of possible problems in anticipating the truth of traditional perspectives; in fact, he allows for situations in which we must give up on our attempts to learn from such perspectives and move to a genetic explanation of how they arose. To this extent he agrees with Habermas that understanding may have to move behind the manifest meaning of a given social consensus to the social and historical conditions that determine it. The danger with which Habermas is concerned, however, is not simply that we will try to anticipate the truth of a perspective or world-view where, it turns out, we cannot learn to see any. His worry is rather that in those cases in which we *do* see truth there may also be ideology, that, in other words, the claims from which we *do* learn may be connected to relations of force and domination in ways that remain obscure to us as long as we rely on hermeneutic understanding alone. On his view, exposing such relations rather requires going beyond the hermeneutic focus on meaning to what he calls a "reference system" comprised by the relations of power and conditions of social labor within a society:

> *Social actions can only be comprehended in an objective framework that is constituted conjointly by language, labor, and domination.* The happening of tradition appears as an absolute power only to a self-sufficient hermeneutics; in fact it is relative to systems of labor and domination. Sociology cannot, therefore, be reduced to interpretive sociology. It requires a reference system that, on the one hand, does not suppress the symbolic mediation of social action in favor of a naturalistic view of behavior . . . but that, one the other hand, also does not . . . sublimate social processes entirely to cultural tradition.[8]

Gadamer's response to this line of argument is to deny the limit Habermas imposes on the ability of hermeneutics to deal with ideological factors. From his perspective, Habermas illegitimately restricts the range of hermeneutic understanding to *expressed* truth, to claims agents explicitly make or values they explicitly uphold. Hermeneutics, however, deals with prejudices and hence not simply with the positions an individual or society can articulate but with the assumptions and expectations those positions include. For example, a hermeneutic understanding of traditional claims about women's needs and interests extends beyond an appreciation of the explicit content of those claims – that women are best suited to domestic tasks and so on – to the complex of implicit views about the appropriate distribution of power and so on that the claims encompass. In thus going beyond a focus on explicit truth-claims to consider the wider content of those claims, hermeneutic understanding can itself reveal their ideological connection to other aspects of the social consensus.

Moreover, Gadamer argues, Habermas's contrast between a linguistic tradition, on the one hand, and the "material conditions" of labor and domination, on the other, makes no sense.[9] If hermeneutic understanding extends to the ideological content of a given social consensus, this is because the so-called extra-linguistic forces that condition it are already part of it. The tradition itself incorporates those forces as part of its self-understanding, whether expressed or unexpressed. They are therefore extra-linguistic only in the sense that their influence on the society's beliefs, norms and values is not yet made explicit. To the extent that they *must* influence the self-understanding of the culture to have any meaning at all, however – that is, to the extent that they "enter our world," as Gadamer puts it[10] – they remain an inextricable part of the tradition itself and are accessible to hermeneutic analysis. The hierarchical power structure that lies behind views about women's proper role is not a structure inaccessible to exposure through language. Indeed, on Gadamer's view, to talk of a hierarchical power structure is already to interpret and therefore to act hermeneutically.

> It restricts the universality of the hermeneutic dimension if one area of intelligible meaning ('cultural tradition") is demarcated against other determinants of social reality that are alone recognizable as its real factors. As if precisely each ideology, as a false linguistic consciousness did not only offer itself as intelligible meaning but allow itself to be understood in its true meaning: e.g., that of the interest of domination.[11]

Finally, Gadamer argues that hermeneutics is not only equal to the task of critical reflection but peculiarly suited to it in as much as its task is just that of revealing complexities in meaning and disclosing different dimensions of a text or other aspect of the tradition. In emphasizing the historicity of understanding, hermeneutics reveals the inexhaustible depths of meaning inherent in such symbolic structures as texts, norms, the meaning of historical actions and the tradition itself. Because these structures are always approached from different historical perspectives, with different purposes and assumptions they always disclose new and different aspects of their meaning. This means, further, that prejudices, commitments and values that are obscured from one point of view can be illuminated from another. In this context, Gadamer speaks of the "productivity of temporal distance" in so far as assumptions that are hidden at one point in history can come to light with the transformation in view provided by historical experience itself.[12] Thus, hermeneutics is not only aware of hidden dimensions of meaning and not only itself capable of revealing them; in fact, the task of revealing hidden dimensions of meaning and, hence, of exposing ideology is precisely its own.

This response to Habermas does not seem to get completely clear on the problem of ideology. The crucial point here is that ideology is not the same as prejudice, that there is a difference between calling a perspective ideological and recognizing its historical and social situatedness. What makes a claim ideological is not merely its connection to an unarticulated source, nor its reliance on unexpressed norms and assumptions. Ideological claims do not simply leave the assumptions behind them implicit; they rather articulate them in such a way that it becomes difficult to disentangle the warranted part of the claims from the unwarranted.[13] For the Western Marxist tradition from which Habermas emerges, the paradigm case of this kind of ideological obfuscation remains Marx's analysis of the buying and selling of labor power. Here the obfuscation results from the appearance of a fair exchange. The owners of two different goods meet on the market, the one to sell his or her labor power for a specified amount of time and the the other to buy the labor power for a specified sum of money. As Marx explains, this transaction appears as "a very Eden of the rights of man:"

> There alone rule Freedom, Equality, Property and Bentham. Freedom, because both buyer and seller . . . are constrained only by their free will. They contract as free agents, and the agreement they come to is but the form in which they give legal expression to their common will. Equality, because each enters into relation with the other, as with a simple owner of commodities and they exchange equivalent for equivalent. Property, because each disposes only of what is his own and Bentham, because each looks only to himself.[14]

The talk of freedom, equality and property here is not a lie. The ideological obfuscation in this case does not consist in a lack of freedom on the part of either partner to the transaction nor in their inequality as owners of commodities nor in the fact that they do not both own commodities. In contrast to the hierarchies of feudal society, seller and buyer here are equal citizens and free both to own property and dispose of it as they wish. The problem is that the characterization of freedom, equality and property conceals as much as it reveals.[15] The talk of freedom obscures the coercion that one partner suffers in as much as he or she must sell his or her labor power in order to survive; likewise, the talk of equality obscures the inequality contained in the economic dependence of one class on the other and the talk of a common right to property conceals the power of the owner of capital to appropriate the products of the labor of others. Thus, as one moves from a surface analysis of the self-understanding of a society to a comprehensive view of the way in which the phenomena in question work themselves out in the society, the peculiar distortion involved in ideology appears in high relief. On a Marxist view one can see the way in which the buying and selling of labor power both conforms to the ideals of freedom, equality and the right to property, as compared to feudal restrictions on all three, and substantively subverts those same ideals by converting freedom into coercion, equality into dependence and the right to property into the power to appropriate the property of others.

Habermas's claim is that because hermeneutics lacks a "reference system," that is, a comprehensive theory of society, it may remain on the surface level and fail to penetrate to the deeper level at which the ideological distortion involved in the talk of freedom, equality and property appears. Here the problem is not simply that the self-understanding of the society rests on prejudices that are as yet unclarified. Instead, its ideological dimension consists in the systematic clouding of the way in which expressed social values and ideals are undermined by the social reality. The "freedom" that appears on the market serves as a mask for the "unfreedom" that continues to exist. Here, the economic conditions that subvert the "bourgeois" ideal of freedom are not prejudices about the meaning of freedom; nor are they ideas about freedom that need to be further explicated. Even if hermeneutic understanding can go beyond a focus on the truth of expressed claims to an analysis of the presuppositions behind them, the problem is that it remains tied to a society's explicit or implicit self-understanding. On Habermas's view, however, what is required for an adequate understanding of the society is an account of how the economic system actually works *whatever* the society's prejudices and self-understanding. And this account of economic conditions requires a *theory* of society which goes beyond the hermeneutic explication of prejudices.

To clarify this critique of Gadamer, both Habermas and Apel turn to psychoanalytic theory since, on their view, it provides an example of the kind of systematic theoretical approach that is required for the critique of ideology. Indeed, the same problem that occurs on the social level with regard to ideology occurs on the individual level with regard to pathologically disturbed behavior. As in the case of ideologically distorted claims, pathological distortions in an individual's self-understanding and ability to communicate with others may remain unclear at a surface level or on the level of ordinary communication. Thus, as long as one remains on this level, hermeneutically clarifying assumptions and implications, the distortion in a patient's expression of purposes and ideas may remain inaccesssible *as* a distortion. The task of psychoanalysis is to show that a given behavior or reaction *is* pathologically conditioned, and in the view of both Habermas and Apel this requires a theoretical, methodologically self-conscious approach for which hermeneutics is insufficient. The ways in which Apel and Habermas defend this view differ somewhat and I shall therefore look at each separately.

APEL'S CRITIQUE OF HERMENEUTICS

Like Habermas, Apel locates the value of Gadamer's work in its critique of positivism and specifically in its success in countering the positivistic devaluation of understanding. On his account, Gadamer's virtue is to have revealed the realm of intersubjective understanding that is presupposed by any "objective science" in as much as scientists must come to an understanding with each other over the meaning of terms, criteria for testing hypotheses and so on. Gadamer shows that the hermeneutic tasks of clarifying meaning and facilitating communication cannot be replaced *in toto* by causal explanations of "verbal behavior," for the norms of such causal explanation are themselves constituted within the domain of intersubjective understanding and consensus. In other words, as Apel puts it, one person cannot do science.[16] Science is a set of social practices adhering to certain standards and following certain norms. These norms and standards are neither arbitrary nor subjective; they issue rather from the growth of a scientific tradition and for Apel, as for Gadamer, this means that they are the result of experience, communication and consensus among scientists. None the less, Apel differs from Gadamer on the issue of how this domain of intersubjective understanding, if it cannot be explained causally as a set of verbal reactions to stimuli, is to be made a scientific theme.

As Apel points out, the strategy of Romantic, Schleiermacherian hermeneutics was to abstract from the question of the truth or rationality of claims and to focus not on evaluating their meaning but on simply understanding them. For him, Gadamer's mistake is to have retracted this step and to have insisted instead on the confluence of application and understanding. He agrees with Gadamer's emphasis on the historicity of interpretation and hence on the delusion involved in supposing the possibility of an objective, value-free "science of meaning." Still, he rejects the consequence that Gadamer draws from this emphasis: namely, that the task of understanding is therefore the mediation of the past with the present or the alien with the familiar. On Apel's view, this account of hermeneutic understanding allies it to the same ideological use or misuse of history that we questioned in chapters 2 and 3. If understanding is the same as application, what prevents interpreters or a culture from employing the past for its own purposes? We saw that Gadamer's answer to this question involved the equation of understanding and dialogue. Opportunism in interpretation is ruled out by the conditions of genuine understanding in which interpreters are concerned with the truth of the subject-matter at issue and are open to the alteration of their perspective that the object may require of them. None the less, Apel argues, the problem of historical opportunism is unavoidable once understanding is internally connected to application:

> In my opinion, the hermeneutic *Geisteswissenschaften* become just as ideologically corrupted through the (existentialist or even Marxist) demand for a binding application of their understanding as they do through the positivistic dismissal of historical engagement as a condition of the possibility of their understanding of meaning.[17]

According to Apel, then, Gadamer is correct to point to the historical situation of interpretation, that is, to the fact that any account of meaning has its roots in the very historical and practical engagement from which not only positivism but the hermeneutic tradition itself wanted to divorce it. Apel denies, however, that this practical and historical engagement leads to an identification of application and understanding and he therefore distinguishes between two forms of engagement which Gadamer equates: that of a judge who must apply a law to a particular case and that of a legal historian who simply has to understand the law. For Gadamer the two tasks are identical: on the one hand, the judge must understand the law before deciding the case; on the other, the legal historian cannot understand the meaning of the law without understanding how it does or will apply to individual cases. In understanding the law against illegal searches, for example, the legal historian must also understand what the law explicitly or implicitly says about the case of wire-tapping or some other case, while in deciding whether the case of wire-tapping or some other case is an instance of an illegal search the judge has to perform the same task: he or she has to understand what the law explicitly or implicitly says about it. Apel counters that the *responsibilities* of legal historian and judge differ: the judge must take responsibility for the "truth and normative bindingness of the meaning to be understood", while the legal historian must take responsibility merely for "the meaning of a text that in its original intention is still simply difficult to understand." He continues:

> The legal historian will certainly not be able to imagine that he could make himself contemporaneous with the public of the text of the "corpus iurus" in the way that Schleiermacher demanded as a precondition for the ultimate identification with the author. Still less, however, may he renounce Schleiermacher's hermeneutic ideal in favor of a conscious actualization of understanding.[18]

It seems to me that Apel misunderstands Gadamer's point here to a certain extent. Although Gadamer thinks the necessity of application follows from the situated character of understanding, he does not think that hermeneutics involves the *conscious* application or actualization of this understanding. His argument is not that given our hermeneutic situation we *should* apply that which we have understood from the past or an alien culture; rather his point, as we have seen, is that in understanding we always *do* apply it. Hence, the application of the meaning of a law is not something that follows an unadulterated understanding of it, an application for which the judge but not the legal historian must take responsibility. The application of understanding is already a structural part of understanding or interpreting a law or any other aspect of the tradition. Thus, it may be that a judge's applicative understanding of a law has normative authority for the meaning that is handed down, that, in other words, the judge can enforce his understanding by handing down a decision on the case in question, while the legal historian may be able to make only suggestions for practice. But Gadamer's argument is that the conditions of understanding do not differ: in each case the law has to be applied if it is to be understood at all.[19]

Despite Apel's apparent misunderstanding of Gadamer's position here, his fear of the ideological consequences of the connection between understanding and application remains justified and, in fact, reiterates the concern I have already expressed about its opportunistic potential. We saw that the dialogic structure of understanding is supposed to dispel this concern but acknowledging the problem of ideology casts doubt on just this solution. The problem here is not simply that our understanding of our society or of another person may be deformed by our failure to recognize the ideological obfuscation that their claims involve. Our *own* understanding may involve ideological components of which we are unaware. In other words, our understanding may involve not only the prejudices that spring from our practical and historical engagement and that our encounter with the object can transform; it may involve the peculiar combination of truth and distortion that, as we have already noted, characterizes both ideology and pathology and, at least in Apel's view, is resistant to hermeneutic penetration. We shall pursue this problem further below. Of importance, here, however, is a second series of objections Apel raises to Gadamer's conclusions.

Apel claims that hermeneutics would be a sufficient ground for social inquiry only if human actions and expressions were a reflection of conscious intentions and motivations. To think that an interpretive understanding alone can suffice for the comprehension of actions, expressions and world-views is to assume that they always make sense and that we can dialogically uncover the assumptions, purposes and values which underlie them. In other words, it is to assume that when we do not understand the meaning of an action or expression immediately, we can enter into a dialogue with the agent or speaker whose action or expression it is and that through doing so its meaning will become clear. Hermeneutics, in short, assumes that problems in understanding are problems of a temporary failure to understand a person's or group's intentions, a failure which can be overcome by continuing the dialogic, interpretive process. Apel, however, points to expressions and actions that cannot be clarified in this way. Following Marx, he claims that history has not been the result simply of the conscious intentions of actors but of causal connections, unconscious motivations and unintended consequences as well. Actions and expressions often spring not from explicit intentions or even explicable reasons but from factors beyond the agents' control. Such actions and expressions therefore cannot be clarified through further communication but can only be causally explained. As Apel puts the point: "A philosophy of history that wanted to understand itself only as the integration of the hermeneutic *Geisteswissenschaften* would here have to founder on the meaningless-factual, the contingent as the simply irrational."[20]

On this basis Apel insists that a hermeneutic understanding must be supplemented with a "quasi-objective explanatory science" for which psychoanalysis provides a model. On the individual level, what is required is a theory of the general factors provoking certain kinds of neurotic behavior and expression. Such a theory is explanatory in so far as it looks for general correlations between, say, early childhood experiences on the one hand, and types of pathological behavior on the other. The theory, however, is only a "*quasi*-objective explanatory science" since its aim is not simply that of predicting occurrences of pathological behavior but rather that of helping patients clarify for themselves the causes behind their actions and hence encouraging their self-reflection and self-knowledge. On the social level, a similar kind of theory is required, a theory of the general factors promoting distortions in a society's self-understanding. Here again, however, the aim of the theory is not prediction but rather the encouragement of undistorted self-understanding so that social subjects can act coherently and rationally, free from the residues of blind causal conditioning.

This difference between a predictive explanatory science and psychoanalysis or the critique of ideology is important because it reconnects the latter two to hermeneutic understanding. In the case of psychoanalysis, the analyst does more than simply locate the cause of pathological actions. If the analysis is to be successful, the analyst also has to make sense out of the connection between the cause and the pathological symptom. But this connection is not simply a contingent one; the relation between cause and effect here is not merely an external connection like that between natural causes and their effects. It is also an internal and symbolic connection. Thus, if one's symptomatic behavior manifests itself in one's continually losing track of one's possessions, this may be not only contingently related to one's having lost one's mother at an early age, for example, it may also be symbolically related to this experience as an experience one continually repeats. Hence, a peculiar feature of psychoanalysis and, by extension, the critique of ideology is that causal explanation on the natural scientific model is not sufficient. Although the actions or expressions under study must be causally explained initially, they must also ultimately make sense and, moreover, make sense precisely according to the hermeneutic model of being able to see the point of what someone has done or said. The goal of the causal theory thus turns out to be that of assisting a hermeneutic understanding; indeed, on Apel's view, its goal is to make possible the hermeneutic dialogue that Gadamer simply assumes. The aim of psychoanalytic treatment is to enable the patient to engage in communication with others as an equal partner in dialogue, offering opinions on the basis of what he or she takes to be true and not on the basis of causal factors he or she cannot control.

Apel's claim that such treatment is beyond the scope of hermeneutics is confusing in three respects. First, as to Apel's position that history is the result not only of conscious intentions but also of unintended consequences and causal connections beyond an agent's control, it should be clear from Gadamer's critique of the work of Ranke and Droysen that this is his position as well. Historical understanding cannot conceive of itself as a reconstruction of agents' intentions because interpreters always read those intentions from the vantage point of a historical perspective, with knowledge of the actual actions performed, their connections to subsequent events, and so on. Historians therefore can never represent the experience or the motivations as the actors lived them but instead reconstruct the historical situation in light of perceived causal connections and unintended consequences. Still, Apel contends that if this is the case, if in attempting to understand history we go beyond the actual intentions of actors, this is not merely because our historical perspective is different from theirs; it is also because human beings do not yet make their history with "will and consciousness" as Marx would have it. Human beings still react as objects to causal factors which they do not control or even perceive. For Apel, then, the problem with Droysen's and Ranke's analysis of historical understanding and, indeed, with all of traditional hermeneutics, is not so much the ontological misunderstanding of the relationship between meaning, intention and understanding that Gadamer makes it out to be; it is rather a misunderstanding of historical conditions. Hermeneutics fails to see either the extent to which individuals react to causal factors rather than acting for themselves or the consequent distortion involved in the intentions and reasons they express.

This clarification of Apel's position leaves two problems with his criticism of Gadamer. He argues that it is possible to see a pathologically or ideologically distorted self-understanding *as* a distortion only if one begins with the assumption that human beings are not only subjects of history but also objects: their actions and expressions may be the effect of causes rather than the outcome of reasoned intentions and hence their real meaning may never become clear through continued dialogue. Indeed, continued dialogue may only further obfuscate the factors at work since it may result in a pathologically or ideologically disturbed consensus in which dialogue participants accept justifications and rationalizations that distort such real meaning. Apel maintains that a quasi-objective explanatory science can resolve this problem by transcending ideology and pathology, but from a Gadamerian point of view the faith he has in the results of such a science is itself problematic. In effect, Gadamer denies that the problem of causally induced action is simply a contingent one and maintains that the transparency of reason and intention to which Apel points as an ideal is utterly chimerical. Human beings are and always will be conditioned by prejudices and elements of their tradition over which they have no control. This is not to say that individuals will be unable to see through any of their prejudices; still it is to say that every dissolution of one prejudice depends upon a conscious or unconscious reliance on a myriad of other prejudices, and that any disentangling of ideological obfuscation is itself one-sided and perspectival. For Gadamer every process of illumination or self-enlightenment rests on a complementary darkening or obscuring of other possible modes of self-understanding. Indeed, on his view it is a mistake to see the "movement of human existence" as a whole on the model of the natural sciences or, in other words, as a "linear progression from mythology to enlightenment." Rather, human life and culture manifest a "relentless tension between illumination and concealment."[21] Hence, there is no one exhaustively correct analysis of the meaning of an action or expression; instead, any analysis, even that of psychoanalysis and the critique of ideology is itself an interpretation that both reveals meaning and, at the same time, obscures other possibilities. As Gadamer writes with regard to history:

> The experience of history is not the experience of meaning, plan and reason and the claim to grasp reason in history could be raised only under the externalizing view of the philosopher of absolute knowledge. In truth, the experience of history returns the hermeneutic task to its own place. It has to decipher the meaning of fragments of history anew, fragments that are limited by, and shipwreck on, the dark contingency of the factual and, above all, on the the twilight into which for each present consciousness the future disappears.[22]

If psychoanalysis and the critique of ideology are themselves interpretations, a third problem with Apel's critique of Gadamer becomes clear: namely, that it is not clear to what extent the transcendence of ideology and pathology through explanatory science is also a transcendence of hermeneutics. Psychoanalytic explanations surely begin with certain assumptions about the relation between early childhood experiences and neurotic symptoms. Moreover, these general assumptions have to be applied to individual cases; that is, they have to make sense out of an individual's history for him or her and therefore they have to be interpreted in light of the individual life. The question, then, is how these premises and interpretive elements within psycho-analytic theory itself justify Apel's understanding of it as a quasi-objective explanatory science? How can it possibly escape the hermeneutic conditions of prejudice and historical situatedness?

Habermas admits that there is problem in his own use of "quasi-objective science" or reliance on a "reference system" of material factors outside of the self-understanding of the tradition. As he asks, "How could such a reference system be legitimated except, in turn, out of the appropriation of the tradition?"[23] How does ideology-critical reflection on the conditions of social labor and domination avoid the influence of the tradition?[24] Why is the claim that a given social self-understanding contains ideological elements not itself simply an interpretation, a situated view that itself relies on certain assumptions, values and expectations? How does it offer more than a particular historical perspective and if it does not how does it escape from the confines of the "hermeneutic situation"?

HABERMAS'S SECOND RESPONSE TO GADAMER

In a second essay on Gadamer's work Habermas attempts to answer these questions by subjecting psychoanalytic theory to a detailed analysis. He begins with the concern Apel voices that a hermeneutic understanding may be itself ideologically affected. The problem here is that in attempting to come to an understanding of its own or of an alien society, hermeneutics relies, as Gadamer would agree, on the categories of its own language. It can extend these categories to encompass foreign or alien meanings; none the less, it cannot leave its own language behind and this means that if the language of interpretation is itself systematically distorted, hermeneutic understanding alone may be unable to recognize it. In this case, the difficulty with ideology is not simply that the respective dimensions of a phenomenon it obscures and reveals may be hard to disentangle but that ideological elements may distort that very attempt to disentangle the various dimensions. Psychopathology raises an analogous problem since the pathology is one that affects a patient's self-understanding. The problem in overcoming forms of pathological behavior is that they issue from a disturbed self-understanding; in other words, they issue from a disturbance within the process of self-reflection itself so that further self-reflection may be powerless to deal with the pathology.

Following Alfred Lorenzer, Habermas views the psychoanalytic treatment of such disturbances as a form of linguistic analysis. Neurotic or pathological expressions and behavior are regarded as elements of a deformed language game that has become privatized and split off from the public language. Such "systematically distorted communication"[25] is explained as the result of early childhood traumas which are repressed and issue in a process of desymbolization. The traumatic experience is desymbolized or withdrawn from the public, accessible sphere of meaning while the gap in the public language game is subsequently filled by the symptomatic behavior. The aim of psychoanalysis is to decode this symptomatic behavior by tracing it back to the childhood trauma thereby creating a lexicon through which desymbolized meanings can be translated back into the public language. Lorenzer describes this process as a form of "scenic understanding." The patient plays out his or her symptomatic scene in the transference situation that the analyst creates by taking on the role of the conflict-producing primary object. The analyst then compares symptomatic scene, transference scene and the original traumatic scene, thereby helping the patient to retrieve lost meaning. Habermas writes:

> The latent meaning of the present situation is made accessible through reference to the unmutilated meaning of the original infantile scene. Scenic understanding thus makes possible a "translation" of the meaning of the pathologically petrified pattern of communication, a meaning that although it determines behavior, has until now been inaccessible to public communication.[26]

From the point of view of a critique of hermeneutics, the importance of this "scenic understanding" lies in its reversal of the relationship between interpretive understanding and genetic explanation. As I have emphasized, Gadamer does not reject the necessity of sometimes moving beyond the hermeneutic focus on truth-claims to an analysis of the prejudices and assumptions behind a speaker's or writer's assertion of them. Nevertheless, he holds that this analysis is oriented by what one takes the truth-claims in question to be. That is, it remains conditioned by our historically situated understanding of what a belief or practice involves, its contrast or similarity to beliefs and practices of our own and the like. It thus remains conditioned by the hermeneutic "initial situation" of the interpreter. Habermas, however, argues that in psychoanalysis interpretation is structured by a theoretical framework used for explanatory purposes. In this case, the genetic explanation of a language deformation is not oriented by our understanding of what the deformation means. Rather, it is only possible to understand the deformation *as* a deformation if we possess a genetic explanation of its development. That is, we can understand the "deep" meaning of the deformed expression only after we have translated it back into the original symptomatic scene and to do this we require an explanatory theory. The explanatory theory thus precedes hermeneutic understanding, or as Habermas puts the point: "The what, the meaning-content of the systematically distorted expression cannot be 'understood' unless the why, the development of the symptomatic scene can be 'explained' through reference to the initial conditions of the systematic distortion itself."[27]

Habermas names two other "points of evidence" for the way in which psychoanalytic explanation supersedes the framework of hermeneutic understanding. First the communication between analyst and patient differs from the balanced, participatory form of dialogue on which Gadamer founds hermeneutics. The analyst does not communicate with the patient as an equal partner in dialogue but rather adopts a quasi-strategic attitude designed to encourage transference and to allow the patient to play out the symptomatic scene. Second the analyst restricts his or her attention to a small, theoretically significant segment of the patient's expressions: namely, to those that exhibit conflicts and provide a glimpse into the original traumatic scene. In Habermas's view, both considerations indicate that scenic understanding is more than the application of a hermeneutically sensitive and open understanding. Rather, it rests upon explicit theoretical assumptions about the nature of psychopathology and its deviation from the structure of normal communication.

But why assume that these explicit theoretical assumptions are "objective," that they transcend hermeneutic limitations and get at the real meaning of an expression rather than simply presenting a different perspective on it? It may be that genetic explanation here precedes the understanding of meaning, but why assume the truth of such genetic explanation? Is it not itself a particular understanding of meaning, a particular interpretation with its own hermeneutic initial situation? Why assume that taking a strategic attitude towards dialogue or restricting one's analysis to a segment of the patient's expression allows one to escape from the limits of an interpretive perspective?

These are questions Gadamer raises in response to Habermas's essay. On his view, it is legitimate for psychoanalysis to appeal to assumptions about normal communication and deviant socialization processes in attempting to identify cases of systematically disturbed communication. But these assumptions are bound to specific cultural prejudices as to what counts as normal; the standard psychoanalysts apply to deviant cases thus has no trans-historical or objective status, nor are their interpretations trans-culturally valid. The standard they use refers only to what individuals at a certain time and place regard as normal communication and their interpretations of individual pathology therefore represent particular views valid for members of a particular society. Moreover, once one moves outside the domain of psychoanalysis to a critique of the self-understanding of the society or tradition at large it is no longer clear what is to provide the standard of normalcy. Here the danger is that one will simply take one's own culture or tradition as normative and claim that the communication of others or outside of one's own group is systematically disturbed. On Gadamer's view, to set oneself up as the arbiter of the "communicative competence" of others in this way can only be elitist. As he points out, differences in political and ethical spheres issue not only from ideological commitments but also from mere differences in opinion resulting from differences in experience and interest. In this context, for one group to claim that opposition to their views is the mark of systematic disturbances in another group's ability to communicate is dogmatically to ignore the simple possibility of difference. In addition, it is to forego the chance of learning from the differences and to give up on the chance of overcoming them through the kind of continued political discussion in which each side tries to see the merit of the positions taken by the other:

> In contrast, hermeneutics still seems to me correct when it maintains that the real meaning of communication lies in the reciprocal testing of prejudices and when it holds to such reciprocity even in regard to the cultural transmission of texts.[28]

According to Gadamer, then, talk of systematically distorted communication makes sense only within a strictly circumscribed sphere: namely, where one is considering disturbances within an individual's "communicative competence" and where the criterion of such disturbances is that they fail to conform to the public language game of the time. But, for one group to convict another of a similarly disturbed self-understanding is, first, to suppose that the account of repression and desymbolization, formulated in connection with the individual's socialization, can be transferred to the level of a group's socialization.[29] Second, it is to suppose that one group has a monopoly on the correct characterization of the public language game of the time. But even if one follows the Marxist account of ideology as simultaneously an expression and distortion of actual social conditions it is not clear that one can view concepts of freedom and equality, for example, as products of symptom formation. Here, Gadamer would argue that a description of the concepts that emphasizes their opposition to slavery and hierarchy, for example, while ignoring the coercion and domination involved in wage labor may reflect a mere difference in emphasis rather than the superior competence of one group over another.

In defending his appeal to psychoanalytic theory, Habermas admits that a criticism of communicative incompetence, applied to one group by another, is not unproblematic. He maintains that the analogy between psychoanalytic and critical theories refers primarily to processes of enlightenment: to the analyst's help in initiating the patient's self-reflection, on the one hand, and the critical theorist's assistance in promoting the self-reflection of social groups on the other. None the less, the theories can be applied to adverserial groups in a secondary way without the crucial confirmation provided by a patient's or group's actual self-enlightenment. As he explains,

I can apply theories such as psychoanalysis (and the Marxist critique of ideology) in order to guide processes of reflection and to dissolve barriers to communication; the authenticity of the recipient in his relations with himself and with others is an indicator of the truth of the interpretation which the analyst (or the Party intellectual) has suggested. But I can also use this same theory to derive an explanatory hypothesis, without having (or taking) the opportunity of initiating communication with those actually concerned. . . . In this case I must remain satisfied with the usual procedures of scientific discourse: for example, whether the patterns of communication identified as pathological are repeated under specified

conditions or change under other conditions, which permit one to assume
that a process of reflection has taken place.[30]

As a scientific hypothesis applied to an adversarial group, a critical theory
does not allow for the confirmation that is possible within the therapeutic
dialogue or in the theoretician's relationship to his or her own political
group. Still, if a critical theory therefore does not permit one group
categorically to convict another of communicative incompetence, it can
orient attempts by the first group to discover obstructions to, and
catalysts for, the self-enlightenment of the second. Of course, this
clarification of Habermas's point does not deal with Gadamer's deeper
concern: namely, that the critical theory is itself only parochially
grounded and that it simply reflects the political prejudices of a
particular group.

Habermas concedes that a critical theory of society is itself historically
situated and hence interpretive; still, he claims that to the extent that it
can theoretically reconstruct the conditions of communicative competence, this historicity need not lead to what he sees as the relativism
inscribed in Gadamer's defense of hermeneutics. He writes:

A critically enlightened hermeneutics that differentiates between insight
and blindness incorporates meta-hermeneutic knowledge of the conditions
of the possibility of systematically distorted communication. It connects
understanding to the principle of rational discourse, according to which
truth would be guaranteed only by that consensus which was produced
under idealized conditions of unconstrained communication free from
domination and which could be maintained over time.[31]

UNCONSTRAINED COMMUNICATION

These "idealized conditions" or the "ideal speech situation"[32] to which
Habermas points as the standard against which the Gadamerian
consensus with the tradition is to be measured is essentially the same
ideal that Apel, following Peirce, calls an "unlimited community of
interpretation."[33] In the view of both Habermas and Apel it fills in what
the hermeneutic dialogue leaves out: a criterion for determining when a
traditional consensus betrays the effects of force and coercion. Systematic
and ideological distortions in the self-understanding of a society are to be
uncovered by moving beyond hermeneutics to a critical theory of society

which takes its bearings from a model of communication in which all parties affected are able to examine disputed claims on an equal basis with equal chances to perform all kinds of speech acts and without fear of force or reprisal.

Gadamer's response to this line of argument is not difficult to anticipate. On his view, not only the self-lucidity to which Apel appeals as the condition of "making" history with "will and consciousness" but also Habermas's ideal of a rational consensus freed from the effects of all prejudice and distortion remain "shockingly unreal."[34] It is important to note that Apel considers the notion of an unlimited communication community simply a regulative ideal while Habermas admits that the kind of uncoerced consensus that he uses as a standard for rationality is a "counterfactual" one.[35] None the less, Gadamer insists, the ideas themselves come straight out of a medieval theory of intelligence represented by the angel "who has the advantage of seeing God in his essence."[36] Against this idea he emphasizes the reciprocal illumination and obfuscation that, as we have seen, he claims is part of all understanding. He denies that there can ever be one correct or absolutely exhaustive way of understanding either oneself or one's culture and argues that any understanding necessarily ignores certain features of a text, culture or situation of action in its very focus on and clarification of others. The same, then, holds of the rational consensus to which Habermas and Apel refer; it too is implicated in a historical process, obscuring as much as it reveals, and hence, can never lay claim to a final, authoritative position on its subject-matter. As Gadamer writes:

> In this domain of historical science one must see the 'result' of the happening of interpretation not as much in progress, which exists only in partial aspects, as in a process opposed to the decline and fall of knowledge: in the revival of language and the re-acquisition of the meaning that is spoken in and through tradition. This is a dangerous relativism only from the standard of an absolute knowledge that is not ours.[37]

For Gadamer, then, the rationality of the tradition cannot be measured against an ideal of either absolute knowledge, complete enlightenment or constraint-free consensus; it is to be evaluated instead within a practical context, as that degree of knowledge, enlightenment and openness of which we are capable at a given time. In contrast to the "counterfactual" norm of an ideal speech situation, Gadamer therefore makes use of the "productivity of temporal distance," to which I have already referred, or, in other words, to the way in which prejudices are overcome and ideologies revealed in the continued course of the tradition itself. Such revelations, however, do not follow a linear path towards total transparency. Rather, since each revelation is simultaneously the closing of another option, Gadamer stresses the finitude and fallibility of our knowledge. Indeed on his account political maturity and responsibility follow not from the possession of a theory of society but rather from an awareness of our hermeneutic situation or historical horizon and hence an awareness, as he puts it, that opinions opposed to our own "could be right."[38]

Habermas's attempt to counter this response to his criticism centers on the program of universal pragmatics, the details of which cannot be spelled out here.[39] In essence, however, he argues that the notion of unconstrained communication is not unreal but rather is implied as a possibility in any act of raising or redeeming "validity claims." The "communicative practice of everyday life" inherently points to the possibility of argumentation or discourse in which speakers examine controversial claims under "idealized" conditions. Competent speakers must be able to defend their assertions, actions and norms of actions if challenged and this means that they must ultimately be able to appeal to reasons. In appealing to reasons, however, they assume that their claims could be substantiated through rational discourse, that is, that their views would win out through the force of the better argument alone. Communication in general, then, points to something like an ideal speech situation in which participants are able to examine the validity of disputed claims under conditions free of all constraints other than those of argumentation itself, conditions which presuppose a sole interest in the possible truth or rightness of claims and a communication community free of relations of implicit or explicit coercion.

This argument is a complex one and has generated debate on many fronts.[40] For the purposes of following his debate with Gadamer, however, one admission that Habermas makes is sufficient. He concedes that his account of the rational structure of communication reflects the influence of the Western tradition. To cite only one aspect of this influence it presupposes the capacity of speakers to distinguish between different kinds of validity claims as well as between the different kinds of defense appropriate to them. But these distinctions are not common to all cultures or historical epochs; Habermas himself points to mythical world-views which remain "undifferentiated," where different kinds of claims are not distinguished in the way we distinguish them and where the necessity we see of redeeming claims through argumentative "discourse" remains undeveloped.[41] How, then, can he claim universality for his analysis of the rationality inherent in communication? Does the communicative competence to which he points not simply reflect the conventions of a specifically Western tradition and is it not therefore hermeneutically circumscribed in its scope?

Habermas's answer to this question is basically that the existence of alternative world-views would count against the universality of the competence to which he points only if we also had no way of assessing their cognitive adequacy. His hypothesis, however, is that the development of a species-wide communicative competence takes place over time and that this can be shown through rational reconstructions of the logic of that development. The point of such rational reconstructions is to show that the modern, differentiated world-view is not *simply* a modern one or the outgrowth *merely* of a particular tradition but rather reflects the result of a learning process.[42] Habermas claims that, for now, this hypothesis constitutes only a research project but argues that its validity cannot be decided in advance, as an impossibility given our historicity. The condition that our world-view reflects the results of a particular historical and cultural process, that we too are bound to tradition, does not show that a universalistic concept of rationality is fictitious. In addition, one would have to show that this tradition is parochial, in other words, that it is not only prejudiced but prejudiced in a way that prohibits universalistic claims. Habermas can thus agree with Gadamer that our idea of rationality, indeed, our connection of legitimate consensus with constraint-free consensus, is the product of a specific historical tradition. This concession, however, does not preclude the possibility that the idea reflects a process of learning or that the specific historical tradition in question represents a higher stage in a species-wide development. The fact that our knowledge is historically conditioned or prejudiced does not mean that the scope of its legitimacy is necessarily limited. The question, rather, is whether the kinds of distinctions we make, the world-view we inhabit and so on can be shown to reflect a higher level cognitive adequacy than other, "undifferentiated" world-views. If it can, then Gadamer's emphasis on the "truth" articulated by others and an openness to the possibility that they "could be right" has, at least, to be balanced with a recognition of the "truths" we ourselves can articulate as the heirs of our own historical tradition. This is the point Habermas stresses in criticizing Gadamer's analysis of the anticipation of completeness:

Gadamer gives the interpretive model of *Verstehen* a peculiarly *one-sided twist*. If in the performative attitude of virtual participants in conversation we start with the idea that an author's utterance has the presumption of rationality, we not only admit the possibility that the interpretandum may be exemplary *for us*, that we may learn something from it; we also take into account the possibility that the author could learn something *from us*.[43]

The point here is that the interpretation of alien cultures by no means always requires "the position of a subordinate." An adequate understanding of Zande witchcraft, for example, does not require us to suppose only that we have something to learn; we can also try to reconstruct the specific developments that distance us from the Azande. In emphasizing only the first direction of communication – what we can learn from the Azande – Gadamer is, on Habermas's view, misled by his model of the dogmatic interpretation of sacred and classical texts. Understanding thus becomes a process of applying their truths to our lives and the aspect of interpretation that involves recognizing the level of learning that separates our lives from those truths is left out of the account. Habermas's approach to the historicity that Gadamer emphasizes is thus two-pronged. He criticizes Gadamer, on the one hand, for failing to acknowledge the extent to which history is not only our cultural heritage but a domain of ideological delusion and, indeed, open force. He criticizes him, on the other, for refusing to allow for a historical learning process that leads to greater insight into binding structures of rationality.

To be sure, Habermas's efforts to substantiate his view have encountered myriad problems. The kind of research projects to which he appeals for "heuristic guide and encouragement"[44] – namely, Piaget's research into the cognitive development of children and Kohlberg's account of moral development – have themselves been charged with Eurocentric and male biases.[45] From a Gadamerian point of view, in fact, it is unclear how Habermas could substantiate his hypothesis in an unprejudiced way. His theory of communicative competence seems rather simply to have taken a certain world-view as the end-state of a developmental–logical process and then read the stages of the development back into the process. The question that arises here is how we can equate the categorial distinctions we find necessary for communication with those necessary for communication in general once we admit the existence of cultures that have done without them. How can we prove our communicative competence to reflect a higher stage in a species-wide developmental process if all the research that we undertake in order to show that it is a higher stage already assumes what is to be proven? How do we escape the vicious circle in which we accept as the principle of research – differentiated as opposed to undifferentiated world-views – precisely that which is at issue: namely, the greater cognitive adequacy of the latter?

It is not clear that Habermas has successfully answered this question. Nevertheless it seems to me that the challenge he presents to Gadamer is very important. In reiterating his emphasis on our historicity, Gadamer provides no proof of his own hermeneutic assumption to the effect that because we are historically situated we can make no universalistic claims. Insight into our historical situatedness is not the end of the story; rather, the question can still be raised as to whether history manifests a development in structures of rationality. Gadamer's unwillingness to allow for such a question in his debate with Habermas reveals the conservative side of his analysis. In my view this is a conservatism that is not substantiated by other insights Gadamer's work offers. Nevertheless we have already seen how it emerges at various points in *Truth and Method* and in the remainder of this chapter I want to indicate how far his opposition to Habermas's universalism pushes him in the same direction.

GADAMER'S CONSERVATISM

In both of his responses to Habermas, "The Scope and Function of Hermeneutical Reflection" and the "Reply" to *Hermeneutik und Ideologie-kritik*, Gadamer criticizes Habermas's appeal to an Enlightenment conception of reflection. As we have seen, Gadamer himself emphasizes the capacity of hermeneutics to see through prejudices and, hence, to overcome a society's mistaken self-understanding. Nevertheless he also criticizes the Enlightenment for an abstract opposition of reflection and tradition or reason and authority. The capacity of reflection to see through prejudices is not the result of any appeal to a suprahistorical concept of reason; it is itself a prejudiced insight. Moreover, it is an insight that, as we have seen, obscures certain possibilities of social or individual self-understanding at the same time that it reveals others. But Habermas suggests that critical reflection sees through distortions in self-understanding and "shakes the dogmatism of life-practice."[46] On Gadamer's view, this faith in reflection simply accepts the Enlightenment's contrast between the on-going authority of a tradition and rational criticism. More specifically, it fails to recognize either the extent to which reflection is itself shaped by the life practice of a tradition or the fact that it can just as easily affirm as undermine that practice. As he continues, "the process of making the prejudicial structure of understanding could culminate in the recognition of authority. It could be that conservatism is advantageous for seeing a truth that is easily hidden."[47]

In fact Habermas does not claim that reflection always dissolves prior convictions or that it can never result in a recognition of authority. His concern is directed at the *dogmatism* of social norms and practices or, in other words, at norms and practices that are adhered to, or pursued in, an unreflective, ungrounded way. Reflection can of course affirm norms and practices; Habermas's point, however, is that if it does so, the norms and practices are now followed not on the basis of authority but because they have been reflectively judged to be appropriate.[48] In other words, reflection "shakes the dogmatism of life-practice" whether it affirms or criticizes a traditional world-view, for if that world-view continues to be accepted it is now because it has been justified with reasons.

But a second part of Gadamer's criticism of Habermas's account of reflection makes it clear that his objection is not primarily that Habermas sees reflection as always undermining traditional norms and practices; the objection is rather that Habermas misunderstands the consequences of reflection in general. Gadamer suggests that the acceptance of authority is not always a question either of coerced obedience or of reflective insight into the legitimacy of the authority. Authority depends rather upon what he refers to as "dogmatic recognition" or, in other words, upon a concession of "superiority in knowledge and insight to the authority" and a belief therefore "that authority is right."[49] The point here is that reflection may lead one to realize that one can find no independent grounds either for legitimating or for criticizing authority, that, indeed, one's understanding of what is legitimate is finite, bound to a historical tradition and hence fallible. But if one's understanding of legitimacy is fallible this means that one cannot criticize authority in any "knowledgeable" or authoritative way. Hence "real" reflection may culminate, not in criticism, but in an understanding of the very basis of authority, on Gadamer's view: namely, to an acknowledgement that one does not oneself have the basis for making a judgment, that one is prejudiced and, therefore, that one has to concede the possibility of superior knowledge and insight to someone else. The acceptance or recognition of authority on these grounds is dogmatic since it does not follow from an insight into the legitimacy of the authority but rather from a concession of putative superiority on the basis of one's Socratic knowledge of one's own ignorance.

Gadamer's view, then, is that critical reflection cannot lead to a legitimate undermining of authority on grounds independent of one's prejudices. Rather it leads to a dogmatic acceptance of authority because it is based on insight into the influence of historical prejudices and hence an understanding that judgments against authority are always fallible. But even if reflection cannot show authority to be certainly illegitimate, neither can it show it to be certainly superior and hence legitimate. Why, then, ought it be accepted dogmatically? Why should it not be rejected dogmatically? Gadamer's thesis here is the fundamentally conservative one that since we are historically finite, since we have no concept of rationality that is independent of the tradition to which we belong and hence no universal norms and principles to which we can appeal, we ought not even to attempt to overthrow the authority of that tradition. This thesis goes beyond his hermeneutic claim that in any attempt to overthrow tradition (whether artistic, epistemological or political) we accept more than we deny and more, perhaps, then we are willing to admit. Here his position is that since we cannot justify revolutionary practice absolutely, through recourse to trans-historically valid principles, we ought to dispense with it entirely.

Even if one rejects Habermas's attempt to found a modern correlate to the Enlightenment's appeal to reason in the universal pragmatics of language, Gadamer's position does not seem to follow. Failure to find axiomatic grounds for our criticism of authority does not mean that we must submit dogmatically to it. We can criticize it for a variety of different reasons, including its own inability to show why we should not. In equating the lack of an ultimate foundation for our beliefs with the necessity of submitting to authority Gadamer reinforces the conservative dimension of his "anticipation of completeness." In *Truth and Method*, as we saw, it usually appears as a condition of the possibility of our modifying or overcoming our prejudices about a text, work of art or the tradition as a whole and involves a provisional acceptance of the truth or authority of a work. This notion of a provisional acceptance is, of course, problematic since it is by no means clear when or how it is to be abandoned. None the less, in Gadamer's comments on Habermas's views such provisional acceptance becomes a political commitment. We must accept the authority of the tradition because we cannot know enough to be certain of our criticism of it.

Gadamer's conservativism here is echoed in remarks he makes on the mediation or fusion of horizons. I argued in chapter 3 that Gadamer uses the notion of mediation in two different ways. In the first instance, mediation simply characterizes the process of understanding and encompasses both agreement and disagreement with what is being understood. Thus, even if I disagree with traditional views of women's needs and interests, my understanding of these views involves a kind of formal mediation with them in so far as I come to terms with them and incorporate my differences with them into my own self-understanding. I bring my own prejudices to the task of interpretation and see the views in question in light of my own concerns. Conversely, my prejudices become less unreflective and more refined through the encounter with views other than my own and the result is a more sophisticated, mediated point of view that incorporates the two previous views as "*aufgehoben*" moments, to use Hegelian language.

This kind of mediation would seem to be part of the methodologically oriented social sciences as well. Indeed, in calling his book *Truth and Method* Gadamer insists that he does not mean to contrast the recognition of truth with methodical social science, but merely to show the extent to which such methodical social inquiry is itself hermeneutic.[50] In other words, it belongs itself to a tradition and rests on certain norms and assumptions; moreover, in "researching" its object it can be described as coming to an agreement with it or bringing two diverse language games into productive relationship with one another. This position notwithstanding, Gadamer attacks Habermas for taking the side of methodical science against hermeneutics and thus the side of methodological "distantiation" or alienation (*Verfremdung*)[51] against hermeneutic mediation. He contrasts distantiation to the hermeneutic appropriation and recovery of the truth found in its object and thus views mediation not as including a critical or distanced approach but rather as contrasting with it. Still, there is no reason why hermeneutics need exclude either criticism or alienation. As Gadamer eludicates his position in *Truth and Method*, hermeneutics is not as much a counterforce to methodical science as, instead, a reflection on the scope and meaning of its results. There he argues that the "objectivity" of the methodical sciences is limited by their own hermeneutic situation and not that hermeneutics opposes the critical attitude they bring with them.

Thus, Gadamer overlays his account of hermeneutics with a conservative thesis that does not necessarily follow from it. This account makes it clear (a) that the mediation or fusion which is part of understanding includes disagreement, and distantiation and (b) that the authority of the tradition is one that may be continually rethought in connection with new truths that are revealed in the dialogue with it. Hence, in contrasting mediation to distantiation and equating the Socratic *docta ignorantia* with subservience to authority, Gadamer pushes his hermeneutic reflections in a direction they need not go. In the final chapter of this book I want to emphasize a different dimension of his work by contrasting it to Richard Rorty's appropriation of it. Although this appropriation develops its cautious and conservative side, in so doing it seems to me to overlook what is more interesting and provocative: the way in which, despite his criticism of Habermas's defense of Enlightenment ideals of truth and reason, Gadamer provides a defense of his own.

5

Hermeneutics and the
"new pragmatism"

For both Habermas and Apel the importance of hermeneutics lies in its critique of a positivistic "unity of science" that attempts to reduce all forms of knowledge to the model of the natural sciences. On their view, Gadamer's merit is to have provided an account of hermeneutic understanding that both indicates the extent to which it deviates from natural scientific explanation and justifies it as an unavoidable component of social scientific inquiry. In this regard, Gadamer's insights into effective history and the force of prejudice are crucial. They show the way in which all forms of knowledge adhere to a set of historically produced norms and conventions and hence the naivety of the claim that the natural sciences provide an unconditioned "objective" view of their subject-matter which it is the task of the social sciences to emulate. Moreover, these insights indicate an important difference between the natural and the social sciences in so far as they reveal the "double hermeneutic" characteristic of the latter, which Gadamer describes as an encounter or dialogue between two sets of prejudices or historical horizons. The successful conclusion of such dialogue is a mutual understanding of the subject-matter at issue that goes beyond both the views of one's text or text-analogue and one's own initial assumptions, prejudices and aims. In stressing this new understanding, Gadamer's hermeneutics attempts to move beyond both the conservatism of simply adopting the views of the "text" and the subjectivism of interpreting it as a verification of one's own prejudices. Hermeneutic understanding rather participates in the self-formation of an interpretive tradition in which each new effort to understand reflects a new education and a new form of the tradition itself.

Both Habermas and Apel criticize this analysis of tradition for its failure to reflect on the possibility of ideological distortion within the tradition's self-formation. As I suggested in chapter 4, the problem they see is really two-fold. On the one hand, that which we are trying to understand may systematically obscure its connections to social relations of power and domination. Hence, in appropriating it hermeneutically as possibly true we may deform our own development, as, it could be argued, women did. On the other hand, our own understanding – that is, the way we appropriate or take seriously that which we are trying to understand – may itself reflect the influence of ideology. In this case, what we learn from others will be deformed by the very language and categories in terms of which we understand it.

We saw that this problem of ideology propels Habermas and Apel beyond hermeneutics. Apel combines hermeneutic understanding with quasi-objective scientific explanation while Habermas turns to a theory of communicative rationality. For both, the solution to the problem involves the capacity to distinguish between a free and open discussion of validity claims and systematically distorted "pseudo"-conversation in which the consensus reached is the product of force. To this extent, both remain "foundationalist" philosophers. Of course the term "foundationalism" can refer to quite different ideas; the foundationalism of Habermas and Apel bears no significant resemblance to that of the logical positivists, for instance. Use of the term here is rather meant simply to emphasize that Habermas and Apel are concerned with the truth of assertions and normative validity of actions and norms of action. They want therefore to counter a position that would reduce ideas of truth and normative validity to matters of differing historical prejudice alone and, on their view, this is just what Gadamer's hermeneutics threatens to do. It fails to provide any basis upon which to adjudicate the validity of a tradition's self-understanding and therefore risks a simple capitulation to it.

Richard Rorty's appropriation of Gadamer's work is very different.[1] In his eyes the merit of hermeneutics is not that it offers a basis for distinguishing the natural and the social sciences, as Habermas and Apel believe; its value is rather that it overcomes false distinctions between all forms of knowledge. It therefore eradicates not only the difference between social and natural science but also the more traditional distinction between the sciences, the humanities and creative enterprises in general. According to Rorty, the notion that forms of knowledge are distinct or that they conform to varying logics is a mistake that follows from the false idea that knowledge "mirrors" the essence of its subject-matter. On this view, there is supposed to be a distinction between natural and social science corresponding to the difference between "nature" and "spirit;" moreover, there is supposed to be a distinction between such creative activities as poetry and a scientific knowledge that represents nature or a human society as it "really" is. The value of hermeneutics, however, is to have shown that any sort of knowledge is bound to a tradition and that it therefore never sees things as they "really" are. All forms of knowledge are rather closer to forms of "making" than to forms of "finding" or discovering and therefore comprise a continuum with creative enterprises in general.[2]

Furthermore, in overcoming the distinction between "objective" knowledge and creativity, hermeneutics for Rorty suggests the problem reflected in any attempt like that of Habermas or Apel to uncover a basis upon which to test knowledge claims. If knowledge is not a representational faculty, if it does not mirror the essence of its subject-matter or things as they "really" are, then there is also no point in looking for the grounds upon which it is justified in making the claims that it makes. Rorty's argument is that the entire epistemological preoccupation of modern philosophy is misguided. Our understanding can be neither enhanced nor justified by the possession of a theory as to the conditions of the possibility of its representing the world; in fact, there is no such possibility that needs to be explained. As Rorty puts this point, epistemological efforts are an instance of "scratching where it does not itch."[3]

In this chapter I shall first examine the new "unity of science" that Rorty gathers from Gadamer's hermeneutics and attempt to articulate the appropriate hermeneutic response to it. I shall then turn to the implications for foundationalist philosophy that Rorty thinks are entailed by this new unity and consider the appropriate hermeneutic response to such a position. My purpose in doing so is to shed light on a different dimension of Gadamer's hermeneutics from that emphasized in the last chapter. On my view, his thought is not as antithetical to Enlightenment concerns as Habermas, Apel and Rorty believe, and remains closer to a foundationalist enterprise than any of them admit.

RORTY'S NEW UNITY OF SCIENCE

In criticizing the attempt to distinguish the logics of the natural and the social sciences, Rorty concentrates his attack on the neo-Wittgensteinian view of Charles Taylor that I briefly reviewed in chapter 4. Since this view is one that Habermas and Apel find in general agreement with Gadamer's position, it will be helpful to examine Rorty's attack on Taylor to understand the very different way in which he appropriates Gadamer's work.

As we saw, Taylor's argument, like that of Peter Winch, is that the actions, practices and norms which the social sciences study are constituted within "semantic fields" or "language games" and that therefore the possibility of understanding them depends upon a familiarity with the relevant games or fields. To mention only one of Taylor's examples, understanding a certain act as a gesture of deference requires seeing it in its relations to the ideas of courtesy and respect, in its contrast to acts of insolence and defiance and, indeed, in its connection to hierarchical relationships and institutions of social power.[4] Without a familiarity with this "web of meaning" within which the act is defined, it cannot be understood as the particular gesture that it is. To this extent, then, understanding the meaning of an action, norm or social practice involves understanding the range of related and contrasting meanings that form its context and, for Taylor, the difference between the natural and the social sciences thus becomes quite clear. The distinguishing mark of the social sciences is that the semantic field that is relevant to understanding is that of the society or community under study whereas the natural sciences have only their own norms and conventions with which to contend. Identifying a particular gesture as an act of deference is legitimate only if the act *could* be one of deference, that is, only if it falls within the proper range or related meanings and only, therefore, if concepts of courtesy, respect, insolence or their equivalents are part of the society to which the actor belongs. Conversely, without this range of related and contrasting meaning the act cannot be legitimately described as one of deference no matter how many behavioral features it shares with what we might call a deferential gesture. The phenomena of the natural world, however, do not possess a complex of meaning they ascribe to themselves. In other words, the natural world is not symbolically structured outside the natural sciences and hence the only semantic field relevant to its investigation is that informed by the needs, purposes and norms of these sciences themselves.

Rorty has two objections to this line of argument. First he denies that the definition of the objects of the social sciences within a set of conceptual interrelations differentiates them from the objects of the natural sciences. In his view, the same claim can be made about fossils, for example, or the migratory behavior of butterflies; in these cases, as well, identifying the phenomena in question rests upon understanding their relation to other phenomena or, as he writes:

> To say that human beings wouldn't be human, would be merely animal, unless they talked a lot is true enough. If you can't figure out the relation between a person, the noises he makes, and other persons, then you won't know much about him. But one could equally well say that fossils wouldn't be fossils, would just be rocks, if we couldn't grasp their relations to lots of other fossils. . . . Anything is, for purposes of being inquired into, constituted within a "web of meanings."[5]

Of course, this objection is not telling against Taylor's position. Taylor does not claim that it is simply the relation of its object to a web of meanings that differentiates social science from natural science. He rather argues that the two are distinguished by the source of the web of meaning to which their objects are related. The semantic field crucial to the identification of the objects of the social sciences is that operative in the community or society under study, while that crucial to the identification of the objects of the natural sciences is that of the scientific community itself. This claim, however, leads to Rorty's second objection to Taylor's position. By claiming that understanding the semantic field to which an action or practice belongs is essential to identifying it, Taylor, according to Rorty, equates the meaning of actions and practices with what their agents or participants say about them. In other words, if Taylor's argument is that a given act can be appropriately described as one of deference only if the language game of deference is one available to the actor then, in Rorty's view, the argument is simply that an act can be one of deference only if the actor him- or herself uses this description of it. To refute the argument Rorty points to "particularly stupid"[6] people and "cases in which the other person's, or culture's, explanation of what it's up to is so primitive, or so nutty, that we brush it aside."[7] He thinks it is a generally sound hermeneutic principle to ask people what they are doing, if possible, since if the explanations are good ones they can save scientists the time of constructing their own. None the less, there is nothing about their constitution within a semantic field that requires us to accept a society's or person's own descriptions of their practices or actions.

In this second objection to Taylor's position Rorty seems to a certain extent to have missed the point again. Just as Taylor does not claim that the constitution of their objects within a semantic field of itself distinguishes the social sciences from the natural sciences, he also does not claim that such constitution requires us to accept a person's or culture's self-understanding.[8] His point is rather that even where a scientific explanation of an action is more sophisticated or intelligent than that offered by the agent, this explanation must still retain some connection to the agent's own intentions and beliefs. Taylor uses the example of negotiation to clarify this point. He argues first that a certain range of conceptions is essential to the practice. Negotiating parties must be able to conceive of themselves as autonomous agents; they must differentiate between free choice and coercion and they must understand the rules for entering into negotiations, breaking off negotiations and the like. These conditions of the possibility of negotiation are implicit in Taylor's claim that actions and practices are defined within a field of semantic relations and distinctions. But second, Taylor denies that negotiating parties must themselves explain what they are doing in the terms used above. They need not describe themselves as autonomous agents and need have no explicit conception of free choice; indeed, they need never use the words "compromise" or "contractual relations." These terms may be ones that only scientists employ but they are legitimate terms to employ only if they are connected to the vocabulary that the agents do use; that is, if they are implicit in the capacity to disagree, concede, come to an agreement, use bargaining chips and so on. Alternatively, where there is no vocabulary for bargaining or compromising, as in traditional Japanese villages, there is also no basis for identifying any practice as one of negotiation. The point, then, is not that parties are negotiating only if they say they are negotiating; the point is rather that the practice involves certain norms and presuppositions which may themselves be described in various ways but from which the practice cannot be divorced without losing the specificity of its meaning.

At issue here is social inquiry's "double hermeneutic" which Habermas and Apel believe Gadamer formulates as dialogue or conversation. Rorty's possible rejoinder to this way of describing the logic of the social sciences takes us to the heart of his position. He not only denies that a culture's self-description is necessarily the best description of its values, norms or practices – a denial with which Taylor can agree. He also denies that any connection is required at all between legitimate social scientific description and the semantic field of action or practice; indeed, he claims that in assuming the necessity of such a connection Taylor reveals his adherence to an outmoded metaphysic. With earlier philosophers of the natural sciences, he supposes that the constitutive element of legitimate description is its representation or mirroring of the nature or real meaning of the object in question. In other words, he supposes that the mark of a good scientific account of an object is that it gets at what the object "really" is.

In Rorty's view such a conception of science overlooks advances that Quine, Kuhn, Feyerabend and others have made in the philosophy of science. As I suggested earlier, the contribution of these philosophers is to have shown that the various natural sciences are themselves constituted within semantic fields or traditions and that therefore what counts as objective knowledge, and what was supposed to provide the model of objective knowledge for the social sciences, itself refers simply to a complex of norms and conventions. For Rorty, this insight means that we have to give up any concept of science as progressing toward an adequate representation of the world as it is "in itself." Following Kuhn, he argues that the history of science rather reflects a series of revolutions between different interpretive paradigms with different criteria of rationality and objectivity that are largely "incommensurable" with one another. The difference between Galileo's experimental natural science and Aristotle's metaphysical approach thus cannot be described in terms of Galileo's having discovered the "key" to nature's "secrets" or finally having found the language in which nature has always wanted to be described. According to Rorty, Galileo rather merely hit upon a way of investigating natural phenomena that worked for certain purposes. By the same token, once we see that the various social sciences also form traditions of norms and conventions, we also have to give up the idea that they get at the "real" meaning of the actions, practices, institutions and norms they study. Again, the way they investigate their object-domain, the kinds of descriptions and terms they use and, indeed, the standards to which they appeal for the confirmation and refutation of theories, all depend on the aims of the science itself. From this point of view an agent's self-description cannot be either more or less accurate than a more scientifically sophisticated one; neither mirror or capture the reality of an action any more than natural scientific explanations capture the nature of the universe. All descriptions rather reflect "ways of coping" that refer simply to the purposes of those who forge them.

In Rorty's view this is the merit of Gadamer's account of tradition and prejudice: not to have articulated grounds for distinguishing the logics of the natural and social sciences but to have forced us to see the pragmatic basis of all inquiry. Thus, while Habermas and Apel stress Gadamer's account of dialogue, Rorty emphasizes the idea of effective-historical consciousness (*wirkungsgeschichtliches Bewusstsein*), a consciousness he explicates as "an attitude interested not so much in what is out there in the world, or in what happened in history, as in what we can get out of nature and history for our own uses."[9] The value of hermeneutics, then, lies in overcoming the outmoded metaphysic to which Taylor remains wedded and Habermas and Apel tie Gadamer's work. The point about effective-historical consciousness is that our understanding is always biased, that we always understand from the perspective of our present concerns and hence that we never understand what our object "really" is.

Despite its affinities with much of what we have discovered about Gadamer's work, this approach to effective-historical consciousness ignores two crucial components of his hermeneutics. First it fails to account for that dimension of hermeneutic dialogue on which Gadamer focuses, not on what we can get out of our inquiry for our own uses but on what we can *learn* from our objects and how we may be changed by what we learn. Hermeneutics is not as subjectivistic as Rorty makes it out to be. As we have seen, Gadamer rather balances the potential opportunism which stems from the influence of prejudices with the openness that understanding requires and which constitutes it as a fusion of horizons. Second, Rorty overlooks Gadamer's emphasis on *die Sache*. In examining the impact of historical prejudices on the social sciences and *Geisteswissenschaften*, Gadamer does not deny that these forms of knowledge get at what their objects really are, as Rorty claims. The different historical vantage points from which texts and text-analogues are viewed reveal different aspects of them; every generation of interpreters participates in different dialogues and arrive at new mediations with their objects. Still, it is crucial for Gadamer's view that these dialogues remain dialogues over *die Sache* and that the different dimensions revealed are facets of it. The important point about effective-historical consciousness, then, is not only that inquiry is always oriented by our concerns; although Gadamer makes this point, his argument is also that inquiry is always inquiry into a subject-matter and that the consensus reached about this subject-matter can reveal something "true" about it. Such truth is not final or exhaustive; none the less it still makes sense to describe understanding as a comprehension of meaning even if this meaning can also change. I now want to see how this account of understanding in the social sciences and humanities affects the validity of Rorty's appeal to Gadamer for a critique of epistemology.

RORTY'S CRITIQUE OF EPISTEMOLOGY

Rorty characterizes "epistemologically-centered philosophy" as the search for a neutral foundation upon which to justify our beliefs and adjudicate between existing theories or interpretations. Since the seventeenth century this form of philosophy has defined knowledge as the correct depiction of reality, a mirror of the way things "really" are with regard to the physical universe, the social world or the constituents of moral action. Accordingly the epistemological project has been that of showing the possibility of such accurate representation. The question it asks has been how the ideas and images within the human mind can be shown to correspond to an external world. In order to answer this question Locke looked to the association of ideas in the mind, Kant to synthetic *a prioris* and modern analytic philosophy, having undermined the notion of "internal representation," to language. The concern of all, however, remains the same; it is to justify our beliefs by discovering the conditions of the possibility of their corresponding to the way things are. In Rorty's view, the problem with this epistemological concern is rooted in the conception of knowledge with which it begins, a conception in which knowledge involves acquaintance with an outer domain of "reality" opposed to an inner domain of impressions and ideas in need of justification. Rorty claims that this conception of knowledge can be traced back to the Greek idea of knowledge as a form of direct familiarity with objects as well as to the "ocular metaphor" which this idea occasions. Nevertheless he insists that both idea and metaphor are "optional" and, moreover, that "if this way of thinking of knowledge is optional, then so is epistemology, and so is philosophy as it has understood itself since the middle of the last century."[10]

To indicate what is wrong with these optional metaphors and assumptions, Rorty turns to a consideration of the dispute between Cardinal Bellarmine and Galileo. For, as he explains, "Much of the seventeenth century's notion of what it was to be a 'philosopher' and much of the Enlightenment's notion of what it was to be 'rational' turns on Galileo's being absolutely right and the Church absolutely wrong."[11] On this Enlightenment reading, Bellarmine's appeal to scripture to limit the scope of Copernican theory is seen as absolutely illegitimate in so far as it introduces into a purely scientific matter such religious and cultural considerations as preserving the church and maintaining the traditional structure of Europe. In other words, it imposes non-scientific values on purely scientific concerns and thus fails to understand the distinguishing marks of rational knowledge as opposed to faith. Rorty points out, however, that the distinction between scientific and non-scientific matters is itself a historical product. Indeed, before Galileo's defenders used it to refute Bellarmine the distinction simply did not exist. It is not written in the sky nor does it mirror reality as it is; rather it is a distinction that was hammered out only through the debate between Galileo and Bellarmine itself. But if the distinction is already part of Galileo's position it obviously cannot also be used to justify it. To be sure, Bellarmine's appeal to scripture seems to us to err in conflating science and religion; according to Rorty, however, this is so, not because we are right to distinguish between them and Bellarmine wrong not to; it is so rather because we are Galileo's heirs:

> We are the heirs of three hundred years of rhetoric about the importance of distinguishing sharply between science and religion, science and politics, science and art, science and philosophy and so on. . . . But to proclaim our loyalty to these distinctions is not to say that there are "objective" and "rational" arguments for adopting them. Galileo, so to speak, won the argument and we all stand on the common ground of the grid of relevance and irrelevance which modern philosophy developed as a consequence of this victory.[12]

Thus, because of our heritage, we take science and scientific values to be distinct from religion and religious values. Indeed Rorty claims that we can even say that it was a "splendid thing" that Galileo developed these distinctions[13] presumably because they have had great pragmatic value in subduing the forces of nature and improving the quality of life. None the less, these pragmatic consequences give us no reason to think that Copernican theory mirrors reality or that Galileo discovered *the* correct method for understanding nature. In Rorty's view, we can say only that Galileo created a vocabulary that happened to work better than a religious or metaphysical one given certain purposes that are also the purposes we have.

But if our allegiance to distinctions between scientific concerns and non-scientific ones is a matter of heritage and not of "rationality" in any absolute sense, then the kind of distinction that philosophers make in general between matters of cognitive knowledge and matters of opinion has to be discarded. From Rorty's perspective, the logic of the dispute between Galileo and Bellarmine does not differ in any significant way from that "between say Kerensky and Lenin or that between the Royal Academy circa 1910 and Bloomsbury."[14] Given our heritage, we take modern science to be an advance over superstition and, for similar reasons, we may take democracy to be an advance over totalitarianism. Still, on Rorty's view, we have no grounds for our beliefs in either case; in each instance we can appeal only to our history and not to that which is actually rational or right in a non-historical sense.

Of course, the dispute between Bellarmine and Galileo seems not only easily resolvable to us; it also seems easily resolvable by reference to the way things "really" are, whereas we tend to deny that political or literary disputes can be resolved in the same way. But Rorty claims that this appearance has simply to do with the greater amount of agreement to be found on the Galileo–Bellarmine issue than on either the Kerensky–Lenin or the Royal Academy–Bloomsbury debate. Moreover, it is not to say that such consensus will continue to exist. Rorty imagines an age in which morality, physics and psychology are all considered "equally objective" because the same degree of consensus is to be found in each. Conversely, literary criticism, chemistry and sociology are considered non-cognitive disciplines because no consensus is similarly forthcoming. In his view, it follows that "the application of such honorifics as 'objective' and 'cognitive' is never anything more than an expression of the presence of, or the hope for, agreement among inquirers."[15]

The notion of objectivity for Rorty then is not to be seen as the reflection of a successful process of mirroring reality but simply as an expression of, or hope for, consensus. But if this is all the idea of objectivity means then, not only the distinction between knowledge and opinion but the epistemological concern with the foundations of knowledge in general appear dispensable. Since no form of knowledge is objective in the sense that it represents the way things "really" are and since it reflects instead simply a conventional idea about the way they are, the traditional epistemological problem of explaining the possibility of representing "reality" turns out to be no problem at all. Our knowledge does not represent reality and hence the conditions of the possibility of its doing so need not be explored. Rather, what we take to be established knowledge and firm fact is the product of an inheritance; it refers to those distinctions and standards of investigation that have been "hammered out" over the course of history for certain purposes that we continue to have. Moreover, these distinctions as well as the evidence to which we look and the standards of rationality on which we depend cannot themselves be justified except by reference to other distinctions we make, other evidence and other standards on which we rely. Thus our heritage conditions even the epistemological checks we make on our knowledge and the criteria to which we appeal in order to establish the facts.

Rorty's critique of epistemology leads to a rejection of foundationalist concerns in favor of what he calls "edification." If we cannot show the way in which our beliefs conform to the way things are, if, in fact, the very idea that they are supposed to conform to the way things are is what has misled philosophy, then on Rorty's view we ought to give up our epistemological preoccupations and become creative. That is, we ought to give up the attempt to justify our beliefs and instead enter into dialogue with others in which we explore other options, try out new modes of self-description and discover the parochial character of our own assumptions. To a philosophical culture concerned with the conditions of the possibility of representing reality Rorty thus opposes a post-philosophical culture concerned with fostering conversation. In this culture philosophers are no longer epistemological police investigating the legitimacy of every belief and placing constraints on cognitive possibilities. They are rather "cultural critics"[16] or "informed dilettantes" who can charm "hermetic thinkers" out of their "self-enclosed practices"[17] and encourage discussion. The point of such discussion is not to discover the one correct way of viewing reality but simply to continue the conversation. "Keeping a conversation going" becomes "a sufficient aim of philosophy" and wisdom is therefore seen not as the ability to uncover the grounds of knowledge but rather as "the ability to sustain a conversation."[18]

In emphasizing the historical nature or tradition-bound character of our norms and beliefs, Rorty obviously follows Gadamer's own stress on prejudice and effective history. Moreover, like Gadamer, he argues that we cannot escape the traditions to which we belong or "step outside our skins"[19] to compare our notions of reality to the way it is in itself. Our understanding is rather a conditioned and historical one and for both Gadamer and Rorty this means that it no longer makes sense to try to justify it as correct or rational by pointing to "reality," the transcendental conditions of knowledge or the moral law as extra-traditional "proofs" of the adequacy of our views. But Rorty suggests that Gadamer's hermeneutics is useful not only in helping us to see through the mistakes of epistemology; he also refers to it in setting the new agenda of edification. As he puts it, hermeneutics is "what we get when we are no longer epistemological."[20]

Hermeneutics is not the name for a discipline, nor for a method of achieving a set of results which epistemology failed to achieve, nor for a program of research. On the contrary, hermeneutics is an expression of hope that the cultural space left by the demise of epistemology will not be filled.[21]

Rorty thus allies hermeneutics with poetry in the effort to create and appreciate new ways of acting and speaking. Hermeneutics, he claims, edifies by "making connections between our own culture and some exotic culture or historical period, or between our own discipline and another discipline which seems to pursue incommensurable aims in an incommensurable vocabulary." Poetry, for its part, edifies "by thinking up new such aims, new words or new disciplines" and by reinterpreting "our familiar surroundings in the unfamiliar terms of our new inventions." In either case the activity is educational rather than justificatory; it does not atempt to legitimate our beliefs but rather tries to "take us out of our old selves by the power of strangeness" and "aid us in becoming new beings."[22]

The term "edification" is Rorty's translation of the German *Bildung* which Gadamer discusses at the beginning of *Truth and Method*. Below I shall assess Rorty's interpretation of this concept. At this point, however, I want to pursue Rorty's own reflections further since, despite their explicit reliance on Gadamer's work, they seem to me to lead to an irrationalism that is quite at odds with its overall thrust.

RORTY'S IRRATIONALISM

We have seen that for Rorty the traditional scorn directed at the kinds of arguments Cardinal Bellarmine used in his debate with Galileo is an accident of history. Galileo "won" the debate and we are his heirs. Nevertheless epistemology has failed to discover any foundation upon which the two competing theories or beliefs could be adjudicated in an unprejudiced way. Instead the distinctions to which we are committed, such as that between science and superstition or that between empirical observation and religious dogma, are founded simply on the growth of our scientific tradition itself. Rorty is aware that this analysis seems to sanction relativism. If there is no neutral grid of "objective" reason to which we can appeal, if the compelling quality of the reasons to which philosophers of science have traditionally appealed is a quality that is simply historically created, then these circumstances seem to indicate that Bellarmine's position is as "good" as Galileo's or at least that we have no more reason to follow Galileo than we do to follow Bellarmine.

Rorty denies this consequence. The claim that there is no neutral algorithm for deciding between beliefs in any given area is not equivalent to the claim that we cannot decide between beliefs. To deny the existence of such an algorithm is to argue merely that the reasons for or against a particular view cannot be determined in advance by reference to notions of truth, reality or the moral law. They are rather determined in the course of conversation, with regard to the concrete advantages or disadvantages a given point of view has. Our reasons for taking up one scientific, political or even aesthetic perspective as opposed to another are thus pragmatic rather than dogmatic; they are reasons debated in dialogue and open to revision or rejection depending upon what other options are advanced. In rejecting epistemology, then, we need not claim that Bellarmine's view is as "good" as Galileo's; it follows merely that there is no "philosophical" or foundationalist way of defending Galileo. We can only refer to purposes we have and advantages Galileo's perspective has with regard to these aims. This means that issues are decided in discussion, in view of the importance of specific purposes and plans and hence in terms of what makes sense to the participants to the discussion themselves. The philosopher as the ultimate arbiter of validity has no place.

Rorty not only claims that this pragmatic conception of adjudication is non-relativistic; he also denies that it leads to irrationalism. That it *seems* irrationalist is clear; if the merits of competing theories or beliefs can be decided only in conversation and only by the participants themselves, the question that Habermas and Apel ask re-emerges: how can we be sure that the arguments and perspectives in play are not distorted by ideological connections of which the participants themselves may be unaware? For Rorty this question is the question of how we can simply assert our beliefs or use them in conversation if we cannot verify their rationality. As he puts it,

> when the pragmatist says "All that can be done to explicate 'truth,' 'knowledge,' 'morality,' 'virtue' is to refer us back to the concrete details of the culture in which these terms grew up and developed," the defender of the Enlightenment takes him to be saying "Truth and virtue are simply what a community agrees that they are." When the pragmatist says "We have to take truth and virtue as whatever emerges from the conversation of

Europe," the traditional philosopher wants to know what is so special about Europe. Isn't the pragmatist saying, like the irrationalist, that *we* are in a privileged situation simply by being *us*? . . . What if the "we" is the Orwellian state?[23]

Rorty's answer to this question begins with an explicitly Habermasian turn: if truth and virtue are to be defined as "whatever emerges from the conversation of Europe" then this conversation must be an "undistorted" one. But Habermas's error, in Rorty's view, lies in his attempt to specify the conditions of this kind of conversation for, here, Rorty claims, "Habermas goes transcendental and offers principles." In contrast, Rorty argues that by "undistorted" we can mean only "employing *our* criteria of relevance where we are the people who have read and pondered Plato, Newton, Kant, Marx, Darwin, Freud, Dewey, etc."[24] In another context, Rorty admits that a position like this, one which cites as the criterion of undistorted conversation a familiarity with the canon of Western thinkers *we* find significant, is "frankly ethnocentric."[25] None the less he denies that any other solution is possible. The epistemological attempt to justify our beliefs or tradition as a whole has been shown to be not only misguided but absurd; hence we only put our beliefs and values forward in conversation without presuming to be able to offer an absolute defense of them.

It is clear, however, that this response is insufficient to dispel worries about irrationalism. One could certainly have read all of the theorists that Rorty cites and remain an ideologue; that is, one could certainly interpret them in one-sided and opportunistic ways, even if one is not oneself aware of the partiality and opportunism involved. Moreover, our criterion of relevance in assuming that the theorists cited are the necessary theorists to have read may itself be an ideological one. As we have seen, these suspicions are precisely those that fuel Habermas's turn to "principles;" the fear he and Apel share is that Plato, Newton, Kant, Marx, Darwin, Freud, Dewey, etc. may be appropriated in a distorted way and, indeed, that the conversation in which they have participated has not been open to all on an equal basis. To concede a "frank ethnocentricism" here is not enough, then, for the question is why such frank ethnocentricism cannot be frankly irrational. If we cannot justify our norms or values, if the Western thinkers cited are important to read only from a parochially Western point of view, why should we be any more frankly ethnocentric than frankly ethnophobic? Indeed, if there is no reason for their importance other than the fact that they have traditionally been taken to be important why should we not move away from tradition and fill in the "etc." by adding Hitler and Stalin? Rorty admits that the only answers he can give to such questions are circular. As he writes, "The pragmatist cannot answer the question 'what is so special about Europe?' save by saying 'Do you have anything non-European to suggest which meets our European purposes better?'"[26] But the problem here is that a different kind of pragmatist could ask a similar question: namely, "Do you have anything non-Orwellian or non-Fascist to suggest which meets our Orwellian or Fascist purposes better?"

Rorty concedes this point as well, suggesting that without foundationalist guarantees it may be impossible "not to sin against Socrates" and hence that his notion of "the conversation of mankind" cannot really substitute for the idea of reason.[27] This conclusion notwithstanding, he simply denies that we can recapture the Age of Enlightenment and argues that conversation is therefore all we have. Indeed, what he finds significant not only in Gadamer's work but in that of Dewey and James as well, is that all face this situation squarely. We Westerners have certain values and commitments that we take seriously, commitments to the freedom and equality of persons, to toleration and respect for the rights of others and so on. We can no longer defend these by appealing to supposedly universal norms of personhood, dignity and rights. Rather we can defend them only as commitments we will continue to think it important to have as long as we are not shown otherwise, where by "being shown otherwise" we mean shown through a discussion we would consider reasoned and productive. Again, however, there is no way of justifying our commitment to such reasoned discussion or to the vision of the "ideal speech situation" it seems to involve. The commitment is simply part of the conversation of the West as we Westerners understand it.

But the question remains as to why this view is not simply irrational. If we cannot justify out commitment to certain values in a non-circular way, that is, if we cannot justify our tradition by appealing to any universal norms or values outside of it, why does it make any more sense to assert it than to criticize or even abandon it? In an essay called "Solidarity or Objectivity?"[28] Rorty shifts ground slightly and argues that we can have only a pragmatic justification of our tradition, one that takes the form of comparisons between it and societies that do not embody such virtues as toleration, free inquiry and respect for persons. Such comparisons, he claims, lead to the suggestion that nobody who had experienced both a free society and a totalitarian one would prefer the latter. But, on pragmatic grounds themselves, this claim seems false, for one's preferences in this case would have to depend on one's situation and aims. If those aims include wealth and power over others, a closed society in which one had total control over the press, the political process and the economy might well be preferable to a democratic society of which one were simply a member.

Perhaps because he recognizes the possibility of this kind of objection, Rorty goes on to suggest not that no one could prefer a closed society but that *we*, at least, cannot prefer one. We have grown up in a certain culture; we have formed certain expectations; we are committed to certain values; and we cannot abandon any of these because we identify ourselves in terms of them. Hence, Rorty argues that "We Western liberal intellectuals should accept the fact that we have to start from where we are and that this means that there are lots of views which we simply cannot take seriously."[29] But even if this is the case, even if there are views that we cannot take seriously, why should we not perceive this circumstance as a defect? Why should we applaud the tradition to which we belong? If the only basis we have for applauding it is our allegiance to it why should we not rather at least try to question that allegiance?

This question is similar to the one I raised with regard to Gadamer's account of the "dogmatic recognition of authority" in chapter 4. It will be recalled that Gadamer emphasizes the Socratic *docta ignorantia*: crucial to the possibility of understanding others or the tradition to which we belong is a consciousness of our own ignorance, a recognition that we do not have all the answers and can learn from others and the past. In his debate with Habermas this conception becomes a justification for a submission to the tradition. Gadamer's point is that critical reflection cannot either justify or undermine our loyalty to the authority of our tradition since it rather leads us to recognize our finitude and fallibility. We must concede superior insight to traditional norms and values, then, because we cannot know enough to reject them. Rorty also thinks we must assert our tradition, on his view because we are irrevocably part of it. It is perhaps of some interest that Gadamer and Rorty do not mean the same tradition. Gadamer's concern is the preservation of the "high culture" stemming from our Greek heritage while Rorty's object is the preservation of American liberal political culture. From our point of view it is of greater interest that in both cases the defense of tradition depends upon the lack of absolute foundations. For both Gadamer in his traditionalism and Rorty in his liberalism, we must accept the tradition because we cannot get outside of it to test its rationality according to a concept of reason independent of it. The same question, however, keeps recurring: namely, why *should* we accept the tradition on that basis? Even if we are conditioned by it and, at any given time, accept far more of it than we would perhaps like to admit, why should efforts to criticize it, revise it and even jettison parts of it not be just as plausible as its dogmatic recognition? To use Rorty's language, if we cannot justify our tradition, why is it not at least as rational (or irrational) to strive for the kind of conversion or escape from our tradition that he doubts we can have?

Despite the similar questions that can be asked of Rorty and Gadamer in this regard, it seems to me that Gadamer's position offers options that Rorty's cannot. I argued in chapter 4 that Gadamer's remarks on the dogmatic recognition of authority are inconsistent with other aspects of his hermeneutics. Indeed, we saw that Gadamer's concept of reaching an understanding with one's tradition incorporated both agreement and criticism. In addition to his substantive concept of the consensus that issues from understanding, in which consensus means agreement with the tradition over a given issue, Gadamer also offers a Hegelian sense of consensus, in which it involves a synthesis of positions into a more refined and articulated point of view. In this case, reaching an understanding with one's tradition does not mean accepting it for fear of unjustly criticizing it. Rather it incorporates critique as the element in understanding that integrates what has been understood as an *aufgehoben* moment of a better view. Hermeneutic understanding thus involves a discriminating integration of the past and an ability to separate justifiable from unjustifiable aspects of traditional claims. This dimension of hermeneutics is further developed in Gadamer's investigations of *Bildung* and practical reason, and it is to these analyses that I shall therefore turn in the final section of this chapter.

BILDUNG AND PRACTICAL REASON

As I mentioned earlier, Rorty uses Gadamer's notion of *Bildung* to characterize a break with epistemologically centered philosophy. *Bildung*, for Rorty, describes an interest in edification and self-formation that contrasts with an interest in certain knowledge. The point of an edifying philosophy is not to discover either foundations for our beliefs or a basis upon which to criticize them. Neither is its concern a final, irrevocable understanding of "truth" or the way the world is. Its point is rather to foster an awareness of different possibilities of coping with the world, of different life-options and, indeed, of new modes of self-description. From the point of view of edification what is important is not "the possession of truths" but our own development. The point is not to justify or ground the assumptions we already have but to consider new ones, to compare our ways of thinking to different alternatives and to recognize the cultural "provincialism" of our own ways of thinking. To be edified is to be aware that our views do not derive from "the" truth or "the" moral law; they rather represent simply the best way of coping that *we* can thus far imagine.[30]

Rorty's account of *Bildung* is substantiated by much of what Gadamer himself says about the concept. As Gadamer describes *gebildete* or cultured individuals they are those who have moved beyond the narrow scope of their private interests and concerns and taken up the concerns of the community to which they belong. To be *gebildet* in this way is to have overcome selfishness, to have learned to postpone immediate gratification and make the interests of one's group, profession or the like one's own. But the *gebildete* person is one who has moved even beyond the limits of the interests of his or her community or group to adopt an interest in world history, different cultures and the past. To this extent Gadamer's analysis of *Bildung* reflects the same emphasis on discovering new modes of self-description and a recognition of diversity that Rorty emphasizes.

Rorty's use of the concept of *Bildung* is also supported by Gadamer's analysis of experience, to which I referred in chapter 1. We saw that for Gadamer experienced people are those who have learned from events in their lives and have learned because they were aware of their fallibility. That is, they have learned because they were open to the possible refutation of their beliefs and prejudices and could therefore revise or supplement them in a productive way. Experience, then, is primarily "an experience of negation,"[31] a discovery that one's beliefs are inadequate to the subject-matter at issue and hence that one must modify one's point of view. In describing this kind of experience Gadamer turns to Hegel's account of dialectic and particularly to the moment of sublation or *Aufhebung* in which one recognizes the partiality or one-sided nature of one's knowledge and moves to a more comprehensive view. We have seen that this notion of *Aufhebung* is crucial to Gadamer's account of understanding in depicting the transformation of both one's own prejudices and those of one's object that occurs in dialogue. What is important here, however, is the extent to which Gadamer differs from

Hegel, who he thinks errs in just the way that Rorty would argue that he errs. In Hegel's work the dialectical process in which knowledge claims are both negated as sufficient in themselves and preserved in a higher synthesis is supposed to culminate in absolute knowledge, in a final synthesis that has reconciled thought to its object and therefore requires no further transformations or modifications. For Gadamer and Rorty, however, both experience and edification lead in the opposite direction: not to absolute knowledge but, as Gadamer puts it, "to that openness to experience that is set free by experience itself:"

> The truth of experience always contains the relation to new experience. Hence, the person who one calls experienced has not only become experienced *through* experiences; that person is also open *for* experiences. The termination of his experience, the completed being of that which we call experience, does not consist in one's already knowing everything and already knowing everything better. In contrast, the experienced person rather proves to be the radically undogmatic person, the person who, because he has had so many experiences and has learned from experiences, is especially able to have new experiences and to learn from experiences.[32]

Gadamer's account of experience thus contains the same opposition between openness and dogmatism that Rorty stresses in his analysis of edification. In studying other cultures, performing scientific experiments, writing poetry and examining one's own history, what one learns is not a series of unrelated and irrevocably true facts. Rather, to the extent that one can avoid an epistemological orientation, to the extent, in other words, that one can transcend questions involving the soundness of one's method or the validity of one's findings, what one achieves is a capacity for future learning, for new ways of thinking, speaking and acting. One learns that one's own historical horizon is part of an endlessly articulated and shifting universe of horizons and that to try to fix this universe in a final, immutable form or hierarchy is to miss the point. Gadamer claims that "The truly experienced person is one . . . who is aware that he is not master of time or the future"[33] and Rorty echoes him in characterizing edifying philosophers:

> These writers have kept alive the suggestion that, even where we have justified true belief about everything we want to know, we may have no more than conformity to the norms of the day. They have kept alive the historicist sense that this century's "superstition" was the last century's triumph of reason, as well as the relativist sense that the latest vocabulary,

borrowed from the latest scientific achievement, may not express privileged representations or essences, but be just another of the potential infinity of vocabularies in which the world can be described.[34]

Despite these similarities, it seems to me that Rorty has overlooked an important dimension of Gadamer's position, one which emerges from a closer examination of his analysis of *Bildung*. We have seen that both *Bildung* and experience involve the virtue of openness and thus preclude an epistemological concentration on "the truth," favoring instead a sensitivity to the multiplicity of possible "truths." For Rorty, edification or *Bildung* therefore "replaces knowledge as the goal of thinking."[35] Yet, despite the opposition that Gadamer himself establishes between *Bildung* and an objective knowledge of facts, on his view *Bildung* remains more than an education into the pluralism of "ways of coping." Indeed, the connection between *Bildung* and a certain kind of knowledge remains fundamental; in this regard, Gadamer argues that it is connected to notions of tact, judgment and taste. To be sure, modern science's monopoly on criteria of knowledge excludes just such notions as these from the cognitive domain and stamps them as purely subjective phenomena. But Gadamer's argument is that this is a mistake, that tact, taste and judgment instance a practical knowledge of how to discriminate between good and bad, right and wrong, important and unimportant and so on. In other words, they reflect a capacity for recognizing truth which perhaps cannot be reduced to a method and for which there are no clear rules but which remains a form of knowledge equal to modern science itself.

If someone is tactful this means that he or she knows what to say and what not to say. Similarly, if someone has taste this means that he or she knows what is beautiful or appropriate and what is not. In this context, Gadamer insists that taste goes beyond an eye for fashion or a conformity to the norms of a particular group; indeed, he sounds somewhat Habermasian in maintaining that taste rather involves "real normative power" in so far as "it knows itself to be certain of the agreement of an ideal community."[36] The person with taste, then, may be ahead or behind contemporary notions of style. Still, that he or she has taste is manifest in the ability to see how things go together and where lines are to be drawn. The same holds of judgment. As Gadamer uses the term it goes beyond the ability to draw correct logical inferences and, again, is rather a form of knowledge that can differentiate between the appropriate and inappropriate, the good and the bad, the right and the wrong. As

Gadamer writes, "Whoever has sound judgment is not enabled primarily to judge particulars under universal viewpoints; instead, he knows what is important."[37]

To the extent that *Bildung* is connected to these notions of tact, taste and judgment it involves not just an awareness of different modes of self- and world-description but an ability to discriminate. The *gebildete* person is one who has learned not only in the sense of knowing certain facts but in the sense of being better able to distinguish between the important and unimportant, the beautiful and the ugly and so on. The recognition of the variety of life-forms or "ways of coping" that is part of *Bildung* is more than an awareness of what exists but rather leads to an increase in sensitivity and selectivity. *Bildung*, for Gadamer, is a "genuine historical idea;"[38] that is, it reflects a process of historical preservation in which one both learns about facts and events but, more importantly, learns how these are to be appropriately integrated into one's life and self-understanding. *Bildung* then does not so much replace "knowledge as the goal of thinking" as, instead, reveal the limits of a certain kind of knowledge: namely, an objective knowledge of facts modelled on the natural sciences. If tact, taste and judgment cannot be codified as methods, if the concept of *Bildung* itself provides no clear principles or criteria for selection and discrimination, all remain part of a practical knowledge concerned not simply with recognizing "truths" but knowing how to live, what to incorporate into one's life and self-understanding and what to reject.

To a certain extent there may be little difference between Rorty's and Gadamer's views on this cognitive dimension of *Bildung*. In contrasting edification and knowledge, Rorty may mean, as Gadamer does, to oppose *Bildung* simply to that objective knowledge which is supposed to issue from the application of reliable methods and which is illustrated by modern natural science. Following Gadamer, Rorty's point would then be that such knowledge represents only one possibility for edification and that by taking it as the model of knowledge in general we undermine the cognitive potential contained in history, literature and those human sciences that are not methodologically formulated. Rorty seems to make just this point in apparently endorsing the view he ascribes to Heidegger, Sartre and Gadamer, that "objective inquiry is perfectly possible and frequently actual – the only thing to be said against it is that it provides only some, among many, ways of describing ourselves, and that some of these can hinder the process of edification."[39]

Nevertheless, it is significant that Rorty never describes edification itself as a form of knowledge and that for him modern natural science rather continues to represent the paradigm for knowledge in general. In fact we have seen that Rorty denies any important difference between the natural sciences and any other mode of cognition. Hence, if the rules and methods on which natural scientific knowledge rests turn out to be thoroughly historical, if the objectivity it achieves turns out to be nothing more than "conformity to the norms of justification . . . we find around us,"[40] as Rorty insists, then the conclusion is clear: we must rid ourselves of a reliance on knowledge altogether or at least of a reliance on it as something approaching justified true belief. This century's knowledge is the next century's superstition, whether we are talking about Zande witchcraft, representational art or quarks. Thus, the notion of knowledge as either requiring justification or capable of it has to be discarded.

But this analysis of knowledge is not consistent with Gadamer's own. For him, the fact that natural scientific knowledge is not objective in any ahistorical sense does not mean the concept of knowledge in general is an outmoded shibboleth. Rather, it remains essential to distinguish between the natural sciences and other modes of knowledge on his view. Because Rorty can see no important difference between the natural and social sciences or, indeed, between the sciences, the humanities and creative enterprises in general, his disillusionment with the objectivity of the one leads to a dismissal of the possibilities of recognizing truths contained in the others as well. *Truth and Method*, however, is devoted precisely to disconnecting other forms of knowledge from the natural sciences. Indeed, its point is that the imposition of the methods of the natural sciences on different, *dialogic* forms of inquiry obscures the insights that these other forms of inquiry *can* achieve. Rorty takes the historicity of the natural sciences to be a limitation on the truth they can attain and, furthermore, takes this limitation to indicate a similar constraint on all forms of human investigation. But Gadamer's suggestion is that the truth of the insights achieved in these other forms of inquiry never depended on their being "objective" or ahistorical. The aim of *Truth and Method* is precisely to clarify forms of inquiry that remain forms of knowledge even though they are bound to specific traditions and historical epochs.

This suggestion indicates a crucial difference between the views of Rorty and Gadamer not only on the distinction between the natural and human sciences but on the role of epistemology in general. Like Rorty, Gadamer rejects a philosophy reduced to epistemology and envisions a different function for it. For Rorty this other function is that of promoting conversation and edification. In a post-epistemological age, philosophers will be "all-purpose intellectuals,"[41] not attempting to ground or legitimate the views of others but simply adding their own to the general discussion. Philosophy, then, will no longer involve the search for foundations but will be simply the attempt to see "how things hang together" or, better, "how all the ways of making things hang together hang together."[42] Gadamer seems at first to make a similar point when he looks not to a post-epistemological age but to a pre-epistemological age, in which philosophy still has a systematic and integrative function. Here the point of philosophy is not to show the conditions of the possibility of our scientific representations of the world, but to show how our beliefs fit together and how they can be made to integrate initially alien views. As he writes, the point of such a philosophy is "to join together science and man's knowledge of himself in order to achieve a new self-understanding of humanity."[43]

But Gadamer's explicit reference to scientific knowledge here suggests how far his view of philosophy is from Rorty's. For Gadamer the problem with modern philosophy's epistemological orientation is not its attempt to offer a justification or account of our knowledge. Rather, the problem is that it restricts this "giving of accounts" (*Rechenschaftsangabe*) to a legitimation of scientific knowledge. The validity of natural science is both taken as a given and held up as a model for all other forms of knowledge. Epistemology's task, then, is to show the conditions of the possibility of this validity and to extend these conditions to show the possibility of similarly rigorous knowledge in other fields as well. To this restricted notion of a "giving of accounts" Gadamer contrasts the older tradition of practical philosophy for which philosophical justification does not refer simply to the project of uncovering the conditions of the possibility of properly scientific knowledge but is rather concerned to show how different forms of knowledge suit our needs and aims in general. Philosophical justification in this practical, Aristotelian form does not reflect just a concern with the objectivity of our knowledge of "facts;" indeed, scientific knowledge no longer serves as the model of knowledge but can rather be seen as tied to a technical form of know-how, the purpose of which is not to set the agenda for reason in general but to facilitate social aims and purposes.

The source of Gadamer's notion of "giving an account" here is not only Aristotle's concept of practical reason but Husserl's attempt to ground the validity of scientific knowledge in the projects of the life-world.

Indeed, for Gadamer, as for Habermas and Apel, the real danger of the epistemological emphasis on the conditions of the possibility of scientific knowledge is a concomitant obfuscation of the practical–political dimension of social life. On Gadamer's view, modernity is characterized by a faith in science which assumes that all problems are technical problems amenable to technical solutions and dependent upon advances in science. Indeed Gadamer argues that the "expert" has replaced the "man of practical wisdom." Social decisions are not the result of reasoned discussion in an informed public sphere but instead the decisions of small groups of experts who have mastered a great deal of technical information and therefore claim to be able to act in the name of everyone else. Gadamer argues that such a society of experts is also a "society of functionaries." What becomes important is not the capacity to make responsible decisions on one's own but rather the willingness to adapt to decisions others have made for one, decisions that, in addition, largely follow the logic of technological imperatives. The course of technological and scientific advance is no longer guided by public consensus on aims and goals; rather, the reverse is the case: goals and purposes are themselves dictated by technological demands and possibilities. Human beings are thus threatened, on Gadamer's view, with a loss of identity; their actions are not the actions of responsible citizens but those of cogs in a machine, the point of which is to assure the continued smooth functioning of the scientific, technical and economic apparatus. The effect of this reversal of the roles of practical–moral deliberation and scientific–technical reason, however, is an increase in "social irrationality" that Gadamer thinks goes a long way towards explaining such phenomena as the "final solution" and the nuclear arms race.[44]

As a "giving of accounts," then, Gadamer thinks that philosophy must take a wider view of its role and need not disintegrate into the theory of science. Neither, however, need it become the cultural dilettantism that Rorty advocates. Rather, if it is to give up its epistemological function it is because it interprets this function too narrowly. For Gadamer, philosophy's task remains that of integrating our knowledge within a cohesive whole, of aiding public consensus on common aims and purposes and thus giving direction to the scientific and technological apparatus. This conception of the role of philosophy may be enough to indicate the difference between Rorty's and Gadamer's view. But Gadamer goes even further, for the tradition of practical philosophy that he wants to resuscitate takes its orientation not from aims and purposes we may happen to have but from a conception of "the good." The function of philosophy is thus not simply to show how the different ways of "making things hang together hang together." Its aim is rather "to understand the world in the same way as one understands one's own behavior when one has known something as good."[45] Philosophical justification, as Gadamer conceives of it, does not reflect a concern either with the objectivity of our knowledge of "facts" or with the conventionality of our descriptions, norms and beliefs. Its concern is rather with living well. Its point is to help us toward a conception of "the good life" from which individual goals as well as scientific and technical knowledge will themselves be directed. Indeed, Gadamer argues that this orientation towards "the good" remains a "need of reason:"[46] What is required is the formation of a new consensus on the appropriate aims of human social life and hence what Gadamer calls a new recognition of "solidarity." As he writes:

> Just as we in the overstimulated process of progress of our technological civilization are blind to the stable, unchanging elements of our social life together, so could it become with the re-awakening consciousness of the solidarity of a humanity that slowly begins to know itself as humanity. This means that it knows itself to belong together, for better or for worse, and that it must solve the problems of its life on this planet. And I therefore believe in the re-awakening of solidarities that could enter into a future society of humanity.

And, he continues, it is these "new normative and common solidarities" that are necessary if practical reason is to "speak again."[47]

In the context of this call for a new recognition of solidarity, Gadamer's discussion of tact, taste and judgment acquire added importance. I noted earlier that Gadamer associates the sureness of taste and judgment not with the existing norms of one community or another but with the norms of an "ideal community." Such a community, it is now clear, is one that incorporates the solidarity of its members, one that is aware, in other words, of the common fate of its members, takes its orientation from a conception of "the good" and thereby allows practical reason to "speak."

Gadamer does not say enough about this conception of "the good." Moreover, the problem of ideology that Habermas and Apel bring to bear on this analysis remains an important one, for it is not clear that the conditions for an informed public consensus on "the good" exist. Gadamer points to the resistance of certain Latin cultures to the modern emphasis on technological progress as a potential source for a renewed practical reason. None the less, as Richard Bernstein points out, he fails to consider the threat to the emergence of such a practical reason exerted not simply by the reversal of practical and technical reason but by the continued existence of the conditions of social power and domination:

> Ironically, there is something almost *unhistorical* in the way in which Gadamer appropriates *phronesis* [practical reason]. Except for some occasional remarks, we do not find any detailed systematic analysis of social structure and causes of the deformation of *praxis* in contemporary society. Insufficient attention is paid to the historical differences that would illuminate precisely how *praxis* and *phronesis* are threatened and undermined in the contemporary world. Since Aristotle clearly saw the continuity and interplay of ethics and politics, one would think that this a movement necessitated by Gadamer's own appropriation of *phronesis*. But although Gadamer acknowledges this to-and-fro movement, he stops short of facing the issues of what is to be done when the *polis* or community itself is "corrupt" – when there is a breakdown of its *nomoi* and of a rational discourse about the norms that ought to govern our practical lives.[48]

This criticism of Gadamer's analysis notwithstanding, the difference between his and Rorty's views of the relation between philosophy, epistemology and science could hardly be more striking. Rorty sees no danger in throwing out all "giving of accounts" and in simply substituting an interestingly diversified discussion. Nor does he see faith in technological progress or the conditions of social domination as a threat to the possibility of practical reason. From his perspective, the so-called voice of practical reason is simply another addition to the general "conversation of mankind," as are the voices of expert and functionary. One person's "practical reason" is another person's "social irrationality" and the decision between these two can only be a pragmatic one about which philosophy has no more to say than anything else. In contrast to this reduction of reason to whatever emerges from humanity's general conversation, however, Gadamer retains something like a deabsolutized Hegelian conception: reason develops historically and develops precisely through the attempts of communities to form a collective conception of "the good."

Gadamer's remarks on freedom are particularly telling in this regard. Following Hegel, he claims that no higher historical principle is thinkable, that whether human beings become more or less free as history continues "the principle that all are free can never again be shaken."[49] Freedom, then, is not a principle that only *we* find crucial; rather, on Gadamer's view, even though the reality of freedom may exist only sporadically, recognition of the principle that all are free marks a stage of historical advance that cannot be reversed. Hence, far from giving up on the notion of a reason that can transcend conventional bounds, as Rorty does, Gadamer tries to preserve it while recognizing the demands of history. He admits that all criteria of rationality are historically produced, that they reflect the experiences of different traditions and that the Enlightenment conception of an ahistorical Reason in itself makes no sense. None the less, the circumstance that criteria of reason are historical does not mean for him either that it is impossible to differentiate the merits of different "ways of coping" or that we can only frankly assert our own ethnocentricism. Rather, it means that we form ourselves historically and that reason emerges through a dialogue with others in which we become *gebildet*.

In spite of the differences we explored between Habermas and Gadamer it is significant that, in contrast to Rorty, both conceive of history as the domain in which reason is cultivated and in which advances such as that exemplified by the idea of freedom are made. To be sure, neither ignores the reality of historical regressions. For neither, however, is consciousness of our historicity the final word, as it seems to be for Rorty. It is true that we are historical beings; the question is whether we can learn through history to be rational ones as well.

6

Conclusion

Since Nietzsche's time, at the latest, attacks on Enlightenment conceptions of reason and on the idea of an autonomous, rational subject have become common. They have become familiar through the work of Horkheimer, Adorno and Heidegger, among others, and more recently through that of Derrida, Foucault and Lyotard. Against strong conceptions of the invariance, universality and *a priori* character of a reason "in itself," such thinkers have emphasized the conventionality of what counts as rational speech and action at any given time, the embeddedness of reason in language and forms of life and, indeed, the incommensurability of different "language games" which cannot serve to legitimate either each other or themselves.[1] They have also pointed to connections between power and knowledge or, in other words, between what societies take as rational justifications of their beliefs and practices and forms of control within those societies.[2] To the notion of the rational subject, they have contrasted its inextricable situatedness and finitude, and hence replaced an epistemological ideal of certainty with an acceptance of fallibility.

In criticizing the epistemological focus of modern philosophy, Rorty might be said to exemplify these anti-Enlightenment trends. As we have seen, he not only emphasizes cultural and historical differences in conceptions of reason, truth and knowledge but denies that the latter is a representational faculty at all. Different descriptions of ourselves and of the social and natural world are neither "mirrors" of them nor, therefore, in need of justification as such. They are rather modes of "coping" and, moreover, modes of self-creation. Hence Rorty advocates the substitution of edification for epistemology and a healthy ethnocentricism for the tortured concern with justifying our own tradition.

We have seen that Rorty turns to Gadamer as an advocate of this kind

of break-with-reason position. He is not the only thinker to do so.[3]
While he enlists Gadamer in his attempt to dispense with epistemologically centered philosophy, Habermas and Apel criticize Gadamer precisely
for failing to take seriously enough the heritage and projects of the
Enlightenment. Neither proposes a return to the strong Kantian
assumptions about the necessity and *a priori* character of reason. None the
less, as they see it, Gadamer gives up any attempt to adjudicate the
rationality of our beliefs and practices and ultimately sanctions a simple
acquiescence to the norms of the tradition to which we belong. In my
view, both assessments of Gadamer's work are in need of modification.
Indeed, it seems to me that the association of Gadamer's hermeneutics
with a Rortian neo-pragmatism or anti-Enlightenment view is misguided.
Against the Enlightenment and in concert with its many detractors,
Gadamer does emphasize the historical character of our beliefs and
practices; to be sure, he takes his philosophical bearings from an analysis
of historical contingency and of the connection between knowledge and
prejudice. None the less as he delineates this connection it does not mean
that we must give up a concern with reason, with the validity of our
knowledge, but rather that we must preserve the Enlightenment ideal
while rendering it compatible with the cultural and linguistic
embeddedness of our understanding.

   In concluding this book, I would like to review and emphasize those
aspects of Gadamer's hermeneutics that I think lead to this conclusion
and specify more fully what this conclusion means. Crucial here are three
analyses that we have already examined: (a) the account of the dialogic
character of human understanding, (b) the notion of hermeneutic
experience; and (c) the use of the concept of *Bildung*.

THE DIALOGIC CHARACTER OF UNDERSTANDING

If one examines Gadamer's analysis of prejudice and tradition its affinities
with anti-Enlightenment attacks on reason seem clear. On Gadamer's
account, all knowledge of the natural or social world, of ethical demands,
aesthetic value or the requirements of political action is grounded in a
traditional orientation. We never come upon situations, issues or facts
without already placing them within some context, connecting them
with some other situations, issues or facts and, in short, interpreting
them in one way or another. The parameters of these interpretations,
moreover, derive from our circumstances and experience and these

circumstances and experience are always already informed by the history of the society and culture to which we belong. Thus we understand modern art within the framework of a tradition that moves from realism to impressionism and beyond; we understand poetry and drama in the context of a tradition informed by the work of Shakespeare, Milton and so on; and we evaluate ethical–political issues in light of a cultural understanding of the importance of such values as freedom, equality and justice. This means that we never assess the beauty of a painting or worth of an action in light of a suprahistorical standard of rationality but are always indebted to the various aesthetic, scientific and ethical–political traditions to which we belong. To this extent Gadamer's point is at least close to that of such thinkers as Rorty, Foucault and Lyotard: to appeal to supposedly neutral criteria of rational justification is to betray a hopelessly uncritical response to our historical and cultural parochialism. We are situated in a history by the experiences of which we are both constituted and constrained. Those experiences make of us who we are and we cannot transcend them to evaluate them according to standards formulated independently of them.

But what is the result of these reflections? Do they mean that all discussions of rationality are simply arenas for the promotion of different prejudices? Must we simply assert our ideas about beauty, truth and justice without being able to offer a defense of them convincing to anyone who does not already accept them? Do the limits which our historical experiences impose mean that we can never revise our views or learn from the experiences of others?

In equating the logic of understanding with the structure of dialogue, Gadamer suggests that the proper answer to these questions is "no." As he depicts genuine conversation it is rather characteristic of it that all participants are led beyond their initial positions towards a consensus that is more differentiated and articulated than the separate views with which the conversation-partners began. We have seen that there is a significant ambiguity in Gadamer's talk of consensus. On the one hand, it refers to a substantive agreement on issues where by substantive agreement is meant, not a critical synthesis of views but a common idea of what is true or valid. On the other hand, however, consensus refers simply to a "fusion of horizons," an integration of differing perspectives in a deeper understanding of the matters in question. According to this second idea of dialogic consensus, one is required to take account of the positions of others in discussing an issue or subject-matter with them. Here, even if one holds to one's initial point of view one has nevertheless to deal with the objections, considerations and counter-examples that others introduce. In the end, whether one changes one's position or maintains it, the view that results is more developed than the one with which one began and the same holds for the views of all participants. Whether they conclude by agreeing or disagreeing in a substantive sense, their positions are now informed by all the other positions. They are able to see the worth of different considerations, incorporate different examples and defend themselves against different criticisms. In this way their views acquire a greater warrant; they are less blind and one-sided and, to this extent, more rational than they previously were.

With this second, in my view more tenable account of consensus, Gadamer suggests that in themselves dialogue and discussion promote the progress of reason. Like Hegel, Gadamer conceives of the reciprocal integration of initally opposed opinions as a process of sublation (*Aufhebung*) or cancellation and preservation. At the conclusion of a conversation, the initial positions of all participants can be seen to be inadequate positions on their own and are integrated within a richer, more comprehensive view. For hermeneutic understanding it follows that we are not limited to the premises of our tradition but rather continually revise them in the encounters with and discussions we have of them. In confronting other cultures, other prejudices and, indeed, the implications that others draw from our own traditions we learn to reflect on both our assumptions and our ideas of reason and to amend them in the direction of a *better* account. For Gadamer hermeneutics is a form of justification involving the dialogic adjudication of both beliefs and standards of rationality. The difference between Hegel and Gadamer in this regard is not that Gadamer no longer identifies the dialectical or dialogic process with the possibility of an advance on the part of reason; it is rather that Gadamer refuses to foreclose this advance by projecting a point of absolute knowledge at which no further dialogic encounters can develop that rationality. Gadamer therefore calls himself an advocate of the "bad infinite" and maintains that as long as history continues, the absolutely rational position is always one that can be further enriched. As he writes:

> Hegel's *Philosophy of World History* remained caught in the insoluble contradiction of an open progress of history and a conclusive apprehension of its meaning, and it could not be repeated if one were intent on taking historicity seriously.[4]

For Gadamer, then, openness to the constant possibility of developing one's perspective or conceptual framework is a crucial feature of rationality itself, one that he further explores in his comments on hermeneutic experience.

HERMENEUTIC EXPERIENCE

We have seen that Gadamer thinks that the mark of an experienced person is his or her openness to new experiences. As I elucidated this argument earlier it bore important affinities with Rorty's analysis of edification. For both Gadamer and Rorty, the lesson of historical experience is that no "truth" is unalterable and that no account of nature, society or art is valid for all time. Rorty uses this lesson to argue for a break with the emphasis on justifying various ideas of truth. For Gadamer, however, experience remains a form of justification: precisely through an openness to the implications of our experience we acquire both more warranted beliefs and an increased capacity to discriminate between what is warranted and what is not.

Gadamer's point here is close to one that Alasdair MacIntyre makes in a paper entitled "Relativism, Power and Philosophy."[5] MacIntyre's purpose in this paper is two-fold: in opposition to certain arguments against relativism[6] he wants first to assert the possibility of an incommensurability between the world-views of different cultures, and second to show that such incommensurability does not lead necessarily to the impossibility of non-parochial standards for adjudicating between these assumptions. The result of this argument is the same as that I have attributed to Gadamer: recognition of the cultural and historical plurality of forms of life and conceptual schemes does not of itself require scepticism towards the idea of reason.

In making this argument, MacIntyre begins by pointing to an example in which the dilemma of relativism appears very real: a bilingual, seventeenth-century Irish person must choose between Irish- and English-language communities because doing so involves not simply language but incompatible sets of beliefs and ways of life. Merely by choosing whether to speak of "Doire Colmcille" or "Londonderry," for example, this person also chooses a series of political beliefs about the legitimacy of the English role in Ireland. This decision in turn will affect others: whether to speak of "a just act of war" or of "theft," of an original act of acquisition of what so far has belonged to no one or of the illegitimate seizure of common land and so on. MacIntyre's claim here is that despite a range of concepts that may be shared by Irish and English there remains a large core of concepts that are not and that, in fact, are mutually exclusive. This conflict cannot be resolved by finding a neutral language for the bilingual person to speak for, as should be clear at this point, any such language will embody premises and suppositions that belong themselves to some linguistic community and condition its solution to the problem. None the less MacIntyre does suggest a way out of the dilemma, making implicit use of Gadamer's account of a tradition in order to do so.

For MacIntyre the important feature of a tradition involves the establishment of a canonical set of issues and problems together with a series of debates surrounding them. Because these problems are canonical for the members of the tradition, the progress of rationality can be measured in terms of the degree of success the tradition has in resolving them. Of course, all such measurement will be internal to the tradition; the criteria of rational progress will therefore not be "objective" or "neutral" in any Enlightenment sense but will refer rather to assessments performed by members of the tradition and legitimated in terms of its norms of justification. But MacIntyre goes on to argue that the development of a problematic within a tradition will go through certain stages and among these may be a stage at which progress even "as judged by standards internal to that particular tradition" comes to a halt. At this stage contradictions appear which the members of the tradition themselves have to recognize as irresolvable within the tradition's own conceptual framework. MacIntyre claims that such recognition is often promoted by an encounter with another tradition that is able both to explain the first tradition's failure to resolve its problems and to offer a resolution of them.

This argument is similar to the one that Gadamer makes about dialogue: namely, that it is precisely in confronting other beliefs and other presuppositions that we can both see the inadequacies of our own and transcend them. MacIntyre's point is also the same as that which Gadamer makes in his analysis of experience. Any tradition that establishes a set of canonical problems also incorporates standards of truth and rational justification. From the point of view of these standards themselves, the solutions the tradition provides will sometimes appear inadequate and at these times rationality will require an openness to the guidance another tradition may provide. To this extent, reason is not itself tied to any one tradition. What a culture takes as rational or irrational will depend upon its history, assumptions, other beliefs and so on. Yet, when contradictions among these beliefs and assumptions become apparent, rationality *qua* rationality requires a willingness to revise, perhaps radically, traditional views and "metanarratives." As MacIntyre puts this point:

> Rationality, understood within some particular tradition with its own conceptual scheme and problematic, as it always has been and will be, none-theless requires *qua* rationality a recognition that the rational inadequacies of that tradition from its own point of view . . . may at any time prove to be such that perhaps only the resources provided by some quite alien tradition . . . will enable us to identify and to understand the limitations of our own tradition . . .

And as he continues:

> rationality requires a readiness on our part to accept, and indeed to welcome, a possible future defeat of the forms of theory and practice in which it has up till now been taken to be embodied within our own tradition . . .[7]

Such openness to future defeat is what Gadamer means by the openness that issues from the hermeneutic experience of negation. Both MacIntyre and Gadamer define rationality, then, as a willingness to admit the existence of better options. The awareness that one's knowledge is always open to refutation or modification from the vantage point of another perspective is not a basis for suspending confidence in the idea of reason but rather represents the very possibility of rational progress.

BILDUNG

On Gadamer's view, the concept of *Bildung* refers to just this possibility. As we have seen, *Bildung* describes the process through which individuals and cultures enter a more and more widely defined community. The "cultured" individual is one who can place his or her life and concerns within a larger perspective or, to use Gadamer's term, "horizon." That is, he or she is the person who is not only familiar with but interested in issues, problems and ways of life that may be quite distant from his or her own and by being distant put the individual life into perspective. Similarly, the *gebildete* culture is one that understands its place within a larger world-community. To the extent that individuals and cultures integrate this understanding of others and of the differences between them within their own self-understanding, to the extent, in other words, that they learn from others and take a wider, more differentiated view, they can acquire sensitivity, subtlety and a capacity for discrimination. These virtues do not indicate only that a *gebildete* culture has appropriated a certain set of beliefs that it finds more defensible than certain others. In becoming cultured we do not simply acquire better norms, values etc. We also acquire the ability to acquire them. In other words we learn tact, taste and judgment. Perhaps we cannot codify what we have learned as a method for adjudicating between beliefs; none the less, through the historical experience and conversation with others that are part of our self-formation or *Bildung* we can learn to think. And this practical reason thus substitutes for the dogmatism of the Enlightenment.

Of course, the claim that hermeneutics fosters practical reason or an increased capacity to discriminate may appear fantastic in light of existing social problems and global threats. We have seen that Gadamer himself points to the increase in social irrationality which accompanies the hegemony of technical reason over practical deliberation. But he also points to specific historical advances such as the recognition, if not realization, of the freedom of all and asks whether it is "so perverse to think that in reality the irrational cannot hold out in the long run."[8] The ideas of dialogue, experience and *Bildung* are meant to show that it cannot and that we can progress in tact, taste and judgment in such a way as to move towards its eradication. Of course, our capacity for discrimination may itself be systematically undermined by ideological connections of which we are unaware and Gadamer's faith in practical reason may therefore be problematic. Still, if others have used the insight into historicity to jettison the idea of reason itself, Gadamer does not. Our historical situatedness does not only limit what we can know with certainty; it can also teach us how to remember and integrate what we must not forget.

Notes

NOTES TO THE PREFACE

1 See, for example, E. D. Hirsch, *Validity in Interpretation* (Yale University Press, New Haven, 1967); Janet Wolff, *Hermeneutic Philosophy and the Sociology of Art* (Routledge and Kegan Paul, London, 1975); Alasdair MacIntyre, "Contexts of Interpretation: Reflections on Hans-Georg Gadamer's *Truth and Method*", *Boston University Journal*, 27 (1) (1976); David Hoy, *The Critical Circle* (University of California Press, Berkeley, 1978).

2 See, for example, Emilio Betti, *Die Hermeneutik als allgemeine Methode der Geisteswissenschaften* (J. C. B. Mohr, Tübingen, 1962); Jürgen Habermas, *Zur Logik der Sozialwissenschaften* (Suhrkamp, Frankfurt, 1970); Charles Taylor "Interpretation and the Sciences of Man", *Review of Metaphysics*, 25 (1971); Karl-Otto Apel et al. (eds), *Hermeneutik und Ideologiekritik* (Suhrkamp, Frankfurt, 1971); Josef Bleicher, *Contemporary Hermeneutics* (Routledge and Kegan Paul, London, 1980); and Roy J. Howard, *Three Faces of Hermeneutics* (University of California Press, Berkeley, 1982).

3 For Gadamer's influence on theological discussions see, for example, Wolfhart Pannenberg, *Theology and the Philosophy of Science* (Darton, Longmann and Todd, London, 1976), and "Hermeneutics and Universal History" in *Hermeneutics and Modern Philosophy*, ed. Brice R. Wachterhauser (forthcoming, State University of New York Press, New York, 1986). For Gadamer's influence on discussions in jurisprudence see, for example, Josef Esser, *Vorverstandnis und Methode in der Rechtfindung: Rationalitätsgarantieren der Richterlichen Entscheidungspraxis* (Athenäum, Frankfurt, 1970); Joachim Hruschka, *Das Verstehen von Rechtstexten: Zur Hermeneutischen Transpositivitäts des positiven Rechts* (Beck, Munich, 1972); Ronald Dworkin, *Law's Empire* (The Belknap Press of Harvard University Press, Cambridge, Mass., 1986).

4 See, for example, Rüdiger Bubner et al. (eds), *Hermeneutik und Dialektik* (J. C. B. Mohr, Tübingen, 1970); Richard Rorty, *Philosophy and the Mirror of Nature* (Princeton University Press, Princeton, 1979), esp. chs VII and VIII;

Richard Bernstein, *Beyond Objectivism and Relativism* (University of Pennsylvannia Press, Philadelphia, 1983); and Robert Hollinger (ed.), *Hermeneutics and Praxis* (University of Notre Dame Press, Notre Dame, 1985).

5 The partial exception in this regard is Joel Weinsheimer's *Gadamer's Hermeneutics: A Reading of Truth and Method* (Yale University Press, New Haven, 1985). Weinsheimer's aim, however, is to provide a "noncontroversial" account of Gadamer's work and, hence, his book is less a critical interpretation and evaluation of *Truth and Method* than an often illuminating page-by-page paraphrase.

NOTES TO THE INTRODUCTION

1 Michael Sandel, *Liberalism and the Limits of Justice* (Cambridge University Press, Cambridge, 1982).

2 Bernard Williams, *Ethics and the Limits of Philosophy* (Harvard University Press, Cambridge, 1985).

3 For the classic statement of this position, see Carl Hempel, "The Function of General Laws in History", *Journal of Philosophy* (1942); reprinted in Hempel, *Aspects of Scientific Explanation and Other Essays in the Philosophy of Science* (The Free Press, New York, 1965). Also see Ernest Nagel, *The Structure of Science* (Routledge and Kegan Paul, London, 1961); and May Brodbeck (ed.), *Readings in the Philosophy of the Social Science* (Macmillan, New York, 1965).

NOTES TO CHAPTER 1

1 W. Dilthey, "Die Entstehung der Hermeneutik", *Gesammelte Schriften*, 5 (1958–60), p. 326. Essay translated in *Dilthey, Selected Writings*, ed. H. P. Rickman (Cambridge University Press, Cambridge, 1976), p. 235.

2 Hans-Georg Gadamer, *Wahrheit und Methode*, 4th edn (J. C. B. Mohr, Tübingen, 1975), p. 166; English translation, *Truth and Method* (Seabury Press, New York, 1975), p. 156.

3 This is roughly Weber's distinction between explanatory understanding and direct observational understanding. See M. Weber, *Economy and Society*, ed. G. Roth and C. Wittich (University of California Press, Berkeley, 1978), pp. 8ff.

4 See, for example, Theodore Abel, "The Operation Called Verstehen", *The American Journal of Sociology*, 54 (1948), pp. 211-18; reprinted in *Understanding and Social Inquiry*, ed. Fred Dallmayr and Thomas McCarthy (Notre Dame University Press, Notre Dame, 1978), pp. 81-92.

5 See, for example, Charles Taylor "Interpretation and the Sciences of Man",

Review of Metaphysics, 25 (1971), pp. 3-51; reprinted in *Understanding and Social Inquiry*, ed. Dallmayr and McCarthy, pp. 101-31.

6 This is similar to the form of understanding, then, that Weber dismisses prior to distinguishing between explanatory and direct observational understanding.

7 See Alasdair MacIntyre, "Is Understanding Religion Compatible with Believing in It?", in *Rationality*, ed. Bryan Wilson (Harper and Row, New York, 1970), pp. 68ff. MacIntyre's point is slightly different than Gadamer's here, but see Peter Winch's criticism in "Understanding a Primitive Society" (in *Rationality*, pp. 109ff). Winch claims that we can see the point of the practice and, in fact, engage in a similar one when we carry pictures or mementos of those close to us.

8 Hans-Georg Gadamer, "Zur Problematik des Selbstverständnisses", in *Kleine Schriften* (3 vols, J. C. B. Mohr, Tübingen, 1967), vol. I: *Philosophie, Hermeneutik*, p. 71; English translation of essay in Gadamer's *Philosophical Hermeneutics*, tr. and ed. D. Linge (University of California Press, Berkeley, 1977), p. 46.

9 I owe this example to Harry Frankfurt.

10 Gadamer, *Wahrheit und Methode*, p. 363; *Truth and Method*, p. 347. Here Gadamer is discussing the conditions of "real dialogue" with another person and claims that "what has to be grasped is the substantive validity (*sachliche Recht*) of the other's opinion so that we can be united with one another on the subject-matter." To "substantive validity" the English translators have inexplicably added "or otherwise."

11 Ibid., p. 168; p. 158.

12 Chladenius, *Einleitung zur richtigen Auslegung vernünftiger Reden und Schriften* (1742). Quoted in Gadamer, *Wahrheit und Methode*, p. 171; *Truth and Method*, p. 161.

13 See the selections by Spinoza, "Von der Auslegung der Schrift", and Chladenius, "Von Auslegung historischer Nachrichten und Bücher", in *Seminar: Philosophische Hermeneutik*, ed. H.-G. Gadamer and G. Boehm, 2nd edn (Suhrkamp, Frankfurt, 1979).

14 F. D. E. Schleiermacher, "Über den Begriff der Hermeneutik mit Bezug auf F. A. Wolfs Andeutungen und Asts Lehrbuch", in *Hermeneutik und Kritik*, ed. M. Frank (Suhrkamp, Frankfurt, 1977), p. 315.

15 Schleiermacher, "Hermeneutik und Kritik" in *Hermeneutik und Kritik*, p. 92; English translation as "The Compendium of 1819 and the Marginal Notes of 1828", in Schleiermacher *Hermeneutics: The Handwritten Manuscripts*, ed. H. Kimmerle, tr. J. Duke and J. Forstman (Scholars Press, Missoula, 1977), pp. 109-10.

16 Hans-Georg Gadamer, "Hermeneutics as a Theoretical and Practical Task", in Gadamer, *Reason in the Age of Science*, tr. Frederick Lawrence (MIT Press, Cambridge, 1981), p. 130.

17 Gadamer, *Wahrheit und Methode*, p. 167; *Truth and Method*, p. 147.

18 Ibid., p. 169; p. 150.

19 See Frank's introduction to *Hermeneutik und Kritik*, p. 47. Also see Claus von Bormann, "Die Zweideutigkeit der hermeneutischen Erfahrung", in *Hermeneutik und Ideologiekritik*, ed. K.-O. Apel et al. (Suhrkamp, Frankfurt, 1977), pp. 87-8.

20 Gadamer seems to offer a somewhat different objection to Schleiermacher's theory of interpretation in his essay, "Das Problem der Sprache in Schleiermachers Hermeneutik", in *Kleine Schriften*, vol. 3: *Idee und Sprache: Platon, Husserl, Heidegger*. Here he claims that psychological interpretation focuses on the individual moment of creative thought while grammatical interpretation focuses on the "identifying" moment of language. Rather than largely ignoring grammatical interpretation as he does in *Truth and Method*, Gadamer here claims that it emphasizes the common elements of language that tie a writer to other language-users and thus deny his or her individuality. Gadamer's criticism, then, is that the division between grammatical and psychological interpretation too sharply separates the individual moment of creative thought (the focus of psychological interpretation) from the identifying moment of language (the focus of grammatical interpretation.) As he puts it:

> Obviously it would mean misunderstanding things if, on the one side, one saw the scope of interpretation so much in terms of language that the individual discourse and individual speaker appeared as organs of language or if, on the other side, one conceived of discourse as a fact in the thinker, thus absolutely not as language. Both extremes leave what is decisive unclear: namely, how far individuality and identity permeate language so that language is certainly, on the one side, something essentially common, but still, on the other, essentially different, namely from all other languages or the languages of other times, so that, precisely as so determined for the individual it means both coercion and freedom at once. (pp. 133-4)

In other words, Schleiermacher fails to see the extent to which a common language allows individual expression and therefore thinks he needs psychological interpretation to get behind language to an author's actual intentions. In any case, whether grammatical interpretation is concerned with the idiosyncracy of an author's language or its similarity with the linguistic usage of the time (and it seems clear that it is concerned with both) the aim of hermeneutics as a whole remains that of illuminating the writer's actual thoughts. Schleiermacher seems to think that sometimes language expresses these, while at other times the interpreter must go back behind the inflexibility of language to elicit them. As I have already noted, Gadamer wants to illuminate the novelty of this endeavor with regard to the previous history of hermeneutics.

21 Gadamer, *Wahrheit und Methode*, p. 175; *Truth and Method*, p. 165.

22 L. v. Ranke, *Aus Werk und Nachlass*, ed. W. P. Fuchs and T. Schieder (4 vols, Munich, Historische Kommission bei der Bayerischen Akademie der Wissenschaften, 1964), p. 86.

23 Ranke, *Weltgeschichte*, vol. 9, pp. xiiiff, quoted in Gadamer, *Wahrheit und Methode*, p. 192; *Truth and Method*, p. 180.

24 Ibid., p. 195; p. 183.

25 Quoted in ibid., p. 198; p. 195.

26 Ibid., p. 198; p. 198.

27 Ibid., p. 198; p. 186.

28 Ibid., p. 191; p. 179.

29 Arthur Danto, *Analytical Philosophy of History* (Cambridge University Press, Cambridge, 1965).

30 Ibid., p. 168.

31 J. G. Droysen, "Grundriss der Historik (1858/1868)", in *Historik: Vorlesung über Enzyklopädie und Methodologie der Geschichte*, ed. R. Huebner (Im Auftrage der Preussischen Akademie der Wissenschaften, Munich, 1957) # 41.

32 See R. G. Collingwood, *The Idea of History* (Clarendon Press, Oxford, 1946), and Collingwood, *An Autobiography* (Oxford University Press, Oxford, 1970).

33 Collingwood, *An Autobiography*, pp. 60ff.

34 Gadamer, *Wahrheit und Methode*, p. 353; *Truth and Method*, p. 334.

35 Droysen, *Historik*, p. 15.

36 Droysen, "Grundriss der Historik", # 91.

37 Gadamer, *Wahrheit und Methode*, p. 203; *Truth and Method*, p. 191.

38 Ibid., p. 203; pp. 184-5.

39 Droysen, "Grundriss der Historik", # 9.

40 Ibid., # 10.

41 Danto, *Analytical Philosophy of History*, p. 159.

42 See William Dray, "Historical Explanation of Actions Reconsidered", in *The Philosophy of History*, ed. Patrick Gardiner (Oxford University Press, Oxford, 1974). Also see Dray's *Laws and Explanation in History* (Oxford University Press, Oxford, 1957).

43 Dray, "Historical Explanation of Actions Reconsidered", p. 68.

44 On the relation between Husserl's and Dilthey's uses of the concept of *Erlebnis*, see R. Makreel, *Dilthey: Philosopher of the Human Studies* (Princeton University Press, Princeton, 1975), pp. 275ff.

45 Gadamer, *Wahrheit und Methode*, pp. 337ff.; *Truth and Method*, pp. 317ff.

46 The notion of negative experience is obviously central to some accounts of the logic of the natural sciences, in particular to Karl Popper's claim that the refutation of hypotheses is more telling than their confirmation. (See "Science: Conjectures and Refutations", in Karl Popper's *Conjectures and Refutations: The Growth of Scientific Knowledge* (Harper and Row, New York,

1962). Nevertheless, the idea that experimental results, whether they confirm or refute specific hypotheses, have to be repeatable remains crucial to the natural sciences. Gadamer suggests that the idea is not always directly applicable to the human sciences.

47 Gadamer criticizes Hegel, however, for attempting to move beyond the dialectical experience of change to an absolute knowledge in which the object no longer changes and is completely known. For Gadamer the importance of dialectical experience is that the knowledge acquired from it is never complete. Hence, he claims that the "truly experienced person is one . . . who knows that he is not master of time or the future" and that experience is primarily "experience of human finitude" (*Wahrheit und Methode*, p. 337; *Truth and Method*, p. 320).

48 Ibid., p. 208; p. 195.

49 Ibid., p. 208; pp. 195-6.

50 Ibid., p. 61; p. 59.

51 Ibid., p. 59; p. 57.

52 W. Dilthey, *Der Aufbau der geschichtlichen Welt in den Geisteswissenschaften* (Suhrkamp. Frankfurt, 1970), p. 170.

53 But also see David Hoy, *The Critical Circle* (University of California Press, Berkeley, 1978), p. 172, n. 13. While emphasizing the negativity of *Erfahrung* and its definition as a learning experience, Hoy also claims that it is "repeatable" and indeed that only as such is learning possible. The difference from *Erlebnis* is that *Erlebnisse* are "unique, nonrepeatable and often ineffable." This way of distinguishing *Erlebnis* and *Erfahrung* as the non-repeatable and the repeatable does not conform to Gadamer's use of the terms. Gadamer claims that "strictly taken" an *Erfahrung* can only be had once (*Wahrheit und Methode*, p. 336; *Truth and Method*, p. 317). He admits that experiences of negation can be confirmed, as one can confirm the "reversal of consciousness" that changes the Great War into World War I. None the less for Gadamer the important points are: first, that experience need not always be confirmed to qualify as learning experience; second, that in any case, the original experience of reversal cannot be repeated; and third, that the emphasis on the repetition of experience misdirects efforts to capture the logic of historical understanding. With regard to *Erlebnis* Gadamer focuses on two functions that the concept has for Dilthey. First, *Erlebnisse* provide an indubitable ground of certainty for the *Geisteswissenschaften* and, second, they serve as the center around which the meaning of a particular life-history develops. In neither case are *Erlebnisse* "ineffable." Hoy's confusion on these points does not seem to have affected his generally trustworthy treatment of Gadamer's work.

54 Gadamer, *Wahrheit und Methode*, p. 211; *Truth and Method*, p. 198.

55 Also see Makreel, *Dilthey: Philosopher of the Human Studies*, pp. 305ff.

56 Dilthey, *Der Aufbau der geschichtlichen Welt*, p. 178.

57 Ibid., p. 166.
58 Ibid., p. 166.
59 Ibid., p. 264.
60 Gadamer, *Wahrheit und Methode*, p. 224; *Truth and Method*, p. 210.
61 Ibid., p. 219; p. 205.
62 For a slightly different critique of Dilthey, see J. Habermas's discussion in *Knowledge and Human Interests*, tr. J. Shapiro (Beacon Press, Boston, 1971), chs 7 and 8. Habermas agrees with Gadamer's objection to the implicit positivism in Dilthey's attempt to ground the logic of the *Geisteswissenschaften*. None the less, he does not think that this positivism should be understood in terms of a conflict between "science and vitalism" (p. 341, fn. 25). Instead he locates it in Dilthey's failure to supersede the limits of biography and autobiography and in the resulting monologism of his conception of understanding. On the relation between theoretical and practical philosophy in Dilthey's work also see M. Riedel, *Verstehen und Erklären* (Klett-Cotta, Stuttgart, 1978), Introduction and chs 1-30. Also see Makreel's defense of Dilthey against Gadamer, in *Dilthey: Philosopher of the Human Studies*, pp. 414–15.
63 M. Weber, *The Methodology of the Social Sciences*, tr. E. A. Schils and H. A. Finch (The Free Press, New York, 1949), p. 84.
64 E. Husserl, *The Crisis of European Sciences and Transcendental Phenomenology*, tr. D. Carr (Northwestern University Press, Evanston, 1970), p. 142.
65 Ibid., pp. 138–9; slightly different translation in Gadamer's "The Science of the Life World", in *Philosophical Hermeneutics*, p. 189.
66 Gadamer, *Wahrheit und Methode*, p. 236; *Truth and Method*, p. 221.
67 Heidegger, *Being and Time*, tr. J. Macquarrie and E. Robinson (Harper and Row, New York, 1962).
68 Gadamer, "Zur Problematik des Selbstverständnisses", in *Kleine Schriften*, vol. 1, p. 74; English translation in *Philosophical Hermeneutics*, p. 49.
69 M. Heidegger, *Being and Time*, p. H12.
70 Gadamer, *Wahrheit und Methode*, p. 243; *Truth and Method*, p. 228.
71 Dilthey, *Der Aufbau der geschichtlichen Welt*, p. 347.
72 Gadamer, *Wahrheit und Methode*, p. 261; *Truth and Method*, p. 245.
73 Heidegger, *Being and Time*, p. H12.
74 Gadamer, *Wahrheit und Methode*, p. 245; *Truth and Method*, p. 230.
75 Heidegger, *Being and Time*, p. H144.
76 Gadamer, *Wahrheit und Methode*, p. 243; *Truth and Method*, p. 228.

NOTES TO CHAPTER 2

1 See David Hoy, *The Critical Circle* (University of California Press, Berkeley, 1978), esp. chs 3 and 4.

2 See *Genre*, 3(1) (1968).

3 E. D. Hirsch, *Validity in Interpretation* (Yale University Press, New Haven, 1967) p. 31.

4 Ibid., pp. 48–9.

5 See Hoy's criticisms in *The Critical Circle*, pp. 28ff.

6 Hirsch, *Validity in Interpretation*, pp. 246ff.

7 Ibid., p. 12.

8 Ibid., p. 26

9 Ibid., pp. 12–13. This admission seems to indicate that Hirsch is concerned to locate a meaning to which all readers could agree rather than to delineate substantive connections between meaning and an author's intention. In his *The Aims of Interpretation* (University of Chicago Press, Chicago, 1976, pp. 90ff) Hirsch's argument is different (despite his claims to the contrary). Here he argues that the normative principle of the author's intention is an ethical ideal and, indeed, a special case of the categorical imperative. To overlook an author's intention is not simply to overlook the only principle that can gain general adherence but also to use his or her words for one's own ends and thus to treat the author as a means.

10 Hirsch, *Validity in Interpretation*, p. 203.

11 Ibid., p. 49.

12 See, for example, Stanley Fish, *Is There a Text in this Class?* (Harvard University Press, Cambridge, 1980), esp. the Introduction, "Literature in the Reader: Affective Stylistics" and "Is There a Text in this Class?". Also see the essays by Fish, George Poulet, Michael Riffaterre and others in Jane P. Tompkins (ed.), *Reader Response Criticism* (Johns Hopkins University Press, Baltimore, 1980).

13 But see Jean Grondin, *Hermeneutische Wahrheit? Zum Wahrheitsbegriff Hans-Georg Gadamers* (Forum Academicum, Königstein/Ts., 1982), pp. 103ff.
Grondin thinks that the concept of games is crucial to understanding Gadamer's account of the "happening of truth" (*das Wahrheitsgeschehen*) in general. Richard Bernstein agrees with this assessment. See his *Beyond Objectivism and Relativism* (University of Pennsylvania Press, Philadelphia, 1983), pp. 121–2. In my view, the relevance of games to understanding needs further explication and grounding.

14 Hans-Georg Gadamer, *Wahrheit und Methode*, 4th edn (J. C. B. Mohr, Tübingen, 1975), p. 102; English translation, *Truth and Method* (Seabury Press, New York, 1975), p. 95. This feature of games suggests an obvious analogy with the Wittgensteinian conception of language games (which Gadamer himself notes in the Foreword to the second edition of *Wahrheit und Methode* (p. xxiv, n. 1; *Truth and Method*, p. 500, n. 12)) and particularly with the use philosophers have made of this conception for understanding social practices. In "Interpretation and the Sciences of Man", *Review of*

Metaphysics, 25 (September, 1971), pp. 3–51; reproduced in *Understanding and Social Inquiry*, ed. Fred Dallmayr and Thomas McCarthy (Notre Dame University Press, Notre Dame, 1977), pp. 101–31), Charles Taylor denies that participation in a social practice can be understood simply in terms of the subjective attitudes or intentions of those who participate. Practices rather involve sets of norms and principles to which agents must already submit in order to participate. Thus, for example, the practice of negotiation encompasses a range of attitudes, beliefs and assumptions: notions of bargaining, good-faith agreements, compromise, individual autonomy and so on. These are not ideas that agents have the option of either possessing or not possessing in negotiating. Whether they have an explicit language for them or not, they are embodied in the practice of negotiation itself. In other words, negotiating, like playing a game, involves accepting a certain set of rules, completing certain tasks and making certain strategic moves. To a large extent, then, it itself determines the actions of those who expect to profit from it. Taylor writes:

> The actors may have all sorts of beliefs and attitudes which may be rightly thought of as their individual beliefs and attitudes, even if others share them; they may subscribe to certain policy goals or certain forms of theory about the polity, or feel resentment at certain things and so on. They bring these with them into their negotiations, and strive to satisfy them. But what they do not bring into negotiations is the set of ideas and norms constitutive of negotiation themselves. These must be the common property of the society before there can be any question of anyone entering into negotiation or not. Hence, they are not subjective meanings, the property of one or some individual, but rather intersubjective meanings, which are constitutive of the social matrix in which individuals find themselves and act. (p. 119)

Taylor uses the notion of intersubjective meaning to argue against empiricist social science. His point is that one cannot undertand social practices in terms of "brute data," for example, by asking individuals what they believe, because their beliefs are already *about* the intersubjective meaning, that is, the practice itself. Gadamer makes a similar argument with regard to works of art: here, again, both the artist's intentions and the viewer's or reader's responses are intentions about and responses to the work of art itself.

15 Gadamer, *Wahrheit und Methode*, p. 103; *Truth and Method*, p. 97.
16 See Roy J. Howard, *Three Faces of Hermeneutics* (University of California Press, Berkeley, 1982), p. 143, for a similar delineation of the important characteristics of playing games.
17 Gadamer, *Wahrheit und Methode*, p. 118; *Truth and Method*, p. 110.
18 Ibid., p. 117; p. 109.
19 Ibid., p. 111; p. 104.

20 On this analysis, a playwright's attempt to exercise some control over different productions of his or her work is perfectly legitimate. As we shall see, Gadamer does not directly deny this right; he rather denies that it makes the play's meaning as "determinate" as the playwright would perhaps want.

21 Gadamer, *Wahrheit und Methode*, p. 105; *Truth and Method*, p. 99.

22 Ronald Dworkin, "How Law is Like Literature" in Dworkin, *A Matter of Principle* (Harvard University Press, Cambridge, 1985), pp. 157–8.

23 Ibid., p. 157.

24 See Nelson Goodman, *Languages of Art* (Hackett Publishing Co., Indianapolis, 1976), pp. 6ff.

25 Thus in "Kunst und Nachahmung" (in *Kleine Schriften* (J. C. B. Mohr, Tübingen, 1967), vol. 1: *Philosophie, Hermeneutik*) Gadamer writes that in the "modern industrial world"

> there are no longer things. Each is a piece that one can buy often on a whim until the production of this model comes to an end because it is arbitrarily produced. This is modern production and consumption. It is entirely appropriate that these "things" are now only produced in mass production, that one sells them only through large amounts of advertising and that when they no longer work, one disposes of them. But the experience of things does not come to us through them. Nothing in them, no piece of life or historical aspect, has achieved a presence that resists substitution. This is the way the modern world appears. What thinker, then, can expect that in our representational art things that are no longer real, that no longer constantly survive us and mean nothing to us will be offered for recognition as if we would thereby again become familiar with our world? (p. 26)

26 Gadamer, *Wahrheit und Methode*, p. 131; *Truth and Method*, p. 121.

27 Ibid., p. 108; p. 102.

28 Ibid.

29 Ibid., p. 108; p. 101

30 Goodman, *Languages of Art*, p. 3.

31 Alasdair MacIntyre, "Contexts of Interpretation: Reflections on Hans-Georg Gadamer's *Truth and Method*", *Boston University Journal*, 27(1) (1976), pp. 41-6.

32 Gadamer, *Wahrheit und Methode*, p. 145; *Truth and Method*, p. 135.

33 MacIntyre, "Contexts of Interpretation", p. 44.

34 Gadamer, *Wahrheit und Methode*, p. 109; *Truth and Method*, p. 102.

35 See ibid., pp. 39-96; pp. 39-90.

36 Ibid., p. 126; p. 117.

37 Hans Robert Jauss, *Toward an Aesthetic of Reception*, tr. Timothy Bahti (University of Minnesota, Minneapolis, 1982) pp. 43-4.

38 Hans-Georg Gadamer, "Aesthetic und Hermeneutik", in *Kleine Schriften* (J. C. B. Mohr, Tübingen, 1967), vol. 2: *Interpretationen*, p. 8; English translation in *Philosophical Hermeneutics*, ed. and tr. D. Linge (University of California Press, Berkeley, 1976), p. 104.

39 See Jauss, *Toward an Aesthetic of Reception*, p. 31.

40 Gadamer, *Wahrheit und Methode*, p. 114; *Truth and Method*, p. 107.

41 Ibid., p. 375; p. 358.

42 Ibid., p. 114; p. 107.

43 Hans-Georg Gadamer, "Wahrheit in den Geisteswissenschaften", in *Kleine Schriften*, vol. 1, p. 42.

44 See Gadamer, *Wahrheit und Methode*, pp. 321ff.; *Truth and Method*, pp. 303ff.

45 Ibid., p. 120; p. 112.

46 Hirsch, *Validity in Interpretation*, pp. 253ff.

47 Gadamer, *Wahrheit und Methode*, pp. 288-90; *Truth and Method*, pp. 271–4. Also see Gadamer's description in *Philosophische Lehrjahr* (Vittorio Klostermann, Frankfurt, 1977), p. 216; in English, *Philosophical Apprenticeships*, tr. Robert R. Sullivan (MIT Press, Cambridge, 1985), p. 49.

48 Gadamer, *Wahrheit und Methode*, p. 283; *Truth and Method*, p. 267.

49 Arthur Danto, *Analytical Philosophy of History* (Cambridge University Press, Cambridge, 1968), p. 142.

50 Harold Bloom, *The Anxiety of Influence: A Theory of Poetry* (Oxford University Press, Oxford, 1973), p. 95. Also see Fish, *Is There a Text in this Class?*

51 Hirsch, *Validity in Interpretation*, p. 260.

52 P. D. Juhl, *Interpretation* (Princeton University Press, Princeton, 1980) p. 8.

53 Hans-Georg Gadamer, *Volk und Geschichte im Denken Herders* (Vittorio Klostermann, Frankfurt, 1942), pp. 22–3.

54 See Gadamer, *Philosophische Lehrjahr*, pp. 118-19; *Philosophical Apprenticeships*, p. 99.

NOTES TO CHAPTER 3

1 Hans-Georg Gadamer, *Wahrheit und Methode*, 4th edn (J. C. B. Mohr, Tübingen, 1975), p. 280; English translation, *Truth and Method* (Seabury Press, New York, 1975), p. 263-4.

2 See Edmund Husserl, *Logical Investigations* (Humanities Press, New York, 1970), vol. 1, particularly Investigation 1; and his *Ideas: General Introduction to Pure Phenomenology* (Collier Books, New York, 1962), particularly ch. 3.

3 Hans-Georg Gadamer, "The Hermeneutics of Suspicion", in *Hermeneutics: Questions and Prospects*, ed. Gary Shapiro and Alan Sicca (University of Massachusetts, Amherst, 1984), p. 60.

4 Gadamer, *Wahrheit und Methode*, pp. 86–7; *Truth and Method*, pp. 81–2.

5 Ibid., p. 255; p. 240.

6 Ibid., p. 247; p. 232.

7 Ibid., p. 271; p. 255.

8 Hans-Georg Gadamer, "Rhetorik, Hermeneutik und Ideologiekritik", in

Hermeneutik und Ideologiekritik, K.-O. Apel et al. (Suhrkamp, Frankfurt, 1977), p. 78. Translated as "On the Scope and Function of Hermeneutical Reflection", in Hans-Georg Gadamer, *Philosophical Hermeneutics*, ed. and tr. D. Linge (University of California Press, Berkeley, 1977), p. 38.

9 Gadamer, *Wahrheit und Methode*, p. 261; *Truth and Method*, p. 245.

10 Hans-Georg Gadamer, "Wahrheit in den Geisteswissenschaften", in *Kleine Schriften* (J. C. B. Mohr, Tübingen, 1967), vol. 1: *Philosophie, Hermeneutik*, p. 42.

11 Brice R. Wachterhauser raises the same question in "Must We Be What We Say? Gadamer on Truth in the Human Sciences", in *Hermeneutics and Modern Philosophy*, ed. Brice R. Wachterhauser (forthcoming, State University of New York Press, Albany, 1986), galley pp. 317–19: "How do we choose . . . between a Kant and a Nietzsche on the nature of the moral life or between a Hegel and a Wittgenstein on the proper goal of philosophical thought?".

12 In ch. 4 we shall see that this is the point that Habermas finds so appealing in Gadamer's hermeneutics.

13 Gadamer, *Wahrheit und Methode*, p. 254; *Truth and Method*, p. 239.

14 Ibid., p. 282; p. 266.

15 It might be objected that Gadamer's elliptical remarks on the anticipation of completeness do not warrant the prominence I give them here. Although Betti criticizes Gadamer's view of anticipation, he argues that it is crucial for Gadamer's attempt to separate "true" from "false" prejudices. See Emilio Betti, *Die Hermeneutik als allgemeine Methode der Geisteswissenschaften* (J. C. B. Mohr, Tübingen, 1962), pp. 44ff.

16 See, for example, Paul de Man, *Blindness and Insight: Essays on the Rhetoric of Contemporary Criticism* (Oxford University Press, Oxford, 1971).

17 E. D. Hirsch, *Validity in Interpretation* (Yale University Press, New Haven, 1967), p. 166. This remark indicates what is wrong with Joel Weinsheimer's solution to the problem of subjectivistic misinterpretation. (See Weinsheimer, *Gadamer's Hermeneutics* (Yale University Press, New Haven, 1985).) According to Weinsheimer a true interpretation is one that is indistinguishable from the work itself whereas a false one reveals its own inadequacy by being separable from the work. Weinsheimer follows Gadamer in denying that the work "in itself" can be understood; even a true interpretation is only an interpretation and he therefore also follows Gadamer in emphasizing the variety of true interpretations or, in other words, interpretations that are not distinguishable from the work itself. As he points out, "Johnson's *Macbeth* is clearly different from Coleridge's and both from Wilson Knight's" (ibid., p. 111) but this does not meant that each is simply a subjective interpretation; instead they are all true. Still, it is not clear from this analysis how the critique of subjectivism is to be avoided for, as Hirsch points out, the problem with false interpretations is that they are *not*

obviously false which is to say, in Weinsheimer's terms, that they are not clearly distinguishable from the work itself.

18 Gadamer, *Wahrheit und Methode*, p. 300; *Truth and Method*, p. 283.

19 Hirsch, *Validity in Interpretation*, pp. 227ff.

20 Cleanth Brooks, "Irony as a Principle of Structure", in *Literary Opinion in America*, ed. M. D. Zabel, 2nd edn (Harper and Brothers, New York, 1951), p. 736.

21 F. W. Bateson, *English Poetry: A Critical Introduction*, 2nd edn (Barnes and Noble, New York, 1966), pp. 29ff, and p. 59.

22 Ibid., p. 240.

23 Monroe Beardsley questions whether one need refer to extra-textual evidence to support Bateson's reading at all, since Brooks's "reading is (uncharacteristically) contrived." Brooks speaks of Lucy's being "whirled" as opposed to "rolled" and of "falling back into the clutter of things" thereby creating an impression of lifelessness that is not in the poem (see "Textual Meaning and Authorial Meaning", in *Genre*, 3(1) (1968), p. 171). Quite apart from this question, however, is Hirsch's failure to indicate how extra-textual evidence itself is to be interpreted or understood.

24 Gadamer, *Wahrheit und Methode*, p. 276; *Truth and Method*, p. 259.

25 Ibid., p. 278; p. 262. As Gadamer puts this point later in "Das Problem des historischen Bewusstseins", in *Kleine Schriften* (J. C. B. Mohr, Tübingen, 1977), vol. 4: *Variationen*, p. 146: "One looks for what is right. This holds for the interpreted author as well as for the interpreter. But it requires granting to the other potential correctness – letting he or it count against me."

26 Gadamer, *Wahrheit und Methode*, p. 253; *Truth and Method*, p. 238.

27 Ibid., p. 253; p. 238.

28 Jacques Derrida "Guter Wille zur Macht (I)" in *Text und Interpretation: Deutsche–französische Debatte*, ed. Phillippe Forget (Wilhelm Fink, Munich, 1984), p. 57.

29 In his interesting discussion of the debate between Gadamer and Derrida, Fred Dallmayr argues that Gadamer's hermeneutics itself involves the kind of rupture that Derrida stresses. (See Fred Dallmayr, "Hermeneutics and Deconstruction: Gadamer and Derrida in Dialogue", forthcoming in Dallmayr, *Critical Encounters* (University of Notre Dame Press, Notre Dame, 1987).) On Dallmayr's view, such rupture is most clearly manifest in the transformation of play into art and in the experience of works of art that I discussed in ch. 2. As we saw, both events signal radical alterations, the first in the nature of play and the second in the audience's assumptions and beliefs, and Dallmayr therefore contends that discontinuity is as much a feature of hermeneutics as it is of deconstruction. None the less, it should be pointed out that the discontinuities at issue lead to very different results. As Dallmayr himself explains, Gadamer's focus in delineating the experience of

art is the disruption of "complacent meaning expectations" or, as I said, the audience's prejudices and assumptions concerning a work. Such disruption, however, involves a move *toward* understanding; in defeating one's expectations and assumptions, works of art can push one to a new and better understanding of both the work and the subject-matter with which it deals. Derrida's rupture, in contrast, is a rupture in understanding itself and one that is meant to point to its problematic status in general. But this is the position that Gadamer's hermeneutics means to dispute. In this regard, Dallmayr correctly points to the social and political importance of the "good will" that Derrida criticizes:

> His [Gadamer's] Paris comments presented the "capacity for understanding" as a "basic human endowment which sustains social life" . . . Seen from this perspective, social and political interaction clearly requires ethical engagement or the reciprocal display of "good will" . . . Needless to say [this] is a far cry from the non-engagement and neutral indifference prevalent in liberal societies (a stance present implicitly as a tendency in Derrida's detached theoreticism). ("Hermeneutics and Deconstruction", manuscript p. 39.)

30 See Gadamer, *Wahrheit und Methode*, p. 278; *Truth and Method*, p. 262.
31 Hans-Georg Gadamer, "Und Dennoch: Macht des Guten Willens" in *Text und Interpretation*, p. 61.
32 Many of these are collected in *Kleine Schriften*, 4 vols (J. C. B. Mohr, Tübingen, 1967–77) and translated into English by P. Christopher Smith in *Hegel's Dialectic: Five Hermeneutical Studies* (Yale University Press, New Haven, 1976), and *Dialogue and Dialectic: Eight Hermeneutical Studies on Plato* (Yale University Press, New Haven, 1980).
33 *Wahrheit und Methode*, p. 296; *Truth and Method*, p. 279.
34 See Gilbert Ryle, *The Concept of Mind* (Hutchison, London, 1949), ch. 2, for this distinction.
35 Gadamer, *Wahrheit und Methode*, p. 300; *Truth and Method*, p. 283.
36 Hans-Georg Gadamer, "Hermeneutik als praktische Philosophie", in *Vernunft im Zeitalter der Wissenschaften* (Suhrkamp, Frankfurt, 1976), p. 83; English in "Hermeneutics as Practical Philosophy", in *Reason in the Age of Science*, tr. Frederick Lawrence (MIT Press, Cambridge, 1981), p. 92.
37 Ibid., p. 117; p. 110.
38 Ibid., p. 298; p. 280.
39 Ibid., p. 307; p. 289. For a similar analysis see Roman Ingarden, *Von Erkennen des literatischen Kunstwerks* (Niemeyer, Tübingen, 1968), pp. 49ff.
40 Gadamer, *Wahrheit und Methode*, p. 280; *Truth and Method*, p. 264.
41 Hans-Georg Gadamer, "The Heritage of Hegel", in *Reason in the Age of Science*, p. 50.
42 Gadamer, *Wahrheit und Methode*, p. 315; *Truth and Method*, p. 297.

43 Emilio Betti, *Die Hermeneutik als allgemeine Methodik der Geisteswissenschaften* (J. C. B. Mohr, Tübingen, 1962), p. 49.
44 Gadamer, *Wahrheit und Methode*, p. 363; *Truth and Method*, p. 347.
45 Ibid., p. 364; p. 348.
46 Ibid., p. 350; p. 331.
47 Ibid., p. 366; p. 350.
48 Ibid., p. 268; pp. 252–3.
49 Ibid., p. 271; p. 255.
50 This analysis of Gadamer's use of the concept of the classical is similar to criticisms by Peter Christian Lang in *Hermeneutik, Ideologiekritik, Äesthetik* (Forum Academicum Königstein, 1981), and Hans Robert Jauss in *Toward an Aesthetic of Reception*, tr. Timothy Bahti (University of Minnesota Press, Minneapolis, 1982). Both consider Gadamer's account of the classical dogmatic in so far as it seems to overlook the historicity of understanding that Gadamer himself emphasizes. The classical is that which cannot be reduced to a historical concept because it speaks immediately to each age. As Gadamer writes, it "does not first require the overcoming of historical distance for, in its constant communication, it does overcome it" (*Wahrheit und Methode*, p. 274; *Truth and Method*, p. 257). Lang argues that this depiction of the classical contrasts with Gadamer's own account of experience, which we considered in ch. 1. Whereas the notion of a negative learning experience indicates the openness of our beliefs to refutation and hence the undogmatic character of hermeneutics, Gadamer's concept of the classical has already decided on its "superior truth." "Since a superior truth by itself comes to validity in the experience of the classical, the experience of the classical is determined in advance and can be criticized as dogmatic by the same theory of experience that is grounded by this experience to a decisive degree." (Lang, *Hermeneutik, Ideologiekritik, Äesthetik*, p. 24). For his part, Jauss claims that Gadamer's account of the classical neglects the distance between the present and a text of the past. On Jauss's view, a classical text does not speak immediately to each age; rather, as with any text we must be conscious of the classical text's own historicity. Hence, what is odd about this conception is its apparent ignoring of the very historical change that Gadamer emphasizes. Despite their similarities to my view of Gadamer's recourse to the classical however, I think both of these criticisms miss one important aspect of Gadamer's analysis. For Gadamer, the "superior truth" of the classical is not decided in advance, as Lang insists. Rather he makes it quite clear that the classical is classical because it continues to *prove* its superiority to each new generation of interpreters. Still, this continual proof of its own superiority perverts the Hegelian conception of synthesis in which the classical would rather be incorporated into a new position and would not remain the final word on the subject-matter at issue.
51 Gadamer, *Wahrheit und Methode*, p. 465; *Truth and Method*, p. 446.

52 In "Discourse and Conversation: The Theory of Communicative Competence and Hermeneutics in Light of the Debate between Habermas and Gadamer", *Cultural Hermeneutics*, 4 (1977), p. 327, Dieter Misgeld, while generally supportive of Gadamer's position, writes: "Gadamer . . . assimilates discourse (a conversation) too much to a situation in which we are overcome by the force of what is said, as we are overcome by events in many daily occasions of action in which we do not possess the freedom to distantate ourselves from what happens."

NOTES TO CHAPTER 4

1 See Peter Winch, *The Idea of a Social Science and its Relation to Philosophy*, 3rd impression (Routledge and Kegan Paul, London, 1964), and Charles Taylor, "Interpretation and the Sciences of Man", *Review of Metaphysics*, 25 (1971), pp. 3-51; reprinted in *Understanding and Social Inquiry*, ed. Fred Dallmayr and Thomas McCarthy (Notre Dame University Press, Notre Dame, 1977), pp. 101-31.

2 Anthony Giddens, *New Rules of Sociological Method* (Basic Books, London, 1976), p. 158.

3 Jürgen Habermas, *Zur Logik der Sozialwissenschaften* (Suhrkamp, Frankfurt, 1970), p. 244.

4 Hans-Georg Gadamer, *Wahrheit und Methode*, 4th edn (J. C. B. Mohr, Tübingen, 1975), p. 362; English translation, *Truth and Method* (Seabury Press, New York, 1975), pp. 346-7. Quoted in Habermas, *Zur Logik der Sozialwissenschaften*, p. 255; English translation of sections on Gadamer is "A Review of Gadamer's *Truth and Method*", in *Understanding and Social Inquiry*, p. 337.

5 Habermas, *Zur Logik der Sozialwissenschaften*, p. 256; "A Review of Gadamer's *Truth and Method*", p. 338.

6 Habermas, *Zur Logik der Sozialwissenschaften*, p. 289; "A Review of Gadamer's *Truth and Method*", p. 361.

7 Albrecht Wellmer, *Kritische Gesellschaftstheorie und Positivismus* (Suhrkamp, Frankfurt, 1969), pp. 48–9. English translation is *Critical Theory of Society*, tr. John Cumming (Seabury Press, New York, pbk edn, 1974), p. 47. Quoted in Habermas, "Der Universalitätsanspruch der Hermeneutik", in *Hermeneutik und Ideologiekritik*, K.-O. Apel et al. (Suhrkamp, Frankfurt, 1977), p. 153; English translation as "The Hermeneutic Claim to Universality", in *Contemporary Hermeneutics: Method. Philosophy and Critique*, Josef Bleicher (Routledge and Kegan Paul, London, 1980), pp. 204–5.

8 Habermas, *Zur Logik der Sozialwissenschaften*, p. 289; "A Review of Gadamer's *Truth and Method*", p. 361.

9 Paul Ricoeur agrees with Habermas that Gadamer at least risks retreating into a philosophy of language in so far as he neglects "the trilogy,

work–power–languages." As Ricoeur continues: "language is only the locus for the articulation of an experience which supports it and . . . everything consequently does not arrive *in* language but only comes to language" ("Ethics and Culture, Habermas and Gadamer in Dialogue", *Philosophy Today*, 17 (1973), p. 162). I do not see how this point functions as a criticism of Gadamer, however, since he himself is capable of taking the same position.

10 Hans-Georg Gadamer, "Rhetorik, Hermeneutik und Ideologiekritik: Meta-kritische Erörterungen zu *Wahrheit und Methode*", in *Hermeneutik und Ideologiekritik*, Apel et al., p. 71. English translation as "On the Scope and Function of Hermeneutical Reflection" by G. B. Hess and R. E. Palmer in *Philosophical Hermeneutics*, ed. D. Linge (University of California Press, Berkeley, 1976), p. 31. This translation claims to be a translation of the essay as its appears in *Kleine Schriften* (J. C. B. Mohr, Tübingen, 1967), vol 1: *Interpretationen*. It should be pointed out, however, that at times this translation is so loose that it gives a misleading impression of Gadamer's position. See, especially, the difference between Gadamer's text on p. 65 of *Hermeneutik und Ideologiekritik* and the English translation on p. 27.

11 Gadamer, "Rhetorik, Hermeneutik und Ideologiekritik", pp. 80-1; "On the Scope and Function of Hermeneutical Reflection", pp. 30-1.

12 Gadamer, *Wahrheit und Methode*, p. 275–84; *Truth and Method*, pp. 258–67.

13 For more on such a "critical" conception of ideology, see John Thompson, *Studies in the Theory of Ideology* (Polity Press, Cambridge, 1984), pp. 4ff.

14 Karl Marx, *Capital* (Progress Publishers, Moscow, reproduced from the 1887 edition), vol. 1, p. 172.

15 This ideology-critical aspect of Marx's description of the buying and selling of labor power is underdeveloped by Allen Wood and Richard Miller, both of whom argue that the description is a neutral analysis and that Marx is not claiming that the wage–labor exchange is unjust. See Richard Miller, *Analyzing Marx: Morality, Power and History* (Princeton University Press, Princeton, 1985), pp. 27ff, and Allen Wood, "The Marxian Critique of Justice" and "Marx on Right and Justice: A Reply to Husami" in *Marx, Justice and History*, M. Cohen et al. (Princeton University Press, Princeton, 1980).

16 See Karl-Otto Apel, "The A Priori of Communication and the Foundation of the Humanities", in *Understanding and Social Inquiry*, ed. Fred Dallmayr and Thomas McCarthy (University of Notre Dame Press, Notre Dame, 1977), p. 299.

17 Karl-Otto Apel, "Szientistik, Hermeneutik, Ideologiekritik: Entwurf einer Wissenschaftslehre in erkenntnisanthropologischer Sicht", in *Hermeneutik und Ideologiekritik*, Apel et al. p. 35; English translation as "Scientistics, Hermeneutics and the Critique of Ideology: Outline of a Theory of Science from a Cognitive–Anthropological Standpoint" in *Towards a Transformation of*

Philosophy, Glyn Adey and David Frisby (Routledge and Kegan Paul, London, 1980), p. 65.

18 Apel, "Szientistik", p. 33; "Scientistics", p. 64. For a similar criticism of the conjunction of understanding and application see Dietrich Böhler, "Philosophische Hermeneutik und hermeneutische Methode" in *Text und Applikation: Theologie, Jurizprudence und Literaturwissenschaft im Hermeneutische Gespräch*, ed. Furhmann et al. (Poetik und Hermeneutik 9, Wilhelm Fink, Munich, 1977), p. 483–512.

19 See Hans-Georg Gadamer's "Replik" in *Hermeneutik und Ideologiekritik*, p. 196 for his own comments on Apel's misunderstanding of his position on application, which he describes as a failure to see that application is "an implicit moment of all understanding." In essence, Apel seems to repeat the mistake that Hirsch makes in trying to separate an understanding of meaning from that of significance (see ch. 2 above, pp. 84–5).

20 Apel, "Szientistik", p. 39; "Scientistics", p. 68.

21 Hans-Georg Gadamer, "Hermeneutik als Praktische Philosophie", in *Vernunft im Zeitalter der Wissenschaft* (Suhrkamp, Frankfurt, 1976), p. 99; English translation as "Hermeneutics as Practical Philosophy", in *Reason in the Age of Science*, tr. Frederick Lawrence (MIT Press, 1981), p. 104.

22 Gadamer, "Replik", p. 302.

23 Habermas, *Zur Logik der Sozialwissenschaften*, p. 285; "A Review of Gadamer's *Truth and Method*", p. 358.

24 This is a criticism that Gadamer repeats throughout his discussion with Habermas. Thus, see his more recent remarks on Habermas in "Text und Interpretation" in *Text und Interpretation: Deutsche–französische Debatte*, ed. Philippe Forget (Wilhelm Fink, Munich, 1984), p. 44.

25 Habermas, "Der Universalitätsanspruch der Hermeneutik", p. 133; "The Hermeneutic Claim to Universality", p. 191.

26 Ibid., p. 137; pp. 193–4.

27 Ibid., p. 138; p. 194.

28 Gadamer, "Replik", p. 307.

29 Paul Ricoeur makes the same point. See "Hermeneutics and the Critique of Ideology", in *Hermeneutics and the Human Sciences* (Cambridge University Press, Cambridge, 1981), p. 85.

30 Jürgen Habermas, *Theory and Practice*, tr. John Viertel (Beacon Press, Boston, 1973), pp. 30–1.

31 Habermas, "Der Universalitätsanspruch der Hermeneutik", p. 153–4; "The Hermeneutik Claim to Universality", p. 205.

32 Ibid., p. 154; p. 206.

33 See, for example, Karl-Otto Apel, "Szientismus oder transzendentale Hermeneutik?", in *Transformation der Philosophie* (Suhrkamp, Frankfurt, 1976), vol. 2: *Das Apriori der kommunicativen Gesellschaft*, p. 217; English translation as "Scientistics or Transcendental Hermeneutics?", in *Towards a*

Transformation of Philosophy, p. 125.

34 Gadamer, "Replik", p. 314.

35 See Apel "Szientismus oder transzendentale Hermeneutik?", p. 217; "Scientistics or Transcendental Hermeneutics?", p. 125. Also Habermas, "Der Universalitätsanspruch der Hermeneutik", p. 155; "The Hermeneutic Claim to Universality", p. 206.

36 Gadamer, "Replik", p. 304.

37 Ibid., p. 299.

38 Ibid., p. 317.

39 For an excellent review of this attempt and comments on some problems with it see Thomas McCarthy, "Rationality and Relativism: Habermas's 'Over-coming' of Hermeneutics" in *Habermas: Critical Debates*, ed. David Held and John Thompson (MIT Press, Cambridge, 1982), pp. 57–78. Also see Seyla Benhabib, *Critique, Norm and Utopia* (Columbia University Press, New York, 1985), chs 7 and 8.

40 See the essays collected in Held and Thompson (eds) *Habermas: Critical Debates*.

41 Habermas, *Reason and the Rationalization of Society*, tr. Thomas McCarthy (Beacon Press, Boston, 1984), pp. 48–53.

42 See ibid., p. 68

43 Ibid., p. 134. For a similar criticism seen Apel, "Szientismus oder transzendentale Hermeneutik?" p. 216; "Scientistics or Transcendental Hermeneutics?" pp. 124–5.

44 Jürgen Habermas, "Legitimation Problems in the Modern State", in *Communication and the Evolution of Society*, tr. Thomas McCarthy (Beacon Press, Boston, 1979), p. 205

45 See Thomas McCarthy, "Rationality and Relativism", in *Habermas: Critical Debates*, ed. David Held and John Thompson, pp. 69–72, where he entertains suggestions others have made that the move to abstract thinking which characterizes the cognitive devlopment of the Western child is based on the needs of Western civilization and should not be universalized as a general developmental logic. In other civilizations, concrete thinking, for example may remains more important. Carol Gilligan, *In a Different Voice* (Harvard University Press, Cambridge, 1982), makes a similar claim for women's moral development. In her view, the fact that women typically place lower than men on Kohlberg's scale of moral development simply indicates that their moral development may follow a different trajectory.

46 Habermas, *Zur Logik der Sozialwissenschaften*, p. 283; "A Review of Gadamer's *Truth and Method*", p. 357.

47 Hans-Georg Gadamer, "Rhetorik, Hermeneutik und Ideologiekritik", in *Hermeneutik und Ideologiekritik*, K.-O. Apel et al., p. 72–3; "On the Scope and Function of Hermeneutical Reflection", p. 33 (with modifications and omissions).

48 This is the point that Jack Mendelson finds decisive in "The Habermas–Gadamer Debate", *New German Critique*, 18 (Fall, 1979), p. 62.
49 Gadamer, "Rhetorik, Hermeneutik, und Ideologiekritik", p. 73; "On the Scope and Function of Hermeneutical Reflection", p. 33.
50 Ibid., p. 66; p. 26. See also Gadamer, *Wahrheit und Methode*, p. xvii; *Truth and Method*, p. xvii.
51 Habermas, *Zur Logik der Sozialwissenschaften*, p. 280; "A Review of Gadamer's *Truth and Method*", p. 355.

NOTES TO CHAPTER 5

1 On the differences between Rorty and Habermas see also Richard Bernstein, *Beyond Objectivism and Relativism* (University of Pennsylvannia Press, Philadelphia, 1983), pp. 197ff.
2 See Richard Rorty, "Pragmatism and Philosophy", Introduction to *Consequences of Pragmatism* (University of Minnesota Press, Minneapolis, 1982), reference to Goodman, p. xxxix.
3 Richard Rorty, "Habermas and Lyotard on Postmodernity", in *Habermas and Modernity*, ed. Richard Bernstein (MIT Press, Cambridge, 1985), p. 164.
4 Charles Taylor, "Interpretation and the Sciences of Man", in *Understanding and Social Inquiry*, ed. Fred Dallmayr and Thomas McCarthy (University of Notre Dame Press, Notre Dame, 1977), p. 107.
5 Richard Rorty, "Method, Social Science, and Social Hope", in *Consequences of Pragmatism*, p. 199
6 Richard Rorty, *Philosophy and the Mirror of Nature* (Princeton University Press, Princeton, 1979), p. 349.
7 Rorty, "Method, Social Science, and Social Hope", in *Consequences of Pragmatism*, p. 200.
8 In fact the objection Rorty raises in this regard reflects an old misunderstanding. Similar criticisms were directed at Winch's position by Richard Rudner in *Philosophy of Social Science* (Prentice-Hall, Englewood Cliffs, 1966), and May Brodbeck in "Meaning and Action" in *Readings in the Philosophy of the Social Sciences*, ed. May Brodbeck (Macmillan, New York, 1968). See my "Hermeneutics and the Social Sciences: A Gadamerian Critique of Rorty", *Inquiry*, 28 (September, 1985), pp. 343–4.
9 Rorty, *Philosophy and the Mirror of Nature*, p. 359.
10 Ibid., p. 136.
11 Ibid., p. 328.
12 Ibid., pp. 330–1.
13 Ibid., p. 331.
14 Ibid.
15 Ibid., p. 335.

16 Rorty, "Pragmatism and Philosophy", Introduction to *Consequences of Pragmatism*, p. xi.
17 Rorty, *Philosophy and the Mirror of Nature*, p. 317.
18 Ibid., p. 378.
19 Rorty, "Pragmatism and Philosophy", Introduction to *Consequences of Pragmatism*, p. xix.
20 Rorty, *Philosophy and the Mirror of Nature*, p. 325.
21 Ibid., p. 315.
22 Ibid., p. 360.
23 Rorty, "Pragmatism, Relativism, and Irrationalism", in *Consequences of Pragmatism*, p. 173.
24 Ibid.
25 Rorty, "Habermas and Lyotard on Postmodernity", in *Habermas and Modernity*, p. 166.
26 Ibid., p. 174.
27 Ibid., also see p. 172.
28 In *Post-Analytic Philosophy*, ed. John Rajchman and Cornel West (Columbia University Press, New York, 1985), pp. 3–19.
29 Ibid., p. 12.
30 At first glance, this characterization of edification may seem to conflict with Rorty's stress on the need for a "frank ethnocentrism." In debunking the claims of epistemology to provide a foundation for our beliefs, Rorty argued that we must substitute what, following Hans Blumenberg, he calls "self-assertion" for "self-foundation." In stressing the importance of edification as opposed to a knowledge of "truth," however, Rorty seems to suggest not that we assert our beliefs and values but that we try out new beliefs and values and that we educate ourselves about the diversity of possible "ways of coping." None the less, the contradiction here is only apparent since becoming *gebildet* in Rorty's sense involves precisely recognizing one's defense of one's tradition as a form of self-assertion rather than of self-foundation. In entering into conversation which others one becomes aware that one's own views, opinions and assumptions are simply one's own and that they can claim no greater convergence on reality than those of others. Hence, it is just the education involved in *Bildung* that allows one to see the folly involved in looking for the foundations of one's beliefs and leaves one open to understanding the equal merit of other views.

   Moreover, if the substitution of self-assertion for self-foundation issues from a proper *Bildung*, Rorty's understanding of *Bildung* itself follows from his ethnocentrism: On his view, what is worth preserving in democratic societies is precisely the openness, toleration and pluralism that allows for an edifying recognition of diversity. In other words, it is an opposition to dogmatism of any kind that is crucial to both liberal democracy and *Bildung*. From both perspectives, what is wanted is not pronouncements on truth but the freedom to try out new theories and vocabularies and to discover new ways of thinking about oneself and one's tradition. Hence, his frank ethnocentricism, which asserts the values of liberal democracy is not opposed to his call for edification, which emphasizes openness to change; the former is rather the precondition of the latter. Indeed, if, as Rorty suggests, we must abandon epistemological pursuits for edifying ones, then the assertion of liberal democracy becomes all the more important.

31 Gadamer, *Wahrheit und Methode*, p. 357; 4th edn (J. C. B. Mohr, Tübingen, 1975), p. 35: English translation, *Truth and Method* (Seabury Press, New York, 1975), p. 318.

32 Ibid., p. 339; p. 320.

33 Ibid., p. 339; p. 320.

34 Rorty, *Philosophy and the Mirror of Nature*, p. 367.

35 Ibid., p. 359.

36 Hans-Georg Gadamer, *Wahrheit und Methode*, *Truth and Method*, p. 36.

37 Ibid., p. 29; p. 31.

38 Gadamer, *Wahrheit und Methode*, p. 9; *Truth and Method*, p. 12.

39 Rorty, *Philosophy and the Mirror of Nature*, p. 361.

40 Ibid.

41 Rorty, "Pragmatism and Philosophy", Introduction to *Consequences of Pragmatism*, p. xxxix.

42 Ibid., p. xl.

43 Hans-Georg Gadamer, "Über die Naturanlage des Menschen zur Philosophie", in *Vernunft im Zeitalter der Wissenschaft* (Suhrkamp, Frankfurt, 1976), p. 123; English translation as "On the Natural Inclination of Human Beings toward Philosophy", in Gadamer, *Reason in the Age of Science*, tr. Frederick Lawrence (MIT Press, Cambridge, 1981), p. 149.

44 See Hans-Georg Gadamer, "Was ist Praxis? Die Bedingungen gesellschaftlicher Vernunft", in *Vernunft im Zeitalter der Wissenschaft*, pp. 59–60; English translation, "What is Practice? The Conditions of Social Reason", in *Reason in the Age of Science*, p. 73–4.

45 Hans-Georg Gadamer, "Philosophie oder Wissenschaftstheorie?", in *Vernunft im Zeitalter der Wissenschaft*, p. 135; English translation, "Philosophy or Theory of Science?", in *Reason in the Age of Science*, p. 159

46 Hans-Georg Gadamer, "Über das Philosophische in den Wissenschaften und die Wissenschaftlichkeit der Philosophie", in *Vernunft im Zeitalter der Wissenschaft*, pp. 15 and 17; English translation, "On The Philosophical Element in the Sciences and the Scientific Character of Philosophy", in *Reason in the Age of Science*, pp. 7 and 9.

47 Gadamer, "Was ist Praxis?", pp. 75–6; "What is Practice?", pp. 86–7.

48 Richard J. Bernstein, *Beyond Objectivism and Relativism*.

49 Hans-Georg Gadamer, "Hegels Philosophie und ihre Nachwirkungen bis heute", in *Vernunft im Zeitalter der Wissenschaft*, p. 52; English translation,

"Hegel's Philosophy and its Aftereffects until Today", in *Reason in the Age of Science*, p. 37. See also his "Über das Philosophische in den Wissenschaften", in *Vernunft im Zeitalter der Wissenschaft*, pp. 17ff.; "On The Philosophical Element in the Sciences", in *Reason in the Age of Science*, pp. 9ff.

NOTES TO CHAPTER 6

1 See, for example, Jean-François Lyotard, *The Postmodern Condition: A Report on Knowledge*, tr. Geoff Bennington and Brian Massumi (University of Minnesota Press, Minneapolis, 1984), pp. 39ff.

2 See, for example, Michel Foucault, *Power/Knowledge: Selected Interviews and Other Writings, 1952-1977* (Random House, New York, 1980), chs 5 and 6.

3 Also see David Hoy's interpretation of the anti-epistemological thrust of hermeneutics in which he agrees with Rorty's account in "Must We Mean What We Say: The Grammatological Critique of Hermeneutics", in *Hermeneutics and Modern Philosophy*, ed. Brice R. Wachterhauser (forthcoming, State University of New York Press, Albany, 1986), galley pages 453-4.

4 Hans-Georg Gadamer, "The Heritage of Hegel", in Gadamer, *Reason in the Age of Science*, tr. Frederick Lawrence (MIT Press, Cambridge, 1981), p. 40.

5 Presidential Address delivered before the Eighty-First Annual Eastern Division Meeting of the American Philosophical Association, New York, New York, 29 December 1984; in *Proceedings and Addresses of The American Philosophical Association* (APA, Newark, Delaware, 1985).

6 See D. Davidson, "The Very Idea of a Conceptual Scheme", in *Post-Analytic Philosophy*, ed. John Rajchman and Cornel West (Columbia University Press, New York, 1985).

7 MacIntyre, "Relativism, Power and Philosophy", p. 19.

8 Hans-Georg Gadamer, "Hegels Philosophie und ihre Nachwirkungen bis heute", in *Vernunft im Zeitalter der Wissenschaft* (Suhrkamp, Frankfurt, 1976), p. 51; English translation, "Hegel's Philosophy and its Aftereffects until Today", in *Reason in the Age of Science*, p. 36.

Index